T0369588

OXFORD TEXTUAL PERSPECTIVES

Intercultural Explorations and the
Court of Henry VIII

GENERAL EDITORS

Elaine Treharne   Greg Walker

Intercultural Explorations and the Court of Henry VIII

NADIA T. VAN PELT

OXFORD
UNIVERSITY PRESS

OXFORD
UNIVERSITY PRESS

Great Clarendon Street, Oxford, OX2 6DP,
United Kingdom

Oxford University Press is a department of the University of Oxford.
It furthers the University's objective of excellence in research, scholarship,
and education by publishing worldwide. Oxford is a registered trade mark of
Oxford University Press in the UK and in certain other countries

© Nadia T. van Pelt 2024

The moral rights of the author have been asserted

All rights reserved. No part of this publication may be reproduced, stored in
a retrieval system, or transmitted, in any form or by any means, without the
prior permission in writing of Oxford University Press, or as expressly permitted
by law, by licence or under terms agreed with the appropriate reprographics
rights organization. Enquiries concerning reproduction outside the scope of the
above should be sent to the Rights Department, Oxford University Press, at the
address above

You must not circulate this work in any other form
and you must impose this same condition on any acquirer

Published in the United States of America by Oxford University Press
198 Madison Avenue, New York, NY 10016, United States of America

British Library Cataloguing in Publication Data
Data available

Library of Congress Control Number: 2023942308

ISBN 9780192863447
ISBN 9780192863454 (pbk.)

DOI: 10.1093/oso/9780192863447.001.0001

Printed and bound by
CPI Group (UK) Ltd, Croydon, CR0 4YY

Links to third party websites are provided by Oxford in good faith and
for information only. Oxford disclaims any responsibility for the materials
contained in any third party website referenced in this work.

For John J. McGavin
with gratitude

SERIES EDITOR'S PREFACE

Oxford Textual Perspectives is a series of informative and provocative studies focused upon texts (conceived of in the broadest sense of that term) and the technologies, cultures, and communities that produce, inform, and receive them. It provides fresh interpretations of fundamental works, images, and artefacts, and of the vital and challenging issues emerging in English literary studies. By engaging with the contexts and materiality of the text, its production, transmission, and reception history, and by frequently testing and exploring the boundaries of the notions of text and meaning themselves, the volumes in the series question conventional frameworks and provide innovative interpretations of both canonical and less well-known works. These books will offer new perspectives, and challenge familiar ones, both on and through texts and textual communities. While they focus on specific authors, periods, and issues, they nonetheless scan wider horizons, addressing themes and provoking questions that have a more general application to literary studies and cultural history as a whole. Each is designed to be as accessible to the non-specialist reader as it is fresh and rewarding for the specialist, combining an informative orientation in a landscape with detailed analysis of the territory and suggestions for further travel.

Elaine Treharne and *Greg Walker*

FOREWORD

Seldom has a royal court invited such intensive study as that of Henry VIII, or become so prominent in popular culture. This book is nevertheless committed to offering a fresh perspective on Tudor court culture by using continental sources to contextualize, nuance, and at times, *challenge* long-held perspectives that have been formed through the use of well-studied, Anglophone sources. As such, this book offers additional cross-language and transcultural perspectives to explore and help re-examine information that, in isolation, can be easily—and indeed has been—taken at face value, but which when read in a wider context can suggest alternative meanings. In Chapter 1, which focuses on music, this approach leads to a more complete understanding of the entourage that Katherine of Aragon brought with her to England. It furthermore reveals the Tudor court in 1501 to have been a more intercultural place than the English records suggest, and importantly shows that the African presence in this context was greater than has hitherto been assumed. I reveal, for example, that before the now-famous trumpet player John Blanke first appeared in the Tudor court records, another Black trumpeter can be situated at sea with Katherine of Aragon, and at the festivities celebrating her marrying Arthur Tudor. At a methodological level, this discovery suggests that further cross-language studies of the English court records and those of Castile, Aragon, and the Habsburgs may yield more information about the mobility of court staff, and will perhaps reveal the presence of other persons of African descent now 'hidden' behind generic group payment references in the English chamber books.

This book also introduces source material which can inform current understandings of Tudor court culture, such as, for example, material from the Archivo General de Simancas, and Spanish account books kept by Gonzalo de Baeza, the treasurer of Queen Isabella of Castile, which provide insight into the make-up and expenses of her household and that of the royal children. Such evidence provides exciting additions to current Tudor scholarship, and, for example, proves that Katherine of Aragon brought an '*enana*' ['dwarf'] in her train when she travelled to England. In Chapter 2, this serves to contextualize understandings of foolery in the context of the royal court, in a study exploring the political and diplomatic meanings of Ambassador Chapuys's bringing a fool to Katherine of Aragon's deathbed. This chapter addresses the expectations and preconceptions contemporaries would have had of court fools. Might a fool also be able to act as a spy? What were fools thought to be capable of doing or delivering? And could the performance of a fool express political messages at various levels, that is, could both the *actions* of the fool and the fact of the fool's *presence* simultaneously express different political purposes for both the performer and their patron?

In Chapter 3, French- and German-language festival books and Venetian ambassadorial accounts complement and contextualize Anglophone sources detailing the meetings—and shared feasts—between the Habsburg emperor Charles V and Henry VIII. Building on an extensive body of studies in food history in which the banquet is understood as a performative 'multimedia' event, this chapter acknowledges other international instances of presenting, ritualizing, and accepting food and their underlying preconceptions of ritual power, hospitality, spectacle, and trust. And, acting in the realization that a full reconstruction of a banqueting event with all its separate media forms cannot be created, instead an attempt is made to contribute to the understanding of how Henry VIII, through hospitality and consumption, invested in his relationship with the most powerful man in Europe, and ensured that other parties were made sufficiently aware of his efficacious foreign relations. The chapter furthermore provides 'food for thought' regarding a more systematic inclusion of food and performance history within 'general' studies of Tudor history.

Where some discussions, such as that of Tudor banqueting in diplomatic settings, can benefit from additional perspectives, some aspects of Tudor history are so dramatically undersourced that they need, at fundamental levels, to be supplemented with fresh evidence, and revisited via additional methodological approaches in order to enhance productive scholarship. This represents a lacuna in research that cannot be solved overnight, but it can at least be addressed in order to redress the balance, and suggestions are made for productive steps in that direction. Thus, Chapters 4 and 5 jointly take as a case study the ways in which scholarship has created a historical narrative about Anne of Cleves,

Henry's second foreign queen, which is both hyperfocused on her physical appearance, and dismissive of her political or diplomatic relevance. Chapter 4, 'Fashion Victims', employs a sartorial lens as a tool to address the former issue. It reveals that descriptions of Anne of Cleves made in ambassadorial letters and other correspondence, and in Hall's *Chronicle* are best understood as part of a genre of writing in which a foreign princess and her entourage were represented in a formulaic way, as is shown through examples of Italian, Polish, Habsburg, English, and Spanish brides at courts where modes of attire were worn that differed from those favoured in their home countries. These descriptions, we will see, say more about this genre of writing than about the princess brides in question.

The book ends (Chapter 5) by introducing new source material to the field, in the form of an extant charter which has been hiding in plain view at the Gelders Archief in Arnhem, the Netherlands. This charter, currently unstudied in Tudor history, consolidated the *per verba de futuro* betrothal of Anne of Cleves and Francis of Lorraine. It provides new insights into the stakeholders of the match, in which Anne of Cleves's mother, Maria of Jülich-Berg, turns out to have been pivotal, contrary to what previous scholarship has suggested. Interestingly, studying the charter as an object reveals that its physical characteristics would have made it very clear to anyone who saw it, including persons who did not read Low German, that Anne had not been consulted when this match was made, and she had not necessarily agreed to it. This would have made it very easy to consider the Cleves–Lorraine match not binding, from which follows that if this charter had been produced at the English court, it would have barred Henry VIII's annulling his marriage to Anne. Anne of Cleves's not urging for the charter to be produced tellingly shows her awareness of marital politics, and her ability to make an informed choice as to what would give her the best options of survival at the Tudor court. Acknowledging that manuscript sources in Low German may present some scholars in the field with a language barrier, this chapter suggests how to make use of such material regardless of one's understanding of the language in which it was written.

The material engaged with in this book is not exhaustive, and readers will notice that, because the book is driven by the wish to explore different methodological streams of research for the opportunities they represent in relation to the current discourse, at times choices had to be made as to what to include. This also meant that while writing this book, I have made excursions into 'side-projects' sparked by the research and reading done for this project.[1] Together, the chapters in this book have been designed to make an attempt—where possible—at unravelling the habits and customs which underpinned and determined Tudor court culture, including ceremony and ritual, and the performance of many cultural practices that are not always recognized as 'performance', but which could have that use, especially in an intricately political environment such as the Tudor court.[2] Additionally, I offer a number of 'intercultural explorations' through addressing primary source material written in Spanish, German, or French, and which represents additional perspectives to the well-known and intensively quoted perspectives that have contributed to defining the field. I show that however quintessentially 'English' the court of Henry VIII may have been, it was also a place of cultural and intercultural encounters that is best understood when studied in dialogue across languages, geographical barriers, and scholarly disciplines. Indeed, the primary evidence employed in this book aims to give a nuanced account of Tudor court matters from a range of perspectives to help question what we know, or think we know, about the Tudor court.

As will be evident from the chapters that follow, this book gratefully makes use of the excellent resources offered by Records of Early English Drama, an international project based at the University of Toronto, and of the Tudor Chamber Books project, a collaborative effort between the University of Winchester, the National Archives, and the University of Sheffield Digital Humanities Institute. It also studies additional sources that supplement and contextualize the REED and Chamber

---

[1] Notably, K.P.S. Janssen and Nadia T. van Pelt, 'Royal epistolary courtship in Latin? Arthur Tudor's "love letter" to Katherine of Aragon at the Archivo General de Simancas and Francesco Negri's *Ars Epistolandi*'. *Renaissance Studies* (2023), https://doi.org/10.1111/rest.12864; and Van Pelt, 'John Blanke's wages: No business like show business'. *Medieval English Theatre* 44 (2023), 3–35.

[2] Full bibliographical overviews are offered per chapter, but here I should already mention the important work done in Janette Dillon, *The Language of Space in Court Performance, 1400–1625* (Cambridge: Cambridge University Press, 2010); Christina Normore, *A Feast for the Eyes: Art, Performance & the Late Medieval Banquet* (Chicago, IL: University of Chicago Press, 2015); and Greg Walker, *Writing Under Tyranny: English Literature and the Henrician Reformation* (Oxford: Oxford University Press, 2005).

Book material. These range from ambassadorial correspondence to account books, but also include legal records, royal warrants, marital contracts, and travel accounts. As observed, an important element of this book lies in the introduction of fresh perspectives and new source material, as well as revisiting previously studied material. Therefore I have sought to, when possible, introduce readers to the relevant web links for manuscript resources when an archive has digitized part of their collections, to make more tangible and interactive for readers anywhere in the world the discovery of fresh source material, as well as the chance to revisit known materials.[3] In this approach, I follow the footsteps of John J. McGavin and Greg Walker's *Imagining Spectatorship* (2016) in which the bibliography section presents primary sources of different form and format (editions, images, manuscripts, and web resources), breaking with the conventional, hierarchical ordering of information that prioritizes physical archival sources over digitized ones.[4] The COVID-19 pandemic has taught us that we cannot always physically access an archival document, and by offering links to scans of manuscript sources, the study of early texts can be made a more inclusive, and less privileged act. I hope to encourage readers of this book, especially student readers, to use the links to digitized (archival) material interactively; to not take any author's word—including my own—for claims made, but to, whenever possible, return to the original, to see for themselves what is written in the original material, and what constitutes the product of interpretation.

[3] Please note that in this book URLs are provided in the footnotes for primary source material, but that DOI links to secondary source material are only given in the Bibliography. Also note that, despite the book's preference for (digitized) archival material, this book has also made use of calendars or registers, such as the *Letters and Papers* and *Calendar of State Papers*. When in this book I referred to a digitized primary source of which I was also aware that it had been calendared, I have cited both so as to enable comparison.
[4] John J. McGavin and Greg Walker, *Imagining Spectatorship: From the Mysteries to the Shakespearean Stage* (Oxford: Oxford University Press, 2016), Bibliography, 185–97.

CREDITS

Portions of Chapter 1 of this book originally appeared in Nadia T. van Pelt, 'John Blanke's Wages: No Business Like Show Business', *Medieval English Theatre* 44 (2023), 3–35. These portions are reprinted with permission from the editors of *Medieval English Theatre*, for which I am most grateful.

Chapter 2 of this book originally appeared as, 'Katherine of Aragon's Deathbed: why Chapuys Brought a Fool', *Early Theatre* 24:1 (2021), 63–87. https://doi.org/10.12745/et.24.1.4357 I am grateful to the editors of *Early Theatre* for their permission to reprint this work.

All quotations from *The Receyt of the Ladie Kateryne*, ed. by Gordon Kipling, EETS no. 296 (Oxford: Oxford University Press, 1990), are by permission of the Council of the Early English Text Society.

All quotations from Antonio de la TORRE and E.A. de la TORRE, *Cuentas de Gonzalo de Baeza, Tesorero de Isabel la Católica* (2 vols; Madrid: Consejo Superior de Investigaciones Científicas, 1955–1956), and all quotations from Antonio de la TORRE, (ed.), *La Casa de Isabel la Católica* (Madrid, Consejo Superior de Investigaciones Científicas, 1954), are by permission of the Consejo Superior de Investigaciones Científicas.

Citations from William Tydeman, ed., *The Medieval European Stage, 500–1550* (Cambridge: Cambridge University Press, 2001) © Reproduced with permission of The Licensor through PLSclear.

Every effort has been made to trace the copyright holders for quoted material. Where this has not proved to be possible, I ask the copyright holder to contact Oxford University Press, and we will attempt to rectify this for any future editions.

ACKNOWLEDGEMENTS

As with any book project, massive debts were incurred, and I would like to express my heartfelt thanks to everyone who has been a part of this. None of this would have been possible if it weren't for the staff at TU Delft Library, in particular Will Roestenburg, who have been exceptionally helpful and encouraging. I would also like to thank the staff at Gelders Archief, Arnhem, for helping me with my research on site, and for making digitally available the Arnhem Charter so that this can now be accessed by the wider public. For guiding me through the Librije in the Walburgiskerk in Zutphen, I thank Jan Bedaux; it was a great privilege to visit this beautiful library and access its well-preserved treasures; the 1519-printed edition of Erasmus's *Moriae Encomium* referred to in Chapter 2 was read there.

I am very grateful to those who have read and responded to parts of this book, in particular to Greg Walker, who read all of it, and made very generous suggestions which have greatly helped me improve this book, and Sarah Carpenter, Clare Egan, Wim Hüsken, and John J. McGavin who read parts of it, and kindly shared their expertise and wisdom. Meg Twycross and Elisabeth Dutton gave extremely helpful feedback that provided me with tools, early on in the project, that enabled tackling some of its more challenging aspects. Gratitude is also extended to Elaine Treharne, to the anonymous reviewers at Oxford University Press, and to Jo Spillane for her guidance during the publication process. Chapter 2 was previously published as an article in *Early Theatre* (2021), and I thank Nicole Lamont and Michael Angell for kind suggestions during its editing process. Erin Kelly is thanked for her encouragement and her vote of confidence. At TU Delft, I thank Sören Johnson for lively discussions and moral support.

To Peter Greenfield I owe thanks for his kindly sharing *REED: Hampshire* material prior to publication; Hilary Doda and Zoe Screti are thanked for sharing with me their photos of archival material, which was incredibly generous. Anna Augustyniak, Elisa Fuhrmann, Renske Janssen, and Éloïse Ruby should also be mentioned here: thank you for all your help. A special mention goes out to Laura Marienus for her invaluable work on the transcription of the Arnhem manuscript. And to my old English teacher, Kevin Schuck, who opened the door to a second language in which I could write.

Some of the material in this book was presented at conferences and symposiums and I am grateful for the rigorous and helpful feedback given; I would like to particularly acknowledge the Medieval English Theatre conference series, at which I was given the opportunity to try out ideas and methodologies in a convivial context.

Finally, I would like to thank Danny for his unwavering support and sense of humour; and, of course, my parents, Krijn and Thérèse. Their taking me along to castles and museums when I was a child led to an enduring fascination with anything medieval and early modern.

CONTENTS

LIST OF ILLUSTRATIONS

LIST OF ABBREVIATIONS

AGS	Archivo General de Simancas
BL	The British Library
Casa	TORRE, Antonio de la, (ed.), *La Casa de Isabel la Católica* (Madrid, Consejo Superior de Investigaciones Científicas, 1954)
CSPS	G.A. Bergenroth et al., eds., *Calendar of State Papers, Spain*, 19 vols (London: 1862–1954).
CSPV	Rawdon Brown et al., eds., *Calendar of State Papers, Venice*, 38 vols (London: 1864–1947)
Cuentas	TORRE, Antonio de la, and TORRE, E.A. de la, (eds.), *Cuentas de Gonzalo de Baeza, Tesorero de Isabel la Católica* (Madrid, Consejo Superior de Investigaciones Científicas, 1955–1956), vol. 1 and 2
EEBO	Early English Books Online
EETS	The Early English Text Society
EMH	*Early Music History*
ET	*Early Theatre*
GldA	Gelders Archief, Arnhem
HJ	*The Historical Journal*
JMH	*Journal of Medieval History*
JSA	*Journal of the Society of Archivists*
JWCI	*Journal of the Warburg and Courtauld Institutes*
LP	*Letters and Papers, Foreign and Domestic, of the Reign of Henry VIII, 1509–47*, ed. J.S. Brewer, J. Gairdner and R.H. Brodie (21 vols, 1862–1932)
METh	*Medieval English Theatre*
Normore, *Feast*	Christina Normore, *A Feast for the Eyes: Art, Performance & the Late Medieval Banquet* (Chicago, IL: University of Chicago Press, 2015)

ODNB	*Oxford Dictionary of National Biography*
P&P	*Past & Present*
PPE Henry	N.H. Nicolas, ed., *The Privy Purse Expenses of King Henry VIII* (London, 1827)
PPE Mary	Frederick Madden, ed., *Privy Purse Expenses of the Princess Mary* (London: W. Pickering, 1831)
REED	Records of Early English Drama
Receyt	Gordon Kipling, ed., *The Receyt of the Ladie Kateryne*, EETS, o.s. 296 (Oxford: Oxford University Press, 1990)
RQ	*Renaissance Quarterly*
RR	*Renaissance and Reformation*
RS	*Renaissance Studies*
Rutland	William Jerdan, ed., *Rutland Papers: Original Documents Illustrative of the Courts and Times of Henry VII and Henry VIII, selected from the private archives of His Grace the Duke of Rutland* (London: Camden Society, 1842)
SCJ	*Sixteenth Century Journal*
TNA	The National Archives
TKVNM	*Tijdschrift van de Koninklijke Vereniging voor Nederlandse Muziekgeschiedenis*

A NOTE ON NAMES

Readers of this book will notice that most of the names of the 'main players' on the stage of the European courts referred to in this book are presented using the English variations of the names. We see this in Charles V, Francis I, Isabella of Castile, and Ferdinand of Aragon. But also, for example, in the decision to refer to Jadwiga Jagiellonka as Hedwig Jagiellon, and to refer to Sebastian Giustinian in the understanding that this was not how he would have been addressed in Venice. When an original form of a name has been more dominant in current scholarship, the frequently used form was used to make it easier for readers to connect what they have read elsewhere to what is presented here (e.g., note that I refer to Katherine of Aragon's sister as 'Juana', not 'Joanna'). For relatively lesser-known persons of interest, I have used the names as they are presented in the primary sources, thus, for example, Richard Berde, instead of Richard Beard.

A NOTE ON CAPITALIZATION

Throughout the book, the word 'Black' is spelled with a capital when it refers to people or studies. The word 'white' is not capitalized. When directly quoting sources, I retain the original capitalization throughout. Furthermore, when 'Black' or 'white' can be identified as a name or moniker, it is capitalized, such as for example in Jean Blanchetête [Jean Whitehead].

| 1 |

Queen's Trumpet or Second Fiddle

Forging alliances

This book explores cross-language and transnational perspectives pertaining to interactions at, or with, the court of Henry VIII. The first chapter, however, must take us back one generation earlier to the court of Henry VII, and addresses Katherine of Aragon's (1485–1536) arrival in England as the intended bride for Arthur Tudor (1486–1502). As such this chapter provides a framework that helps us better to understand the princess's later fulfilment of the role of Henry VIII's queen, and sheds light on Iberian influences within the Tudor court. Furthermore, the chapter serves as a methodological case study to show how engaging with Spanish as well as Francophone Burgundian sources alongside the better-known English records, can offer new perspectives on aspects of Tudor court culture which have so far been taken for granted. This approach provides a foundation for the remainder of the book.

I will first set the scene. The house of Tudor was a 'new' royal dynasty, established after Henry VII's victory over Richard III at Bosworth in 1485. In order to consolidate the status of his house, Henry sought to form alliances with the established monarchies in Europe, such as with Isabella of Castile (1451–1504) and Ferdinand of Aragon (1452–1516), who had themselves started as 'New Monarchs', to use Steven Gunn's term, at the beginning of their reigns, having had to fight for their

Intercultural Explorations and the Court of Henry VIII. Nadia T. van Pelt, Oxford University Press.
© Nadia T. van Pelt (2024). DOI: 10.1093/oso/9780192863447.003.0001

crowns just as Henry had.[1] Wasting no time in arranging his two-year-old son's marriage to that of one of the young daughters of Spain, later known as Katherine of Aragon, Henry initiated preliminary contracts and opened negotiations as early as 1488.[2] A breakthrough was reached in 1489, and in March of that year Isabella and Ferdinand signed the Treaty of Medina del Campo.[3] On this festive occasion the English delegates were treated to 'jousts and bull fights', as reported by the diplomat Roger Machado, perhaps of Portuguese descent, who served Henry VII on a number of foreign missions.[4] Yet outward goodwill aside, it would take another decade of to-ing and fro-ing before the monarchs of Castile and Aragon were prepared to let Katherine sail off to England.[5]

Conditions were to be met by both parties. 'Spanish diplomats, who had to negotiate with the [English] king, recognized his extreme cunning', writes Sydney Anglo.[6] And indeed, bargaining topics between Henry and the *Reyes Católicos*, as Isabella and Ferdinand would be

---

[1] Steven Gunn, 'Henry VII in Context: Problems and Possibilities', *History* 92:3 (2007), 301–17 (305).

[2] See, for example, Sydney Anglo, 'The London Pageants for the Reception of Katherine of Aragon: November 1501', *JWCI* 26:1/ 2 (1963), 53–89 (53). A temporary agreement was signed by Queen Isabella and King Ferdinand on 6 July 1488. MINISTERIO DE CULTURA Y DEPORTE Archivo General de Simancas, Patronato Real, Capitulaciones con Inglaterra, PTR, LEG, 52, 135 (6 July 1488). Available at: http://pares.mcu.es/ParesBusquedas20/catalogo/description/2207858 [Accessed on: 22.03.2023]. Readers will find a fine example of the signatures of the *Reyes Católicos* halfway down the page on the right side.

[3] MINISTERIO DE CULTURA Y DEPORTE Archivo General de Simancas, Patronato Real, Capitulaciones con Inglaterra, PTR, LEG, 52, 29 (approx. on or after 27 March 1489). Available at: http://pares.mcu.es/ParesBusquedas20/catalogo/description/2207751 [Accessed on: 22.03.2023].

[4] *CSPS* vol. 1, #33 (1489). See also, Adrian Ailes, 'Machado, Roger [Ruy]', *ODNB*, Oxford University Press (version 23 September 2004). https://doi.org/10.1093/ref:odnb/17527

[5] Katherine's departure was a strong political bargaining point. In a 1498 letter, de Puebla writes that the English king and queen were hoping to receive Katherine in the following year, supposedly to start her cultural assimilation by learning the English language and customs, but, he warns, underlying these suggestions was Henry's readiness to start a war with France that, considering the recent peace between the *Reyes Católicos* and the king of France, would not be in their interest. MINISTERIO DE CULTURA Y DEPORTE Archivo General de Simancas, Patronato Real, Capitulaciones con Inglaterra, PTR, LEG, 52, 144. Available at: http://pares.mcu.es/ParesBusquedas20/catalogo/description/2207867 [Accessed on 22.03.2023]. Catalogued in: *CSPS* vol. 1, #227 (25 September 1498).

[6] Sydney Anglo, 'Ill of the Dead. The Posthumous Reputation of Henry VII', *RS* 1:1 (1987), 27–47 (28).

titled by Pope Alexander VI in 1496,[7] included, among other things, the treatment of Spanish merchants in English territories, and—with eerie foresight—the specifications of Katherine's dowry lands to be supplied by Henry should Katherine become a widow. Furthermore, Katherine's place in the Spanish line of inheritance needed to be formally addressed before the alliance could be cemented by marriage. The tenuous relationship that both royal houses had cultivated with France was also on the agenda. Isabella and Ferdinand were, however, particularly worried about the stability of the English throne, and about potential pretenders to the crown, such as Perkin Warbeck, whose execution led Dr Rodrigo Gonsales de Puebla—a diplomat resident in England—to write to his patrons: 'There have always been pretenders to the crown of England; but now that Perkin and the son of the Duke of Clarence have been executed, there does not remain "a drop of doubtful Royal blood", the only Royal blood being the true blood of the King, the Queen, and, above all, of the Prince of Wales.'[8] Henry VII, it seems, had lived up to the expectations of the *Reyes Católicos* and could now look forward to welcoming his new daughter-in-law.

Burgundian-style splendour

Political expectations aside, Henry also needed to meet implicit social expectations that came with Katherine's imminent arrival in England. Only a few years before, in October 1496, Katherine's sister Juana of Castile (1479–1555) had married the Burgundian Archduke Philippe 'le Beau' (1478–1506), the son of the Holy Roman Emperor Maximilian I (1459–1519). The ceremony and festivities took place in Lier in what is now Belgium. The marital 'deal' had been closed in the understanding that Margaret of Austria (1480–1530), who was Philippe's sister, would marry the Spanish crown Prince Juan (1478–97) to further strengthen the Spanish–Burgundian connection. And indeed, shortly after Juana's arrival, the Spanish fleet that had delivered her to her new husband,

---

[7] Olivia Remie Constable, *To Live Like a Moor: Christian Perceptions of Muslim Identity in Medieval and Early Modern Spain* (Philadelphia, PA: University of Pennsylvania Press, 2018), 5.

[8] *CSPS* vol. 1, #249 (11 January 1500); See also, S.B. Chrimes, *Henry VII* (New Haven, CT: Yale University Press, 1999), 73.

4 | INTERCULTURAL EXPLORATIONS AND THE COURT

sailed off to bring Margaret across the seas to Spain.[9] Juan and Margaret were married in the spring of 1497 in the cathedral of Burgos.[10]

Meanwhile in the Low Countries, Juana had been enthusiastically welcomed by the city of Antwerp, which she passed through on her way to Lier, and had in December 1496 enjoyed a warm civic reception in the city of Brussels where she was honoured with an elaborate *joyeuse entrée* [joyous entry] featuring 'twenty-seven tableaux vivants'.[11] And now that Henry VII was welcoming Juana's sister, it was unthinkable that he would organize a wedding event that was any less impressive than the one hosted by his Burgundian neighbours. As Tess Knighton observes, 'many of those amongst Catherine's Spanish retinue (including a number of musicians serving in the royal household) would also have attended Juana's wedding, and the Tudor king would undoubtedly have been compared with the Burgundian duke, and the English effort measured against the Flemish'.[12]

[9] For the various documents pertaining to this 'double wedding', see ADN, B. 432, in Jules Finot, ed., *Collection des Inventaires des Archives Communales Antérieures a 1790* (Lille: Imprimerie de L. Danel, 1899), vol. 1, part 1, 329. Please note that as the pages of the *Collection des Inventaires* are not numbered, the reader is asked to take the page number as the document page number (counting from title page). For Margaret being brought to Spain using the ships that carried Juana to Flanders: MINISTERIO DE CULTURA Y DEPORTE Archivo General de Simancas, Patronato Real, Capitulaciones con Inglaterra, PTR, LEG, 52, 40 (28 March 1496). Available at: http://pares.mcu.es/ParesBusquedas20/catalogo/description/2207762 [Accessed on: 22.03.2023]. For an English summary: *CSPS* vol. 1, #128. (28 March 1496). See also, Björn R. Tammen, 'A Feast of the Arts: Joanna of Castile in Brussels, 1496', *EMH* 30 (2011), 213–48 (213).

[10] Antonio Rumeu de Armas, ed., *Itinerario de los Reyes Católicos, 1474–1516* (Madrid: Consejo Superior de Investigaciones Científicas, 1974), 233.

[11] Paul Vandenbroeck, 'A Bride Amidst Heroines, Fools and Savages: The Joyous Entry into Brussels by Joanna of Castile, 1496 (Berlin, Kupferstichkabinett, Ms. 78D5)', *Jaarboek Koninklijk Museum voor Schone Kunsten Antwerpen* (2012), 153–94 (153); Laura Weigert, *French Visual Culture and the Making of Medieval Theatre* (Cambridge: Cambridge University Press, 2015), Chapter 1, 26–73; Wim Blockmans and Esther Donckers, 'Self-Representation of Court and City in Flanders and Brabant in the Fifteenth and Early Sixteenth Centuries', in Wim Blockmans and Antheun Janse, eds., *Showing Status: Representation of Social Positions in the Late Middle Ages* (Turnhout: Brepols, 1999), 81–111, esp. 94–6 and 99–107; Gordon Kipling, 'Brussels, Joanna of Castile, and the Art of Theatrical Illustration (1496)', *Leeds Studies in English* 32 (2001), 229–53; Tammen, 'A Feast of the Arts', 214.

[12] Tess Knighton, 'Northern Influence on Cultural Developments in the Iberian Peninsula during the Fifteenth Century', *RS* 1:2 (1987), 221–37 (222); Gordon Kipling, *The Triumph of Honour: Burgundian Origins of the Elizabethan Renaissance*, Publications of the Sir Thomas Browne Institute, General Series 6 (The Hague: Leiden University Press,

The likely pressure caused by this significant threat to Henry's public image was enhanced by the fact that the inhabitants of the Burgundian courts were what we might now call 'trend setters', whose cultural practices and expressions had long been followed by other European courts. Henry VII intended, to cite Kipling's words, to 'stage a festival that would present his court as the equal in magnificence and status to any court in Europe'.[13] And in order to do so, he too saw himself influenced by Burgundian ceremonial culture and fashion. A chronicle text that has preserved an impression of the Tudor–Aragon wedding, titled *The Receyt of the Ladie Kateryne* suggests that this influence was apparent across a number of festive aspects, perhaps most obviously in the organization of the joust. Jousting had been a popular chivalric sport at the court of Edward III,[14] but was now refashioned to reflect the very latest and most 'spectacular . . . dramatic possibilities of the tournament'.[15]

Another event that stands out was a performance featuring a state-of-the-art pageant car of the type that had been previously used in the 'Franco-Burgundian *entremet*' but had not yet been seen in the context of the English court.[16] The car was built to represent a mountain and

1977), 9: 'If Henry were to rank with the princes of Europe, his household would have to provide the plays, tournaments, pageantry, music, and *entrements* necessary to a Burgundian wedding celebration. Only then could Henry hope to match the style of Joanna's wedding to Philip the Handsome at Brussels, or even that other more famous celebration, the wedding of Margaret of York to Charles the Bold at Bruges (1468)'.

[13] Gordon Kipling, ed., *The Receyt of the Ladie Kateryne*, EETS, o.s. 296 (Oxford: Oxford University Press, 1990), xxv. All quotations from *The Receyt of the Ladie Kateryne*, ed. by Gordon Kipling, EETS no. 296 (Oxford: Oxford University Press, 1990), are by permission of the Council of the Early English Text Society.

[14] See for example Philip E. Bennett, Sarah Carpenter, and Louise Gardiner, 'Chivalric Games at the Court of Edward III', *Medium Ævum* 87:2 (2018), 304–42; Sydney Anglo, 'Financial and Heraldic Records of the English Tournament', *JSA* 2:5 (1962), 183–95; Sydney Anglo, 'Archives of the English Tournament: Score Cheques and Lists', *JSA* 2:4 (1961), 153–62.

[15] *Receyt*, xxv.

[16] *Receyt*, xx. Note that the use of the word *entremet* is here understood to mean performances of spectacle. In Chapter 3 the word will be used in a broader sense, acknowledging L.B. Ross's assertion that the term was used to refer to a number of different things: 'Between the thirteenth and fifteenth centuries, some authors appear to use this word in a more restricted meaning to indicate fantastic sculptures, at least in part edible, adorning the table of noble banquets on special occasions: for example, cooked peacocks and swans painted over with saffron to simulate gold or silver leaf, or rendered lifelike by dressing in their own plumage. But others seem to give it a more inclusive interpretation, as they

was so large that it could hold twelve 'fresshe lords, knightes, and men of honour, moost semely and straunge disguysid'.[17] A smaller hill carried twelve 'like disguysid ladis, and on in the topp arrayed aftir the maner of the Princes of Hispayne', who all held musical instruments, such as 'clavycordes, dusymers, clavysymballes, and such othir'.[18] The writer of the *Receyt* remarks that both pageant cars were paraded from the lower end of Westminster Hall until they reached the king and queen, and that the performers 'pleayed upon ther instrumentes all the wey ... so swetly and with such noyse that in my myend it was the furst such plesaunt myrthe and propertie that ever was herd in Englond of longe season'.[19]

The *Receyt* author's description, although somewhat hyperbolic, conveys an image of the artistry and entertainment value of such a performance, in which the harmony of the music complemented the visual harmony of the Burgundian-style pageants, both showcasing the Tudor court's cultural refinement and a healthy dose of international competition. The symbolic reference to a successful and harmonious union between the two royal houses, embodied by the mountain of men and the mountain of ladies, and the homage at the address of the Spanish princess—the 'disguysid ladis' had, after all, been 'arrayed aftir the maner of the Princes of Hispayne'—is reminiscent of the kind of pageants performed for Katherine as she was traversing London and being welcomed by the city.[20] On such occasions, the foreign princess was lauded, and the match between two countries was celebrated, but there could be no mistaking on whose honour such celebration reflected.

The *Receyt* presents Katherine as a recipient of Henry VII's favour and gifts, and at times, bluntly put, as a participant in a Tudor show. Yet, while travelling over land to La Coruña where she was to embark on her sea journey to England, Katherine had made stopovers in cities where she had been honoured in her own right. Anxious to please *la señora*

associate it with both culinary art and courtly spectacles.' L.B. Ross, 'Beyond Eating: Political and Personal Significance of the *Entremets* at the Banquets of the Burgundian Court', in Timothy J. Tomasik and Juliann M. Vitullo, eds., *At the Table: Metaphorical and Material Cultures of Food in Medieval and Early Modern Europe* (Turnhout: Brepols, 2007), 145–66 (146).

[17] *Receyt*, 67.
[18] *Receyt*, 67.
[19] *Receyt*, 67.
[20] Anglo, 'The London Pageants', 53–89.

Princesa de Gales as she is referred to in the documents, the city officials of Zamora contacted her *Camarero Mayor* [major-domo] in order
to confirm the visit and to establish suitable entertainment to please
the princess, and on Saturday 19 June 1501 she finally arrived. She was
welcomed in the city with gifts, and rich foods, and entertained with
bullfights to honour her stay.[21] Although no documents are extant nar-
rating the exact procedure of the visit, Ladero Quesada has suggested
that it would have followed regular protocol: the princess would have
been received outside the city walls, welcomed through speeches by the
relevant authorities, after which the princess would go in procession
through the festively decorated streets of Zamora, filled with citizens
and people from nearby regions.[22] At the Plaza de San Juan where the
town hall can be found, the captain García Alonso formally presented
his troops, after which the princess would have visited the church of San
Pedro where the relics of the city's patron saint would be venerated. A
banquet, gift-giving, and a bullfight would have followed.[23] Taking the
role Katherine performed individually in Zamora as a comparative element, one may wonder if perhaps the expectations held by the Princess
of Wales and her parents were more aligned with the actual unfolding
of the wedding events than the *Receyt* suggests. In other words, what is
the *Receyt* not telling us?

A note on source material

The *Receyt* was written as a festival book, and as such, the views found
in the *Receyt* offer a perspective dictated by the genre in which they were
conveyed. As Helen Watanabe-O'Kelly reminds the reader:

> Festival books often present the event they are describing—the
> solemn entry, the wedding celebration, the tournament—as one of
> the great deeds, the *res gestae*, of the prince who is the central figure.
> The whole purpose of these works is to present events from the

---

[21] M.F. Ladero Quesada, 'Recibir princesas y enterrar reinas (Zamora 1501 y 1504)',
Espacio Tiempo Y Forma. Serie III, Historia Medieval 13 (2000), 119–37 (131). See also,
p. 124.

[22] Ladero Quesada, 'Recibir princesas y enterrar reinas', 124.

[23] Ladero Quesada, 'Recibir princesas y enterrar reinas', 124.

standpoint of whoever has commissioned the festival book and give them the desired official interpretation.[24]

In order to further interpret the event, readers can refer to Anglophone sources such as *The Traduction & Mariage of the Princesse* (1500), a book of ordinances devised for the wedding,[25] and the financial accounts in the Chamber Books of Henry VII,[26] which illuminate the efforts made in preparation for the event, and offer glimpses of gifts and honours bestowed on delegates and participants from overseas, suggestive of an extension of respect given towards the foreign princess. However, even when these additional sources are consulted, many questions remain unanswered.

In what follows, the case study of Katherine's musicians will be used to show how non-Anglophone source material can be used to better understand the well-known English sources, and to complement, question, and at times problematize ideas about Katherine's entourage that have so far been taken for granted. Given that Katherine's musicians had been hand-picked by Queen Isabella to accompany her daughter abroad, and were funded by her household, this chapter relies on a number of sources pertaining to the house of Castile, such as Gonzalo de Baeza's *Cuentas* and Alonso de Morales's *Data*, which comprise the financial accounts of Queen Isabella, and *La Casa de Isabel la Católica*, detailing the make-up of staff in the queen's household. Furthermore, a variety of sources from the Archivo General de Simancas, as well as other Spanish archives are included. Francophone Burgundian source material further contextualizes this evidence.

The primary records discussed in this chapter offer the names and available additional information about a number of musicians who travelled with Katherine on her way to her new country. These sources furthermore reveal that the court of Henry VII in 1501 during the wedding festivities was both a more international place than may be expected, and a more culturally and ethnically diverse place than has

---

[24] Helen Watanabe-O'Kelly, "'True and Historical Descriptions'? European Festivals and the Printed Record,' in Jeroen Duindam and Sabine Dabringhaus, eds., *The Dynastic Centre and the Provinces* (Leiden: Brill, 2014), 150–9 (152).

[25] *The Traduction & Mariage of the Princesse* (London: Richard Pynson, 1500; STC (2nd edn.) / 4814), EEBO. https://eebo.chadwyck.com/home.

[26] *The Chamber Books of Henry VII and Henry VIII, 1485–1521*, eds. M.M. Condon, S.P. Harper and L. Liddy, and S. Cunningham and J. Ross. https://www.tudorchamberbooks. org/.

thus far been assumed. To be precise, it can be demonstrated that the African presence at the Tudor court was greater than has so far been thought, and that the well-known trumpeter John Blanke was not the first Black musician to perform in this context.[27] This chapter introduces to Tudor studies the high-paid trumpet player Alfonso or Alonso de Valdenebro, also known as Alonso '*el Negro*', and situates him at sea with Katherine of Aragon in 1501, on his way to England.[28] This information challenges previously held presumptions about the make-up of Katherine's entourage, as well as about the status of her members of staff.

Katherine's musicians at play

The earliest English-language reference to Katherine's musicians performing on English soil can be found in the Plymouth 1501–02 Receivers' Accounts, incorporated in the Records of Early English

[27] John Blanke has received much attention in publications and public engagement efforts such as the educational pages of the National Archives and the John Blanke Project. See for example, Michael Ohajuru, 'The John Blanke Project', in Gretchen H. Gerzina, ed., *Britain's Black Past* (Liverpool: Liverpool University Press, 2020), 7–25. John Blanke was first identified by Sydney Anglo as the Black trumpet player visually represented on the Westminster Tournament Roll in Anglo, The Court Festivals of Henry VII: A Study Based Upon the Account Books of John Heron, Treasurer of the Chamber' *Bulletin of John Rylands Library* 43 (1960/1961) 12–45, at 42 and footnote 3. This was repeated in Miranda Kaufmann, *Black Tudors* (London: Oneworld, 2017), Chapter 1, 7–31, and in Miranda Kaufmann, 'John Blanke (*fl.* 1507–1512)' *ODNB*, Oxford University Press, https://doi.org/10.1093/ref:odnb/107145. See also, K.J.P. Lowe, 'The Stereotyping of Black Africans in Renaissance Europe', in T.F. Earle and K.J.P. Lowe, eds., *Black Africans in Renaissance Europe* (Cambridge: Cambridge University Press, 2005), 17–47 (39–40); Peter Fryer, *Staying Power: The History of Black People in Britain* (London: Pluto Press, 2018), 4.
[28] Within the field of early music studies, Tess Knighton has importantly noted Alonso to be 'one of four trumpeters who travelled to England with Katherine of Aragon in 1501'. Knighton, 'Instruments, Instrumental Music and Instrumentalists: Traditions and Transitions', in Tess Knighton, ed., *Companion to Music in the Age of the Catholic Monarchs* (Leiden: Brill, 2017), 97–144 (116); See also: Tess Knighton and Kenneth Kreitner, *The Music of Juan de Anchieta* (London: Routledge, 2019), 19. Note that Knighton refers to the musician as 'Alfonso', which can be observed to be the spelling used in e.g., *Casa*, 94–6, and *Cuentas*, vol. 2, 78. I refer to the musician as 'Alonso', following, e.g., MINISTERIO DE CULTURA Y DEPORTE Archivo General de Simancas, Cámara de Castilla, CCA, CED, 6, 101, 4 (15 May 1503), and *Cuentas*, vol. 2, 583. I do so in the understanding that he may equally have been known to the people around him as 'Alfonso'. Studies of Tudor history have not yet referred to Alonso. I hope through this interdisciplinary lens to introduce new information and contexts to the study of the courts of Henry VII and Henry VIII.

Drama. Katherine and her entourage had originally been expected to reach English shores at Southampton, where a welcoming committee was awaiting them. The winds and currents had, however, unexpectedly carried the princess and her servants to Plymouth, where the city officials had been unprepared for her arrival.[29] Therefore, any entertainment to be had was likely to have presented itself rather at the last-minute and would need to be provided by local musicians resident in Devon, and by the musicians who had come fresh off the ship. Katherine's providing her hosts with musical entertainment is revealed by a payment to two of 'the prync*es* ys mylstrell*es*'.[30] Some further diversion was provided by one of her high-ranking countrymen referred to as the 'erle' of Spain,[31] as evidenced by a payment that reads: 'It*em* to the Erle ys mylstrell*es* of Spayne xx d'.[32] Presumably the same musicians were rewarded for their services as documented in Henry VII's book of payments, which refer to 'the pr*i*ncesse stylmynstr*elles*', and to 'therle of Spayn trumpett*es*'.[33] The word 'minstrel' has in the past caused confusion, as it can be interpreted to mean 'servant'. Richard Rastall has, for example, noted that 'the word "minstrelsy" covered

[29] For Alcaraz's message to Queen Isabella informing her of Katherine's arrival at Plymouth: MINISTERIO DE CULTURA Y DEPORTE Archivo General de Simancas, Patronato Real, Capitulaciones con Inglaterra, PTR, LEG, 53, 43 (approx. 4 October 1501). Available at: http://pares.mcu.es/ParesBusquedas20/catalogo/description/2207961 [Accessed on: 22.03.2023].

[30] John M. Wasson, ed., *REED: Devon* (Toronto: University of Toronto Press, 1986), 215.

[31] This cryptic entry likely refers to Diego Fernández de Córdoba, who carried the title '*conde de Cabra*' [count or earl of Cabra]. His mother was the Castilian noblewoman doña María de Mendoza. See, Rosana de Andrés Díaz, *El ultimo decenio del reinado de Isabel I a través de la tesorería de Alonso de Morales (1495–1504)* (Valladolid: Secretariado de Publicaciones e Intercambio Editorial, Universidad de Valladolid, 2004), 567, entry 3.625 describing him as his mother's son; 739, entry 4.556 for a reference to his having been to England with the Princess of Wales; 659, entry 4.096 referring to the three dignitaries who were in England with Katherine: '*el arzobispo de Santiago, el conde de Cabra y el obispo de Mallorca*' [the archbishop of Santiago, the count (or earl) of Cabra and the bishop of Mallorca]; 673, entry 4.170 'places' the *conde de Cabra* and Katherine on a ship together sailing for England through payment details to the naval commander Martin Ibañez de Luxarra, which refers to him [Luxarra] as '*Maeste de la nao en que pasó el conde de Cabra a Inglaterra con la Princesa de Gales el año pasado de 1501*'. Note that the *conde* had his own entourage (and hence his own musicians).

[32] Wasson, ed., *REED: Devon*, 215.

[33] *The Chamber Books of Henry VII and Henry VIII, 1485–1521*, ed. M.M. Condon, S.P. Harper and L. Liddy, and S. Cunningham and J. Ross, TNA, TNA, E101/415/3, f. 74v. https://www.dhi.ac.uk/chamber-books/folio/E101_415_3_fo_074v.xml.

many types of entertainment in the Middle Ages—not only the instrumental performance of those known as "the king's minstrels", but the work of the king's fool, his bearward, the keeper of his lions and leopards, and many others'.[34] Rastall's work however also identifies a 'still minstrel' as 'a player of a <u>bas</u> instrument' (emphasis Rastall's).[35] Introducing a different perspective, Eileen Sharpe Pearsall suggested that still minstrels 'functioned primarily as administrators rather than performers'.[36] Pearsall's view has more recently been opposed by Theodor Dumitrescu:

> There is really no good reason to believe that servants described as minstrels were not musicians, and the word 'still' is readily explained as the English term to refer to the standard bas music: soft, indoor instruments, separate in type and function from 'loud'/ haut instruments. The opposition of these English terms is clearly observable, for example, in a 1503 musicians' livery list which groups the 'Stil mynstrelles' just before the 'lowed mynstrelles' (the sackbuts and the shawms).[37]

It is likely that Katherine's 'stylmynstr*elles*' were not administrative staff but instrumentalists of the type that provided indoor dancing music. They can be seen in action on the day of Katherine and Arthur's first meeting, helping to break the ice, and allowing for an activity that enabled the two young people—who had to make do with the rather formal Latin as a common language in which to communicate—to get a sense of each other. *The Receyt of the Ladie Kateryne* records:

> . . . [The] Lord Prince visited the Ladie in her owne chamber. And then she and her ladies let call their mynstrelles, and with right goodly behaviour and maner they solaced theymself with the disportes of

[34] Richard Rastall, 'The Minstrels of the English Royal Households, 25 Edward I—1 Henry VIII: An Inventory', *R.M.A. Research Chronicle* 4 (1964), 1–41 (1). Richard Rastall's valuable book, with Andrew Taylor, *Minstrels and Minstrelsy in Late Medieval England* (Woodbridge: The Boydell Press, 2023) unfortunately appeared too late to be taken into account in writing this chapter.

[35] Rastall, 'The Minstrels of the English Royal Households', 28, footnote 2.

[36] Eileen Sharpe Pearsall, *Tudor Court Musicians, 1485–1547: Their Number, Status, and Function* (Unpublished doctoral thesis, New York University, 1986), vol. 1, 79–80. Cf: Theodor Dumitrescu, *The Early Tudor Court and International Musical Relations* (Aldershot: Ashgate, 2007), 102.

[37] Dumitrescu, *The Early Tudor Court*, 102.

daunsyng, and afterward the Lorde Prince in like demeanure with
the Lady Gulford daunced right plesant and honourably.[38]

In addition to musicians with a particular expertise in creating an atmosphere for dancing or other indoor entertainment, the princess also
brought instrumentalists who could produce louder music, and who
participated in a number of ceremonial, celebrative, and recreational
activities.[39] For example, when Katherine first showed herself to the citizens of London in procession, she moved along with the sounds of '...
such trumpettes, shalmewes, and sakbotes to a great nombre as cam
with the Princes owte of Spayne'.[40] It is highly conceivable that some
of these loud instrumentalists also participated in the wedding ceremony, which took place at St. Paul's cathedral, referred to in the extant
ceremonial ordinances as *The Traduction & Mariage of the Princesse*.
The ordinances prescribed that the 'trompettis' were to signal the presence of the young royalty on their arrival in the public sphere outside
the palace, as they were instructed to 'blowe contynuelly after the first
comynge oute of the princesse out of the great gate of the saide paleys
tyll the tyme she be in the churce upon the haute place'.[41] On leaving the church again, Arthur and Katherine were to be accompanied
with music made by a larger variety of instruments, so the *Traduction*
decreed:

> as sone as the seide prince and princesse shall begynne to departe
> from the saide haute place than shall all the mynstrellis euery man
> after his faculte (...) do their poyntis in musike contynuelly as it shall
> come to their course'.[42]

Katherine's musicians had an important role to play in the princess's
self-representation. But who were they and what do we know about
them? The following section turns to a trumpet player known as 'John

---

[38] *Receyt*, 8.
[39] The Spanish chronicler Andrés Bernáldez famously wrote about a royal entry that
the instruments 'made such a din that if a bird happened to fly past, they made it fall
from the sky into the crowd'. Cf; Tess Knighton and Carmen Morte García, 'Ferdinand of
Aragon's Entry into Valladolid in 1513: The Triumph of a Christian King', *EMH* 18 (1999),
119–63 (126).
[40] *Receyt*, 31.
[41] *The Traduction & Mariage of the Princesse*, EEBO, B1v.
[42] *The Traduction & Mariage of the Princesse*, EEBO, B2v.

de Cecil' who has traditionally been assumed to have entered the English Chamber Books after having been a member of Katherine's entourage. Using Francophone evidence written under the auspices of the Burgundian itinerant court of Philippe le Beau to complement Henry VII's financial records, I problematize this understanding, as well as scrutinizing the meaning of the word 'Spanish' in the English source material.

Jehan de Cécil, *espagnol*

The English chamber records suggest that a new trumpet player was taken on in Henry VII's service in January 1501/2 when a payment was made to 'the new trumpett in Re*ward* xx s'.[43] Coincidentally, a person by the name of 'John de Ceull, trumpeter' is provided with 'banners with the Royal Arms for their instruments' on 22 January 1501/2 following the king's warrant to the Great Wardrobe.[44] The first payment recorded that mentions de Cecil by name appears later in the year on 4 June 1502: 'Item for John de Cecely the trumpet wag*es* xx s'.[45] During de Cecil's royal service at the English court, the instrumentalist participated in a number of high-profile ceremonies. He played at the funeral of Henry VII's queen, Elizabeth of York, for which de Cecil (here spelled 'John decessid') was listed as one of the 'King's Trumpettes', and was given 4 yards of cloth for 'mourning liveries' on 23 February 1502/3.[46] In May 1509 de Cecil appears again as one of the 'King's Trumpets' at King Henry VII's funeral,[47] as well as at King Henry VIII's coronation in

[43] *The Chamber Books of Henry VII and Henry VIII, 1485–1521*, ed. M.M. Condon, S.P. Harper and L. Liddy, and S. Cunningham and J. Ross, TNA, E101/415/3, f. 80v. https://www.dhi.ac.uk/chamber-books/folio/E101_415_3_fo_080v.xml. De Cecil is also addressed in: Nadia T. van Pelt, 'John Blanke's Wages: No Business Like Show Business', *Medieval English Theatre* 44 (2023), 3–35.
[44] Maria Hayward, *The Great Wardrobe Accounts of Henry VII and Henry VIII* (Woodbridge: London Record Society: The Boydell Press, 2012), 260; Andrew Ashbee, ed., *Records of English Court Music: 1485–1558* (London: Routledge, 1993), vol. 7, 16. Note that Ashbee dates the record 22 January and Hayward 23 January.
[45] *The Chamber Books of Henry VII and Henry VIII, 1485–1521*, ed. M.M. Condon, S.P. Harper and L. Liddy, and S. Cunningham and J. Ross, TNA, E101/415/3, f. 97v. https://www.dhi.ac.uk/chamber-books/folio/E101_415_3_fo_097v.xml.
[46] Ashbee, ed., *Records of English Court Music*, 20.
[47] *LP* vol. 1, #20 (11 May 1509); Ashbee, ed., *Records of English Court Music*, 25.

June of the same year.[48] In September 1514 he was one of eight trumpet players 'attending the French Queen [Mary Tudor] into France' where she was to be married to Louis XII (1462–1515).[49]

De Cecil had previously served at the Burgundian court, and was identified by Van Doorslaer as '*Jehan de Cécille, espagnol qui retourna dans son pays*', found in the '*comptes*' of October 1496.[50] Localizing the musician in this context is significant in a number of ways. It shows de Cecil's mobility between the courts of Burgundy and his native country, and suggests that he had experience of other cultures before arriving in England. It also provides evidence for John de Cecil's nationality as perceived by the Burgundian account taker, something which the English sources do not do. Dumitrescu suggested that John de Cecil was one of the 'Spanish players from Katherine's retinue' before taking the job at the Tudor court.[51] Michelle L. Beer, relying on Dumitrescu's work, has however restated his claim with a small but distinctive alteration. She noted that de Cecil was 'one of the Spanish trumpeters in Catherine's *wedding party*' [emphasis mine].[52] And although Beer does not explain why she modified Dumitrescu's claim, a joint reading of Francophone and English source material does indeed suggest that de Cecil likely participated at the wedding, and was afterwards taken on by Henry VII, but also that he had not arrived as part of Katherine's own retinue. He had likely been part of a group of instrumentalists who had been sent on a different mission.

A chronicle extant in the K.K. Hofbibliothek in Vienna records an account of the journey made by Philippe of Burgundy and Juana of Castile in 1501 and 1502. It shows that in early January 1501/2 a group of trumpet players under the patronage of King Ferdinand met with Philippe and Juana in Guîtres, France. The musicians had been sent

---

[48] *LP* vol. 1, #82 (24 June 1509); Ashbee, ed., *Records of English Court Music*, 29.

[49] *LP* vol. 1, #3320 (30 September 1514). Here, the trumpeter's name is spelled 'John Cecylia'.

[50] 'Jehan de Cécille, Spaniard who returned to his country'. G. van Doorslaer, 'Lachapelle musicale de Philippe le Beau', *Revue belge d'archeologie et d'histoire de l'art* 4 (1934), 21–57 (39).

[51] Dumitrescu, *The Early Tudor Court*, 33.

[52] Michelle L. Beer, *Queenship at the Renaissance Courts of Britain: Catherine of Aragon and Margaret Tudor, 1503–1533* (Woodbridge: Boydell and Brewer, 2018), 94. Note that she also generally states, 'They both [Katherine of Aragon and Margaret Tudor] brought musicians with them to their new kingdoms as part of their wedding parties'.

to honour the archducal couple with ceremonial greetings, and, no doubt, in order to contribute to the visual and auditory impact they would make on all persons they encountered while travelling to Spain.[53] The record describing the encounter reveals that Ferdinand's trumpet players were well-recognizable as such, wearing Spanish livery: '*huyt trompettes du Roy despaigne tous habilliez dung manteau de rouge drap a la maniere despaigne, et vne barette sur leur teste de velours vert*'[54] [eight trumpet players of the King of Spain all dressed in coats made of red cloth in the manner of Spain, and on their heads a beret of green velours].

The chronicle account continues to describe how the trumpet players had arrived in France:

> Lesquelz trompettes auoient este enuoyez en engleterre cuidant que Monseigneur deust venir par mer, et auoient este auec la fille du Roy despaigne seur de madame larchiducesse que lon enuoya en engleterre pour espouser le prince de galles filz du Roy dengleterre . . .[55]
>
> [These trumpets had been sent to England thinking that *monseigneur* [Philippe of Burgundy] had to come by sea, and had been with the daughter of the King of Spain sister of *madame* [Juana of Castile] the archduchess who was sent to England to marry the Prince of Wales son of the King of England . . .]

Not having anticipated that Philippe would travel by land, the musicians had made a bit of a detour, but found a silver lining in being able to share with Juana the latest news from her sister ('*nouuelles de sa seur la princesse de galles*').[56] For our purpose, it is unfortunate that the narrative does not specify *how* the group of trumpet players had reached

---

[53] Joseph Chmel, ed., *Die Handschriften der K.K. Hofbibliothek in Wien*, vol. 2: *Handschriften* (Vienna: Carl Gerold, 1841), 583. The source is mentioned in María Elena Cuenca Rodríguez, 'Patrocinio Musical en el Viaje de Felipe y Juana a la Península Ibérica a Través la Crónica de Viena', *Revista de Musicología* 42:1 (2019), 17–42 (29). This account in Chmel is referred to in Nadia T. van Pelt, 'John Blanke's hat in the Westminster Tournament Roll', *Notes & Queries* 68:4 (2021), 387–9, gjab156. Lalaing's record of the voyage confirms Philippe and Juana's staying in 'Guitres' on 5 January 1502. Antoine de Lalaing, *Collection des voyages des souverains des Pays-Bas*, ed. Louis Prosper Gachard (Brussels, 1876), vol. 1, 144.

[54] Chmel, ed., *Handschriften*, 583.

[55] Chmel, ed., *Handschriften*, 583.

[56] Chmel, ed., *Handschriften*, 583.

England. Had they joined the ships carrying Katherine and her retinue across the sea, or had they travelled over land, meeting Katherine on arriving at the Tudor court? The suggestion that they 'had been with the daughter of the King of Spain' (*'auoient este auec la fille du Roy despaigne'*) could imply either.[57]

Joining the sources from the different linguistic areas, it appears that the nine trumpet players sent north by Ferdinand of Aragon corresponded to the 'ix trumpett*es* of Spayn' mentioned in the Tudor Chamber books as categorized separately from other 'loud' instrumentalists referred to as 'the pr*i*ncesse trumpett*es*', 'ij other trumpett*es*', and 'therle of Spayn trumpett*es*'.[58] 'The new trumpett' accounted for as John de Cecil in January 1501/2 explains the reduced number of only eight trumpet players arriving with Philippe and Juana in this same month.[59]

The Vienna chronicle, read alongside the English records, can also illuminate other uncertainties. It shows the missing link between de Cecil's Burgundian service in the 1490s and his arrival at the Tudor court, and also allows for a more confident interpretation of his surname as a toponym. If we can place de Cecil in the service of King Ferdinand's household, this enables us to interpret the word '*espagnol*' as used in the Burgundian archival material of 1496,[60] as both more inclusive than readers today might expect, and, in relation to de Cecil, more geographically specific. Antoine de Lalaing's description of Philippe le Beau's journey to Spain in 1506 describes Ferdinand of Aragon as: '*le roy don Fernande d'Arragon, de Naples, de Cecille* [i.e., 'of Sicily'] *et de Jhérusalem*' [emphasis mine].[61] And indeed, Ferdinand had inherited various kingdoms including those of Naples and Sicily, from which follows that a native of Sicily could have been identified as

[57] The scenario in which the musicians travelled independently from Katherine is favoured in Cuenca Rodríguez, 'Patrocinio Musical', 29: '*ocho de los trompetistas del rey Fernando viajaron a Inglaterra donde se encontraron con* [met with] *la infanta Catalina de Aragón para reunirse con los archiduques*' (emphasis added).

[58] *The Chamber Books of Henry VII and Henry VIII, 1485–1521*, ed. M.M. Condon, S.P. Harper and L. Liddy, and S. Cunningham and J. Ross, TNA, E101/415/3, f. 74v. https://www.dhi.ac.uk/chamber-books/folio/E101_415_3_fo_074v.xml.

[59] *The Chamber Books of Henry VII and Henry VIII, 1485–1521*, ed. M.M. Condon, S.P. Harper and L. Liddy, and S. Cunningham and J. Ross, TNA, E101/415/3, f. 80v. https://www.dhi.ac.uk/chamber-books/folio/E101_415_3_fo_080v.xml.

[60] Van Doorslaer, 'Lachapelle musicale de Philippe le Beau', 39.

[61] Lalaing, *Voyages*, 478.

Spanish. One may thus allow for the possibility that *Jehan de Cécil* was a Francophone nickname or toponym indicating a Sicilian heritage.

Furthermore, being able to place John de Cecil in Ferdinand's service explains why in 1511 the trumpet player was sent along on an English mission with Lord Darcy to support the King of Aragon in his so-called African war.[62] De Cecil's being able to interpret between the English and Spanish parties, smoothing the path for discussions was a clear advantage, but his being a familiar face to Ferdinand will have further motived Henry VIII to send de Cecil on this mission.

What's in a name?

The Vienna chronicle also provides two additional pieces of information that more generally facilitate a better understanding of the English material referring to Spanish trumpet players. First of all, it helps to question what is meant when account takers write '*trompette*' or 'trumpet'. We have seen that the text describing the encounter between the archducal couple and the eight heraldic musicians in Guîtres overtly refers to the trumpet players sent by Ferdinand as '*huyt trompettes du Roy despaigne*' [eight trumpets of the King of Spain].[63] Further on, however, the account offers another description of these musicians as '*beaucop de trompettes et de gros tamburins despaigne*' [many trumpets and large drums of Spain].[64] Here the '*tamburins*' [drums] appear to have been previously implied as part of the group of trumpet players. This is not an unusual phenomenon, and by means of an example we

---

[62] 'Item to John de Sycell. and John de Furnes Trumpet*tes* goyng to the king of Aragon with the lorde Darcy for iij monethes wag*es* after the Rate of xvj d the day þᵉ pece. that is to say. May. Juyn. and July xij li'. *The Chamber Books of Henry VII and Henry VIII, 1485–1521*, ed. M.M. Condon, S.P. Harper and L. Liddy, and S. Cunningham and J. Ross, TNA, E36/215, f. 118. https://www.dhi.ac.uk/chamber-books/folio/LL_E36_215_p118.xml. For the term 'African war', see *CSPS* vol. 2, #54 (15 September 1511) describing how Henry Guildford was knighted by Ferdinand of Aragon for his war efforts. This may have been a symbolic gesture considering that when the English arrived, their help was not needed. The year before, in May 1510, Ferdinand had already written to his Viceroy of Naples that he had 'under the pretext of a war with the Moors, provided every thing that is necessary for a war with France'. *CSPS* vol. 2, #47.

[63] Chmel, ed., *Handschriften*, 583.

[64] Chmel, ed., *Handschriften*, 596.

see the following list in de Baeza's financial records for Queen Isabella's household for 1494:

> Trompetas
> A Diego de Cueva, 2.500 mrs.
> A Françisco de Medina, 2.500 mrs.
> A Fernando de Ysla, 2.500 mrs.
> A Juan de Dueñas, atabalero, 5.000 mrs.[65]
> [Trumpet players. To [name], [amount payable in maravedís]. Note that 'Atabalero' translates as 'kettle drum player'].

This practice in conjunction with the information in the Vienna manuscript, suggests that at least one of the 'ix trumpettes of Spayn' mentioned in the English payment accounts was a drummer.[66]

A further point needs to be made about the descriptor '*despaigne*'. In the context of the signalling musicians in Guîtres the descriptor is used to refer to King Ferdinand's trumpet players. Given that the English records take note of this same group of trumpet players as 'trumpettes of Spayn',[67] it appears that the English record taker also equated Ferdinand's players to 'Spanish' players. This may seem like an obvious point to make, were it not that 'Spain' is a collective term used for the various kingdoms under Isabella and Ferdinand's joint rulership. Queen Isabella had her own household and patronized her own musicians. It appears that the Burgundian and English officials responsible for the accounts referred to in the above did not make the distinction between musicians of Aragon or Castile; it was likely not relevant for their accounts. The casual use of '*despaigne*' might reveal a simplistic

---

[65] *Cuentas*, vol. 2, 74. 'mrs.' is an abbreviation for 'maravedís'. Earenfight writes: 'A maravedí was originally a silver or gold coin, akin to the gold dinar, with a value in 1.91 grams of silver in 1303. By the later Middle Ages, the maravedí was only a unit of account and did not circulate.' Theresa Earenfight, 'The Shoes of an Infanta: Bringing the Sensuous, Not Sensible, "Spanish Style" of Catherine of Aragon to Tudor England', in Tracy Chapman Hamilton and Mariah Proctor-Tiffany, eds., *Moving Women Moving Objects (400–1500)* (Leiden: Brill, 2019), 293–317 (293, footnote 2).

[66] *The Chamber Books of Henry VII and Henry VIII, 1485–1521*, ed. M.M. Condon, S.P. Harper and L. Liddy, and S. Cunningham and J. Ross, TNA, E101/415/3, f. 74v. https://www.dhi.ac.uk/chamber-books/folio/E101_415_3_fo_074v.xml.

[67] *The Chamber Books of Henry VII and Henry VIII, 1485–1521*, ed. M.M. Condon, S.P. Harper and L. Liddy, and S. Cunningham and J. Ross, TNA, E101/415/3, f. 74v. https://www.dhi.ac.uk/chamber-books/folio/E101_415_3_fo_074v.xml.

view of the patronage of instrumentalists, and indeed more widely, of the rulership of joint lands, where account takers not used to a queen regnant might not have expected Isabella to have been a political and military force in her own right.[68]

From this follows that for a more precise understanding of Katherine's entourage it is key to keep in mind that the musicians referred to in the Tudor Chamber books as the 'ix trumpettes of Spayn' were trumpet players of Aragon, who relied financially on Ferdinand.[69] Katherine's musicians, referred to in the English records as 'the princesse trumpettes' were on Isabella's payroll.[70] They were trumpets players of Castile.

At sea with Katherine of Aragon

On 20 February 1502 in Sevilla, Queen Isabella's accountant Alonso de Morales paid out a sum of 271,230 *mrs.* to '*Oficiales y personas en una nómina de la princesa*' who had been to England with Katherine.[71] The list mentions most officials by name, but the musicians who were paid out on this occasion were, unfortunately, only indicated as a group. De Morales's account registers: '*a seis trompetas, 60 escudos de oro / a seis menestriles altos, 60 escudos / a dos atabaleros, 20 escudos*' [to six trumpet players, 60 gold *escudos*/to six players of wind instruments, 60 *escudos*/to two kettledrum players, 20 *escudos*].[72] De Morales's *Data* can be supplemented with information from *La Casa de Isabel la Cátolica*, which records four trumpet players connected to the house of Castile as having been to England ('*fue a Ynglaterra*'). Their names are provided as Alfonso de Valdenebro,[73] Gonçalo de Bustamente, Bernardino de

---

[68] Isabella's *Testamento* offers a full description of her titles and lands: *Testamento y Codicilo de Isabel la Católica* (Madrid: Ministerio de Asuntos Exteriores, 1956), 14–15.

[69] *The Chamber Books of Henry VII and Henry VIII, 1485–1521*, ed. M.M. Condon, S.P. Harper and L. Liddy, and S. Cunningham and J. Ross, TNA, E101/415/3, f. 74v. https://www.dhi.ac.uk/chamber-books/folio/E101_415_3_fo_074v.xml.

[70] *The Chamber Books of Henry VII and Henry VIII, 1485–1521*, ed. M.M. Condon, S.P. Harper and L. Liddy, and S. Cunningham and J. Ross, TNA, E101/415/3, f. 74v. https://www.dhi.ac.uk/chamber-books/folio/E101_415_3_fo_074v.xml.

[71] De Andrés Díaz, *El ultimo decenio*, 620–1, entry 3.853.

[72] De Andrés Díaz, *El ultimo decenio*, 621, entry 3.853.

[73] De Valdenebro was replacing Sancho Lopes de Trevyño who had died. *Casa*, 95–6.

Benavente, and Luys de Sepulveda.[74] It is difficult to say whether these four trumpet players all formed part of the group of six trumpet players paid out by de Morales. Luys de Sepulveda according to the *Casa* was paid out until 1502, and is listed in this account as *'finado'* [deceased],[75] and has been identified by previous research as having died in England.[76] De Bustamente was to be paid out until 1502.[77] *La Casa* specifies that different payment constructions were applied in hiring Bernardino de Benavente and Alfonso de Valdenebro. They were each to be paid their specified wages of 25,000 *mrs.* a year; the former to be paid out until 1503, and the latter was paid out in advance in 1501, and received another payment until 1503 through an *albalá*, a royal letter or certificate in which a favour was granted or something else was provided.[78] This *albalá* may correspond to a financial account written up by Gonzalo de Baeza dated 15 May 1503, to which I will refer to next. The indication of the year 1503 may suggest that the latter two musicians remained in England for a longer period of time than de Benavente and de Bustamente had been intended to remain, although it may also simply be an indication of their having been on the queen's payroll, including other missions or services aside the trip to England. Combining these sources, it is therefore a possibility that Katherine travelled with up to ten trumpet players, and at least two drummers. As for setting out together in Katherine's entourage: since the musicians referred to in *La Casa* and Morales's *Data* were paid by Queen Isabella to do this job, they can be placed in the context of the princess's train rather than in the group of Ferdinand's 'trumpet*es* of Spayn'.[79]

[74] *Casa*, 94–6. Note that Gonzalo de Bustamente's full name was Gonzalo Valero de Bustamente: MINISTERIO DE CULTURA Y DEPORTE Archivo General de Simancas, Real Cancillería de los Reyes de Castilla. Registro del Sello de Corte, RGS,LEG,149504,139 (28 April 1495). Available at: http://pares.mcu.es/ ParesBusquedas2o/catalogo/description/1640445?nm [Accessed on: 22.03.2023]. Ferer places de Bustamente in the context of Katherine's sister Juana's musical entourage as well as that of their mother, Queen Isabel: Mary Tiffany Ferer, 'Queen Juana, Empress Isabel, and Musicians at the Royal Courts of Spain (1505–1556)', *TKVNM* 65:1/ 2 (2015), 13–36 (16).

[75] *Casa*, 95.

[76] Pablo F. Cantalapiedra, *Percusión en la Corte de los Reyes Católicos* (Unpublished dissertation, Universidad Autónoma de Madrid, 2015), 39.

[77] *Casa*, 94.

[78] *Casa*, 94–6.

[79] *The Chamber Books of Henry VII and Henry VIII, 1485–1521*, ed. M.M. Condon, S.P. Harper and L. Liddy, and S. Cunningham and J. Ross, TNA, E101/415/3, f. 74v. https:// www.dhi.ac.uk/chamber-books/folio/E101_415_3_fo_074v.xml.

The *Casa* records do not specify that the four trumpet players patronized by Isabella travelled to England at the same time as Katherine, although given their function and the need for a princess to arrive with a musical entourage, this is to be strongly expected. Here, the *Casa* records can be supplemented with the abovementioned financial account written up by Gonzalo de Baeza dated 15 May 1503. This record uniquely and clearly places an *atabalero* [kettledrum player], and a *trompeta* [trumpet player] in Katherine's travelling entourage, and shows that the name of the *trompeta* corresponds to one of the four trumpet players in the *Casa* records:

> Por otra çedula de la Reyna, fecha a 15-V del dicho año, a Alonso de Valdenebro, trompeta de su Alteza, e a Francisco de Dueñas, atabalero, 10.000 mrs., 5.000 mrs., a cada vno, de que les hizo merçed en enmienda de qualquier cargo que les fuese, por lo que gastaron e daños que rresçibieron en la yda de Yngalaterra con la princesa de Galiz.[80]
>
> [In another one of the Queen's warrants, dated from the 15th May of that year, to Alonso de Valdenebro, the trumpet player of Her Highness, and to Francisco de Dueñas, kettledrum player, 10,000 maravedís, 5,000 maravedís, to each of them, paid in compensation for any service rendered, any expenses and damages incurred on the trip to England with the Princess of Wales].[81]

The account, although drawn up in the standardized language of an expenses payment, is revealing. To unwrap the message: de Baeza's use of the word '*con*' [with] the princess, that is, in her company, suggests that Alonso de Valdenebro and Francisco de Dueñas arrived in England as part of the royal entourage, rather than in advance of Katherine's journey. The short expenses payment account furthermore provides teasing glimpses into the statuses and identities of these musicians. For example, the trumpet player was given double the amount of compensation compared to the drummer. The queen's trumpet players and

---

[80] *Cuentas*, vol. 2, 583.
[81] I am grateful to Dr Anna Augustyniak for this translation and her help with the linguistic conundrums surrounding the early Spanish. Any remaining errors are, of course, my own. As early as 1976, Duggan wrote in an article concerned with Juana of Castile's musical interests: 'the Princess Catherine left to be married in England with her own minstrels, a fool to perform tricks, and at least one drummer and trumpeter to sound her coming', providing as a reference de Baeza's *Cuentas*. Mary Kay Duggan, 'Queen Joanna and Her Musicians', *Musica Disciplina* 30 (1976), 73–95 (76).

drummers appear to have had different statuses, as reflected in their wages or remunerations: an annual tariff of 25,000 maravedís, and 15,000 maravedís respectively.[82] It may also be observed that Alonso is referred to with the elegant title '*trompeta de su Alteza*' [trumpet player of Her Highness] whereas Francisco was here plainly documented as an '*atabalero*' without the honorific marker. Yet, supposed hierarchical differences between the instrumentalists aside, both individuals had been deliberately chosen by Queen Isabella to accompany her daughter. In what follows I elaborate on these two heraldic instrumentalists: what made them suitable or even desirable members of Katherine's entourage in England?

Family matters

The answer to why Francisco the Dueñas had been selected to accompany Katherine on this journey as a drummer can be found in his family's serving the royal family. Both his father and his brother were royal drummers, and can be traced in the *Casa*, de Baeza's *Cuentas*, and Morales's *Data*.

First of all, Morales's *Data* pertaining to 28 February 1496 reveal a payment of 20,000 *mrs.*: '*A Juan de Dueñas, atabalero, para él y sus criados*' [To Juan de Dueñas, kettledrum player, for him and his servants].[83] On the same day, the '*Oficiales del príncipe*' [those serving Prince Juan] list under trumpet players and drummers: '*Juan de Dueñas, atabalero, 11.395 mrs. / Francisco de Dueñas, su hermano, idem*'.[84] These payments were made for work done in the previous year. The double occurrence of this Juan de Dueñas in the records is not an error on Morales's part but, as cross-referencing of sources show, an indication that a father and his two sons played the same instrument at court; Juan senior entertained the queen while Juan junior and his brother Francisco entertained the prince. When Prince Juan died in October 1497, many of the servants

---

[82] *Casa*, 154.

[83] De Andrés Díaz, *El ultimo decenio*, 39, entry 251.

[84] De Andrés Díaz, *El ultimo decenio*, 44, entry 253. '*Su hermano*' can be understood to mean 'his brother', see Real Academia *Diccionario de la lengua Española*, sv *hermano, na*. https://dle.rae.es/.

of his household transferred to that of his mother, the queen.[85] It is therefore not surprising that on 21 March 1498, Francisco de Dueñas was registered as an official of the queen's household *por atabalero*, for an annual salary of 15,000 maravedís, which had been paid out until 1499.[86] And his employment with the royal family did not cease after this. A record from 20 March 1500 shows that on Juan senior's death, Francisco de Dueñas followed his father's professional footsteps and took over his position as a drummer with three pairs of drums.[87] Correspondingly, de Baeza shows that in this year Francisco was referred to as '*fijo de Juan de Dueñas, defunto, atabalero de su Alteza*' [son of Juan de Dueñas, underline{deceased}, drummer of Your Highness] (emphasis added).[88] *La Casa* further emphasizes the family relationship between the two drummers, and the son taking over his father's position as a consequence of the latter's death through the phrasing '*por muerte de su padre*'.[89]

And what happened to Francisco's brother? The *Casa* records show that alongside Francisco, a Juan de Dueñas had also been appointed as a drummer in the queen's service on 21 March 1498, paid out until 1503, the payment also being 15,000 *mrs.* a year.[90] The record refers to him as '*finado*', which can be understood as a euphemism for a '*persona muerta*', that is, deceased person.[91] This is underscored by an account written in Medina del Campo on 6 December 1503 in which the deceased Juan is referred to as Francisco's brother.[92]

Returning to de Baeza's payment of 15 May 1503 made out to Francisco de Dueñas and Alonso de Valdenebro for going to England, it may be observed that this evidence of their working together is not the first such occurrence. The payment documented by de Morales in 1496 through which Prince Juan's staff was paid for services rendered in the previous year showed the two brothers Francisco and Juan de Dueñas working together, but also included Alonso in this musical group.[93] It

[85] *Casa*, 8–9.
[86] *Casa*, 102. The *Casa* records give his name as both 'Françisco' and 'Francisco'. I use the latter spelling, as it is used in de Baeza.
[87] *Casa*, 174.
[88] *Cuentas*, vol. 2, 509.
[89] *Casa*, 102.
[90] *Casa*, 102.
[91] Real Academia *Diccionario de la lengua Española*, sv finado, da. https://dle.rae.es
[92] *Casa*, 104.
[93] De Andrés Díaz, *El ultimo decenio*, 44, entry 253.

seems likely that since both brothers de Dueñas were taken into the queen's service on the same day in 1498 in the same capacity, and given that Alonso de Morales documented two drummers having accompanied Katherine of Aragon to England,[94] one of them being Francisco, and both having previously worked with Alonso de Valdenebro, we can make an educated guess that the second drummer listed by de Morales was likely to have been Juan de Dueñas the younger.

Both drummers would have been introduced at the court by virtue of their father, Juan senior, being the queen's drummer. The esteem he appears to have invited during life can be found in the records. His favour with the king and queen can be found expressed in a document kept at the Archivo General de Simancas (AGS) which records '*Ayuda de viaje*' [gratuity or expenses paid towards a journey or travel] having been granted to María de Dueñas, Juan de Dueñas senior's wife, on 16 November 1500, in the year that she had become a widow.[95] Earlier evidence of de Dueñas senior having been in the queen's favour takes the form of a payment from 1492 which shows that, on behalf of the king and queen, a generous contribution of 30,000 maravedís was made towards his daughter's marriage, in remuneration of many and good services to the queen.[96] Marriage help was a customary form of generosity within the context of the court. The queen's *damas* could receive this such as, for example, María de Cárdenas,[97] but also the *criados reales* [royal servants] were given financial aid towards marriage. For example, in 1500, Mencia Nieto who was a '*criada de la infanta Catalina*' [Katherine's maid], received financial support towards her marriage representing a staggering 250,000 maravedís.[98] In this light, the 30,000 maravedís received by the drummer for his daughter might not seem much. Here, however, it needs to be remembered that the *damas* and the *criadas* working in close proximity to the queen and the

---

[94] De Andrés Díaz, *El ultimo decenio*, 621, entry 3.853.

[95] MINISTERIO DE CULTURA Y DEPORTE Archivo General de Simancas, Cámara de Castilla, CCA, CED, 4, 244, 4. (16 November 1500). Available at: http://pares.mcu.es/ ParesBusquedas2o/catalogo/description/2317120?nm [Accessed on: 22.03.2023].

[96] *Cuentas*, vol. 2, 14.

[97] MINISTERIO DE CULTURA Y DEPORTE Archivo General de Simancas, Cámara de Castilla, CCA, CED, 4, 133, 5 (22 August 1500). Available at: http://pares.mcu.es/ ParesBusquedas2o/catalogo/description/2316089?nm [Accessed on: 22.03.2023].

[98] MINISTERIO DE CULTURA Y DEPORTE Archivo General de Simancas, Cámara de Castilla, CCA, CED, 4, 139, 8. (20 June 1500). Available at: http://pares.mcu.es/ ParesBusquedas2o/catalogo/description/2316126 [Accessed on: 22.03.2023].

infantas had a more intimate position than a (male) drummer would have had. Furthermore, the social status of a drummer can be inferred to have been, compared to other musicians, relatively low. Finally, it was not de Dueñas senior himself getting married, but Queen Isabella extended her generosity towards his family, with a gift that represented two years' annual salaries for a man in his position. This was generosity indeed.

From this follows that Queen Isabella sent her daughter abroad with an entourage that included at least one drummer—but likely two drummers who had come from the same trusted family—whose father had been much-appreciated at court. Trained and prepared by his—or their—father, Francisco de Dueñas had been deemed an appropriate 'heir' to his father's position on his death. Meanwhile, his brother maintained his initial position as a courtly drummer that he had already had before his father's passing. Similar to the English court, the court of Castile, when reconstructed through documents such as de Baeza's, appears to have comprised intricate networks of relations, in which family, as is to be expected, was a strong tie. Insight into relations such as the de Dueñas family and their positions at court enhance our knowledge of the intimate circle surrounding Katherine of Aragon, their expected loyalty, and the trust placed in them by Queen Isabella.

Alonso 'el Negro'

The late Juan de Dueñas senior had been a well-established and appreciated drummer in the service of the queen. Sending at least one, but likely two of his sons, to England to accompany Katherine, seems to have been highly appropriate. Similarly, when choosing Alonso de Valdenebro as one of the trumpet players Isabella made a decision that sought to bring credit to her house. Reasons for selecting this musician would have been multiple. Practically speaking, Alonso de Valdenebro took up a position vacated by Sancho Lopes de Trevyño on the latter's death in 1500.[99] But Alonso's being chosen to take this place would have been based on his

---

[99] *Casa*, 95. Sancho Lopes de Trevyño was listed in the 'oficiales' of the queen paid out in Tortosa on 28 February 1496 for work done in 1495, alongside two other trumpet players: Francisco de Arévalo and Gonzalo de Bustamante (note that the spelling of his name is 'Bustamante' here). De Andrés Díaz, *El ultimo decenio*, 41, entry 252.

experience and qualities. De Baeza's *Cuentas* identify Alonso as one of the four trumpet players serving Prince Juan while in Barcelona:

> A Juan de Salonia, 2.000 mrs.
> A Juan de Çieça, 2.000 mrs.
> A Alfonso de Valdenebro, 2.000 mrs.
> A Françisco de Medina, 2.000 mrs.[100]
> [To Juan de Salonia, 2,000 maravedís, etc.]

We have also already seen Morales's *Data* position him in the prince's service in 1495 as one of the '*Trompetas y atabaleros*', working together with Francisco de Dueñas and his brother Juan junior.[101] Such experiences may have made him a reliable choice for the task given his experience in formal rituals announcing the royal children's presence in itinerant court settings. He could be trusted to move confidently in unknown territory, and presumably exuded sufficient gravitas to accompany and represent a young prince or princess.

Further evidence suggests that when Queen Isabella chose Alonso as one of the musicians to accompany Katherine and to represent her family and country, she may have additionally valued an aspect of his outward appearance: the colour of his skin.[102] An account from 22 November 1495 details Prince Juan's gifting Alonso with money for a horse (paid for by Queen Isabella): '*Alonso, el Negro, menestril de su Altesa, 3.500 mrs., que le mando dar para vn cauallo*'.[103] [Alonso, the Black, minstrel of Her Highness, 3,500 maravedís which are given for a horse]. What can '*el Negro*' tell us about Alonso's ethnic or geographical background? The short answer is: nothing. In the case of Alonso, it is possible that 'de Valdenebro' was a toponym signifying 'Valle de Ebro',

---

[100] *Cuentas*, vol. 2, 78.

[101] They were paid out in 1496. De Andrés Díaz, *El ultimo decenio*, 44, entry 253. Note that in Morales's *Data*, the trumpet player appears as 'Alonso de Valdenebra, *trompeta*' (note the differently spelled ending of his name).

[102] Tess Knighton has observed that, 'Black musicians were employed in the royal and noble households to perform in the heraldic ensembles of trumpets and drums as a symbol of prestige', Knighton, 'Introduction', 16.

[103] *Cuentas*, vol. 2, 276. No surname is mentioned in this payment record, but in these years no other instrumentalists with the name Alonso can be identified at the court. Knighton also interprets the Alonso who was 'rewarded with a horse' to be 'one of four trumpeters who travelled to England with Katherine of Aragon in 1501'. Knighton, 'Instruments, Instrumental Music and Instrumentalists', 116; Knighton and Kreitner, *The Music of Juan de Anchieta*, 19. See Note 28.

which would geographically place him in the area around the river Ebro in the north and north-east of the Iberian peninsula. But '*el Negro*' does not contribute to understanding better Alonso's background or heritage. Olivette Otele has recently reminded readers, quoting Cedric Robinson, that the word '*negro*' as a term does not signify a 'situated-ness' in 'space', that is, 'ethno- or politico-geography'.[104] And although Otele refers to later usage of the word, its way of being uninformative or even evasive regarding a person's background or history also applies to the use of the word around 1500. According to Aurelia Martín Casares, the word '*Negro*' is used in the Spanish documentary evidence to refer to several different groups of people, of which she provides the following overview:

> 1) Sub-Saharan people from different ethnic groups speaking differ-ent native languages (. . .) ; 2) North African Muslims (freed or slaves) of sub-Saharan origin who spoke Arabic; 3) People with sub-Saharan ancestors born in Spain or Portugal, baptised and Castilian-speaking; 4) Moriscos (Spanish Muslims converted by force to Christianity, either free or enslaved) with sub-Saharan blood; 5) People from the Canary Islands who had dark skin and were in most cases slaves; 6) Hindus or Tamils from India brought by Portuguese slave mer-chants; 7) African Americans brought to Spain by their Spanish owners living in the Americas.[105]

These groups represent different geographical areas, religious beliefs, political backgrounds, ethnic backgrounds, languages spoken, and,

---

[104] Olivette Otele, *African Europeans: An Untold Story* (London: Hurst & Company, 2020), 3.

[105] Aurelia Martín Casares, 'Free and Freed Black Africans in Granada in the Time of the Spanish Renaissance', in T.F. Earle and K.J.P. Lowe, eds., *Black Africans in Renais-sance Europe* (Cambridge: Cambridge University Press, 2005), 247–60 (248). Note that in this 2005 quote, Martín Casares uses the term 'sub-Saharan'. Language-use has since then changed. In a more recent study, Onyeka Nubia explains why this term may be less useful to historians: 'The word "sub" comes from the Latin word meaning "under", "beneath or within". The phrase surmises that in some ways the Sahara Desert alchemically changed the anthropology of Africans, so that magically they became two separate peoples sepa-rated by it. . . . when modern scientists, historians, etc. use the term "sub-Saharan" they contend that it is an accurate phrase that defines more than the geographical origins of Africans, in fact, it is a euphemism or "proxy" to describe "dark-skinned Africans". This terminology, generated through the post-colonial praxis, does not help us understand Africans in early modern society.' Onyeka Nubia, *England's Other Countrymen: Black Tudor Society* (London: Zed, 2019), 132.

sometimes but certainly not always implied, social status. Generaliza-
tions cannot be made regarding any of these aspects. However, if we
accept the broad indication that Alonso was a person of colour, then
we can 'place' him in a tradition of heraldic instrumentalists of colour
seen across the European courts.

Juan II, the father of Isabella, 'had at least two *moro* drummers in
his retinue', and Ferdinand of Aragon was served by 'the drummer
Cristóbal el Negro . . . between at least 1476 and 1500'.[106] A slightly
later example of a Black heraldic musician operating in the Spanish
courtly context can be found in the well-known visual representation
of a drummer on horseback in Christoph Weiditz's *Trachtenbuch* (see
Figure 1.1).[107] The image shows a young man playing the kettledrum,
which is fixed to the riding animal. The description above the drawing
says: '*Allso Reitten die herbaucker In spanig Wen der Kaÿser In ain statt
Reitt*' [this is how the drummers in Spain ride when the Emperor rides
into a city].[108]

In Portugal, Black musicians were also found at court, as suggested
by a shawm band depicted in *The Santa Auta Retable: The Encounter
of Prince Conan and St Ursula* (1522–25), kept at the Museu Nacional
de Arte Antiga in Lisbon.[109] Annemarie Jordan suggests that the retable
'probably celebrates the marriage of Catherine [of Austria] to João III
in 1525'.[110] Jordan also notes that chapel musicians of colour worked in
the Portuguese courtly context: 'King João III had a Black chaplain and
singer called D. Afonso who also played the organ.'[111] And also outside

---

[106] Knighton, 'Instruments, Instrumental Music and Instrumentalists', 115–16.

[107] The *Trachtenbuch* can be fully explored through a digital facsimile provided by
the Germanisches Nationalmuseum Digitale Bibliothek, Nürnberg. http://dlib.gnm.de/
Hs22474/168, 168/66 in the overview.

[108] The emperor in question is Charles V, in whose retinue Christoph Weiditz was able
to travel parts of the Iberian peninsula. Albrecht Classen, 'Spain and Germany in the Late
Middle Ages: Christoph Weiditz Paints Spain (1529): A German Artist Traveller Discovers
the Spanish Peninsula', *Neuphilologische Mitteilungen* 105:4 (2004), 395–406 (399).

[109] Rui Pedro de Oliveira Alves, 'The Trombone as Portrayed in Portuguese Iconography During the Sixteenth and Early Seventeenth Centuries', *Scottish Journal of Performance* 2:1 (2014), 55–85 (64); see also, Annemarie Jordan, 'Images of Empire: Slaves in the
Lisbon Household and Court of Catherine of Austria', in T.F. Earle and K.J.P. Lowe, eds.,
Black Africans in Renaissance Europe (Cambridge: Cambridge University Press, 2005),
155–80 (158–9).

[110] Jordan, 'Images of empire', 158.

[111] Jordan, 'Images of empire', 159.

FIGURE 1.1 Christoph Weiditz, *Trachtenbuch*, Germanisches Nationalmuseum Digitale Bibliothek. 168/66. http://dlib.gnm.de/Hs22474/168. Public domain mark 1.0.

the Iberian peninsula, heraldic instrumentalists of colour can be found to have performed in the service of kings. For example, a number of Africans or persons of African descent resided at the court of King James IV (1473–1513), including a 'Moryen *taubronar*' [drummer].[112]

---

[112] Cited in Imtiaz Habib, *Black Lives in the English Archives, 1500–1677: Imprints of the Invisible* (London: Routledge, 2008), 278.

The drummer was given a horse which cost £4 4s., clothing, medical care when he was ill, money 'for paynting of his taubron', as well as funds to spend on his spouse and child. Fryer suggests, 'perhaps the same "Moris barne" whom the king asked specially to see'.[113]

At the Tudor court, a trumpet player by the name of John Blanke, also spelled 'Blak', appears in the court records in a payment of wages in 1507: 'Item to John Blanke the blacke Trumpet for his moneth wag*es* of Nouembre last passed at viij d the Day xx s'.[114] In 1509 he performed alongside John de Cecil as one of the 'kynges trompyttes' at the funeral of Henry VII,[115] as well as at the coronation of Henry VIII.[116] In 1511, he participated at the Westminster tournament held in honour of Henry VIII's and Katherine's first-born son, an event that was commemorated in the Westminster Tournament Roll.[117] In the next year he got married, which we know because Henry VIII signed a Warrant to Sir Andrew Windsor, the keeper of the Great Wardrobe from 14 January 1511/12 which specified,

> We wol and charge you that vnto *our seruau*nt John Blak[e] our Trompeter ye deliuer thes[e] | *par*celles folowing Item[?] [for a] g[owne?] of violet clothe conteyning iiij brode[?] yard*es*[?] to be f[ur?]ed *with*| spanysshe buge . . .[118]

The warrant furthermore refers to 'Jtem a dublet of velwet[?]', a 'p[air?] of s[carl?]et [hose?]' and 'I[te*m*] a [bonet and a Hatte?]', which, we can

[113] Fryer, *Staying Power*, 2–3.

[114] *The Chamber Books of Henry VII and Henry VIII, 1485–1521*, ed. M.M. Condon, S.P. Harper and L. Liddy, and S. Cunningham and J. Ross, TNA, E36/214, f. 109r. https://www.dhi.ac.uk/chamber-books/folio/E36_214_fo_109r.xml For an image of the original: https://www.nationalarchives.gov.uk/wp-content/uploads/2019/02/E-36_214-f109_7-December-1507.jpg.

[115] TNA, LC 2/1, fol. 126; calendared in *LP* vol. 1, #20 (11 May 1509). See also, Ashbee, ed., *Records of English Court Music*, 25.

[116] TNA, LC 9/50, fol. 207v; calendared in *LP* vol. 1, #82 (24 June 1509). See also, Ashbee, ed., *Records of English Court Music*, 29.

[117] Anglo, 'The Court Festivals of Henry VII', 12–45 (42, footnote 3). See also, Sydney Anglo, *The Great Tournament Roll of Westminster: A Collotype Reproduction of the Manuscript*, 2 vols. (Oxford: Clarendon Press, 1968), vol. 1, 85.

[118] TNA, E101/417/6, #50; image at: http://aalt.law.uh.edu/AALT7/E101/E101no417/E101no417no6/IMG_0161.htm. Calendared in *LP* vol. 1, #1025, which reads: "a gown of violet cloth, &c., including a bonnet and a hat, 'to be taken of our gift against his marriage'. A transcription of the warrant is offered in, Nadia T. van Pelt, 'John Blanke's Wages', 3–35. I am grateful to Prof. Dr Meg Twycross for her scholarly generosity in relation to the warrants and petitions transcribed in the article in *METh*.

read, represented 'to be takyn of *our* gift ayenst[?] his mariage[?]'.[119] The warrant specifies that it was 'Yeuen vnder our Signet at our manour at Grenewich'.[120] In previous research, I compare the text of the king's warrant which details John Blanke's wedding present to a very similar warrant written out to Richard Mayre, one of the yeomen of the Ewery two days earlier.[121] The main difference between the warrants appears to be that Richard Mayre was also provided with wedding garments for his wife, whereas John Blanke was not. The implication is that Mrs Mayre, like her husband, worked in the royal household, but that Blanke married someone who was not employed there.[122]

A further piece of documentary evidence pertaining to Blanke's career is a petition kept in the National Archives in which Blanke formally asked the king the following:

> To yeue and graunte vnto hym the same Rowme of Trompet*our* whiche Domynyc Decessed late had / To haue and enioye the said Rowme to y*our* said s*er*ua*n*t from the furste day of Decembre last passed During y*our* moost grac*i*ous pleas*our* w*i*th the wag*e*s of xvjd by the day.[123]

As was customary, the king's signature on the top left hand of the document turned the petition into a warrant.

Persons of colour at the European royal courts

Although the scope of this case study means that this chapter is primarily interested in instrumentalists, it should be noted that royal servants

---

[119] TNA, E101/417/6, #50. See Note 118.

[120] TNA, E101/417/6, #50. See Note 118.

[121] This wedding gift is referred to in Maria Hayward, *Dress at the Court of King Henry VIII* (Leeds: Maney, 2007), 231. For the original document, see TNA, E101/417/6, #57, filed a few documents further on: http://aalt.law.uh.edu/AALT7/E101/E101no417/E101no417no6/IMG_0169.htm. Calendared in *LP* vol. 1, #1023.

[122] See also, Van Pelt, 'John Blanke's Wages', 3–35.

[123] TNA, E101/417/2, #105; image at: http://aalt.law.uh.edu/AALT7/E101/E101no417/E101no417no2/IMG_0158.htm. The document is transcribed (although slightly inaccurately) in Kaufmann, *Black Tudors*, 21. A full transcription of the document is offered in Van Pelt, 'John Blanke's Wages', 3–35. In this article, I contextualize John Blanke's petition by comparing it to other royal servants' petitions asking for positions at court.

in other occupations can also be seen throughout the documentary records, suggesting that royal retinues were really not as 'white' as is sometimes supposed. For example, a 1475 document extant in the AGS refers to the appointment of one 'Juan de Valladolid, *negro, portero de cámara*' [Juan de Valladolid, Black doorman of the chamber],[124] as '*de mayoral y juez de todos los negros de Sevilla y su arrabal*' [head and superior (or judge) of all '*los negros*' of Sevilla and his neigbourhood]. Likely the same Juan de Valladolid was in 1499 paid for services rendered in the role of '*criado de la archiduquesa doña Juana*' [servant of the Archduchess *doña Juana*, that is, Juana of Castile].[125] The Burgundian *Comptes* reveal that Juana's 1501 itinerant household when journeying from the Low Countries to Spain included staff members called Chrétien Blanchetête, Jean Blanchetête, Jean Noiretête, and Guillaume Blanchetête.[126] Although there is no additional evidence to suggest Black presence, the names are suggestive. But whether in these cases one would be more likely to find a person of African descent behind the moniker 'Jean Noiretête' [Jean Blackhead] or 'Jean Blanchetête' [Jean Whitehead], is unclear. Going by the way the names John Blanke or John Blak are used interchangeably, both would theoretically be possible. Perhaps one of these persons named 'Jean' in the *Comptes* corresponds to Juan de Valladolid, but this is just conjecture.

Juana's spouse also employed persons of colour in his royal entourage. For example, during his 1506 journey, Philippe of Burgundy employed among his '*escuirie*' [stables] a 'Nicolas le Morre' earning five sols a day, and a Christophe le *Morre* earning four sols a day.[127] Among the

---

[124] MINISTERIO DE CULTURA Y DEPORTE Archivo General de Simancas, Real Cancillería de los Reyes de Castilla. Registro del Sello de Corte, RGS, LEG, 147511,725 (8 November 1475). Available at: http://pares.mcu.es/ParesBusquedas20/catalogo/description/1596918?nm [Accessed on: 22.03.2023].
[125] MINISTERIO DE CULTURA Y DEPORTE Archivo General de Simancas, Cámara de Castilla, CCA,CED,4,55,4 (15 November 1499). Available at: http://pares.mcu.es/ParesBusquedas20/catalogo/description/2315782?nm [Accessed on: 22.03.2023].
[126] ADN, B. 3459. Jules Finot, ed., *Collection des Inventaires des Archives Communales Antérieures a 1790*, vol. 8 (Lille: L. Danel, 1895), 132. Two of these men are also referred to as members of the 'Etat des gages des officiers de l'hôtel de la Reine' in 1505: here referred to as a 'maître Jehan Blanceteste' and a 'Jennin Noire-teste'. *Collection des Inventaires*, vol. 8, 142.
[127] ADN, both: B. 3463. *Collection des Inventaires*, vol. 8, 146; Lalaing, *Voyages*, vol. 1, 529. The spelling varies in both sources. In Lalaing, both surnames are spelled 'More'. Note that the 'stables' traditionally managed the minstrels, trumpet players and (kettle) drum players. See the etiquette book written by Gonzalo Fernández de Oviedo, *El libro*

'*captaines et archiers de corps*' [captains and archers] a Jacques le More can be found.[128] These names read in isolation do not necessarily have to be indicators of Black presence, but additional staff lists of other years indicate that the name 'le Morre' or 'le More' likely functioned as a descriptor rather than as a surname, as suggested by the aliases or synonyms used by the account taker. For example, the 1505 list of Philippe's staff reveals the name of stable employee, 'Nicolas le Morianno', earning five sols a day, used as an alternative name for 'Nicolas le Morre'.[129] 'Christophe le More' appears twice in the 1506 *Comptes* list as well as in Lalaing, indicating that there were two persons named Christophe referred to by the same nickname.[130] In the 1505 list, one of the men named Christophe is listed as 'Christophe le More' earning four sols, and the other is referred to as 'Christophe le Nègre' earning three sols.[131] It is clear that for the account taker, the indicator 'le Nègre' could substitute 'le More', and that he understood these indicators to refer to the physical attribute of one of the two men named Christophe that, to the scribe, stood out: his skin colour. Ernst van den Boogaard has suggested the likelihood that Christophe le Nègre served Charles V in Valladolid in 1517, and that he appears again in Aachen in 1520 where he may have served as a bodyguard for Charles V as he was crowned emperor.[132] It is furthermore possible that this Christophe is the person depicted in *Portret van een Onbekende Man* [Portrait of an Unknown Man] by Jan Jansz Mostaert (c. 1525–30) (see Figure 1.2).[133]

Charles's sister, Catherine of Austria (1507–78), when queen alongside the Portuguese King João III, took on a great number of Amerindians

de la cámara Real del Principe Don Juan e officios de su casa e servicio ordinario, ed. J.M. Escudero de la Peña (Madrid: Sociedad de Bibliófilos Españoles, 1870), 182–4. Cf; Félix Labrador Arroyo, 'From Castile to Burgundy: The Evolution of the Queens' Households during the Sixteenth Century', in Anne J. Cruz and Maria Galli Stampino, eds., *Early Modern Habsburg Women: Transnational Contexts, Cultural Conflicts, Dynastic Continuities* (Farnham: Ashgate, 2013), 119–48 (123–4).

[128] ADN, B.3463. *Collection des Inventaires*, vol. 8, 147; Lalaing, *Voyages*, vol. 1, 532. In Lalaing the name is spelled 'le Morre'.

[129] For 'Nicolas le Morianno', see: *Collection des Inventaires*, vol. 8, 140.

[130] *Collection des Inventaires*, vol. 8, 146; Lalaing, *Voyages*, vol. 1, 529.

[131] *Collection des Inventaires*, vol. 8, 140.

[132] Ernst van den Boogaard, 'Christophle le More, Lijfwacht van Karel V?', *Bulletin van het Rijksmuseum* 53:4 (2005), 412–33 (420 and 424). See also the Catalogue Entry of this painting at the Rijksmuseum. https://www.rijksmuseum.nl/nl/collectie/SK-A-4986/catalogus-entry. Please note that the Catalogue still lists the painting under its previous name: 'Portret van een Afrikaanse Man' [Portrait of an African Man], whereas the

FIGURE 1.2 *Portret van een Onbekende Man* [Portrait of an Unknown Man], Jan Jansz Mostaert, ca. 1525–30, oil on panel, 30.8 cm × 21.2 cm. Rijksmuseum Amsterdam. Public domain.

and Black Africans, many of whom had been made slaves. Jordan argues, 'Catherine's self-fashioning was part of a deliberate approach undertaken to offer her subjects and court a fitting image of a queen consort, who wielded political power and influence over far-flung domains filled with exotic peoples, flora and fauna.'[134] Perhaps the most well-known African at her court was João de Sá Panasco, who started out as a slave and a court fool, and later became a courtier as a '*cavaleiro*' [gentleman] in the royal household and '*moço fidalgo*' [valet for the king].[135] But we also see many persons of colour employed in Catherine's household with what Silleras-Fernández has referred to as 'downstairs' work, such as cleaning and other labour.[136] The Italian royal courts also employed many Black servants, and enslaved people of colour. 'This custom', Silleras-Fernández suggests, 'was introduced to Italy by the Aragonese kings of Naples, through their close diplomatic ties to important northern Italian patrician houses, such as the Sforza, Gonzaga, and D'Este...'[137]

Long-held preconceptions

It is important to emphasize here the mobility of royals and their ambassadors, entourages, and servants, and the plethora of international connections between the different courts of Europe. Marriages consolidated good or improved tenuous diplomatic relations, facilitated matters of trade, power negotiations, provided the occasions for summits, and so forth. This meant that people were frequently on the move, and there seems to have been no clear limit on how far one might travel for such an interaction. Think, for example, of King Francis I (1494–1547) who, after reaching an alliance with Süleyman the

---

museum now refers to the painting as 'Portret van een Onbekende Man' [Portrait of an Unknown Man].

[133] This is suggested by Boogaard, 'Christophle le More', 421.

[134] Jordan, 'Images of Empire', 156.

[135] Jordan, 'Images of Empire', 160–1.

[136] For 'downstairs', see Núria Silleras-Fernández, '*Nigra Sum Sed Formosa*: Black Slaves and Exotica in the Court of a Fourteenth-Century Aragonese Queen', *Medieval Encounters* 13 (2007), 546–65 (563). For Catherine's household, see: Jordan, 'Images of Empire', 159.

[137] Silleras-Fernández, '*Nigra Sum Sed Formosa*', 562.

Magnificent (r. 1520–66), was said to have sent musicians to Constantinople with his ambassador to please the Sultan.[138] It is in this
context of multiple encounters between royal houses and their staff, that
we need to see the complexity of the roles and statuses of Black musicians as well as other persons of colour working in a courtly context.
In parts of Europe, such as in Spain, Portugal, and Italy, slavery was an
accepted part of life. The many *cartas de horro* [freedom letters] found
in the Spanish archives are a testament to the lives of people who had, up
to obtaining these letters, been enslaved.[139] In England, however, slavery
was not an acceptable legal 'state'. Onyeka Nubia has recently clarified:

> . . . in Tudor England, status was primarily determined by social
> standing, lineage, birth, gender and, to a lesser extent, wealth. During
> the Tudor period, Africans seem to have been free to determine their
> status in the same way as other people. African people's status was

---

[138] Castil-Blaze, *Chapelle-Musique des Rois de France* (Paris: Chez Paulin, 1832), 62–3.
For more on French diplomacy in aid of good relations with Sultan Süleyman the Magnif-
icent: De Lamar Jensen, 'The Ottoman Turks in Sixteenth Century French Diplomacy',
SCJ 16:4 (1985), 451–70. That this tale may be the stuff of legends is suggested by Robert J.
Knecht, who observes that 'This story . . . cannot be traced back further than 1645'. Knecht,
The French Renaissance Court, 1483–1589 (New Haven, CT: Yale University Press, 2008),
219.
[139] For example, 'Carta de horro a favor de Antonio Negro'. MINISTERIO DE CUL-
TURA Y DEPORTE Archivo General de Simancas, Real Cancillería de los Reyes de
Castilla. Registro del Sello de Corte, RGS, LEG, 149008, 315. Available at: http://pares.
mcu.es/ParesBusquedas20/catalogo/description/1621895?nm [Accessed on: 22.03.2023];
'Horro y amparo a Fernando Negro, hijo de María Negra, esclava de Alonso Gómez'. MIN-
ISTERIO DE CULTURA Y DEPORTE Archivo General de Simancas, Real Cancillería
de los Reyes de Castilla. Registro del Sello de Corte, RGS, LEG, 14850, 266. Available
at: http://pares.mcu.es/ParesBusquedas20/catalogo/description/1607536?nm [Accessed
on: 22.03.2023]. Multiple other examples can be found in the archival material that has
been digitally made available through *Pares*. Some studies on slavery in medieval and
early modern Europe that readers can refer to as a starting point: Hannah Barker, *That
Most Precious Merchandise: The Mediterranean Trade in Black Sea Slaves, 1260–1500*
(Philadelphia, PA: University of Pennsylvania Press, 2019); Debra Blumenthal, *Enemies
and Familiars: Slavery and Mastery in Fifteenth-Century Valencia* (Ithaca, NY: Cornell
University Press, 2009); Steven A. Epstein, *Speaking of Slavery: Color, Ethnicity, and
Human Bondage in Italy* (Ithaca, NY: Cornell University Press, 2001); various chapters in
T.F. Earle and K.J.P. Lowe, eds., *Black Africans in Renaissance Europe* (Cambridge: Cam-
bridge University Press, 2005); Dienke Hondius, 'Black Africans in Seventeenth-Century
Amsterdam', *RR* 31:2 (2008), 87–105; Kate Lowe, 'Visible Lives: Black Gondoliers and
Other Black Africans in Renaissance Venice', *RQ* 66:2 (2013), 412–52.

not restricted by government legislation or public policy. It was in the private sphere of English society that their status was determined.[140]

It should be noted here that within English history, Black Presence Studies is still a relatively young field. In the past two decades studies such as Imtiaz Habib's *Black Lives in the English Archives* (2007), Onyeka Nubia's *Blackamoores: Africans in Tudor England* (2013), and his *England's Other Countrymen: Black Tudor Society* (2019), Olivette Otele's *African Europeans* (2020), and Miranda Kaufmann's *Black Tudors* (2017) have taken important steps in visualizing African presence in Tudor England, enriching our awareness of English history. These studies have, however, had to bring to light pervasive misunderstandings and preconceptions that readers have about the statuses of Africans in Tudor England.[141]

It is possible that persons of colour travelling between different countries or royal households may have found themselves changing status, or may have been perceived as holding different statuses by their patrons and by the persons whom they met while in another country. At the Tudor court, Catalina de Motril springs to mind. She was a servant of Katherine's bedchamber who is referred to as 'a woman called Catalina, who was slave to the queen of England, and served her in her chamber' in the investigations surrounding the consummation of Katherine's marriage to Arthur, which suggests that Katherine did indeed bring people with her who had at some point been enslaved.[142] A further piece of evidence consolidating this information can be found in the financial accounts of Alonso de Morales, which reveal that on 20 August 1501 a man by the name of Juan Davalos, inhabitant of Granada, was paid 25,000 *mrs*. '*Por una esclava que de él se tomó para la princesa de Gales*' [for a female slave whom he had given to the

---

[140] Onyeka Nubia, 'Why Diversity in Tudor England Matters', in Suzannah Lipscomb and Helen Carr, eds., *What is History, Now?* (London: Weidenfeld & Nicolson, 2021), 169–77 (171).

[141] Kaufmann, for example, wrote: 'The misconceptions surrounding the status of Black Tudors are part of a wider impression that any African living outside Africa before the mid-nineteenth century, be it in Europe or in the Americas, must have been enslaved'. Kaufmann, *Black Tudors*, 2.

[142] *LP* vol. 5, #362 (31 July 1531). See also, Lauren Johnson, 'Catalina of Motril (fl. 1501–1531)', *ODNB*, Oxford University Press. https://doi.org/10.1093/odnb/9780198614128.013.369157.

Princess of Wales].[143] Morales does not provide the name of the '*esclava*' in question, but the transaction taking place with an inhabitant of Granada—like Catalina—suggests that Katherine had in her entourage one or perhaps two women from that region whom Katherine likely perceived as enslaved. Once arriving in England, however, this status would not have been legally recognized, although this would not necessarily have changed the *infanta*'s perception of her attendant, of course. The presence of Alonso de Valdenebro, a well-paid, high-ranking 'loud' instrumentalist in Katherine's train proves that also within the specific context of the princess's travelling entourage, the perception was not held that persons of colour were necessarily equated with enslaved persons. We can use this additional information to challenge persisting assumptions about the social statuses of persons of African descent in Katherine of Aragon's entourage. Attributions of such assumptions are also persistent. With the new information this can also be challenged. For example, in a 2014 article, it was noted that,

> Of the fifty-one members of Catherine of Aragon's household to make the trip to England with her, two were black. Describing these individuals as 'slaves to attend on the maids of honour', More calls them not 'Tolerable' to look at.[144]

However, although Thomas More did indeed write an eye-witness account of Katherine's arrival in London, in which he referred to the Spanish entourage, calling some of Katherine's members of staff '*pigmei Aethiopes*', and mockingly writing that their faces were '*vix tollerabiles*' [hardly tolerable], More's account did not actually mention 'slaves'.[145] The description referred to by Chapman is actually from a letter from Queen Isabella and King Ferdinand to their ambassador de Pueblo written on 3 October 1500, in which they provide a list of 'Officers and Servants of her Household who are to remain with her [Katherine] in

---

[143] De Andrés Díaz, *El ultimo decenio*, 592, entry 3.768.

[144] Matthieu A. Chapman, 'The Appearance of Blacks on the Early Modern Stage: *Love's Labour's Lost*'s African Connections to Court', *ET* 17:2 (2014), 77–94 (77).

[145] Reproduced with permission from: *The Correspondence of Sir Thomas More*, ed. Elizabeth Frances Rogers (Princeton, NJ: Princeton University Press, 1947), 4. Translation mine. Cf; Habib, *Black Lives*, 275–6.

England'.[146] The list pertains to a smaller party than the entourage that originally set out with Katherine on her journey to England, and from this follows that, in theory, any of the comments made in More's eyewitness account could have referred to persons who would not remain in England with Katherine after the festivities were over. In other words, the people to whose appearances More mockingly referred as '*vix tollerabiles*' may, but certainly do not have to have been, the same people as the individuals referred to as 'slaves' on Isabella and Ferdinand's list.[147]

I will now briefly return to Tudor studies' best-known heraldic instrumentalist, John Blanke. Some scholars have suggested (with varying degrees of certainty) that the trumpet player may have arrived in England as part of Katherine's crew.[148] This would be an attractive thought were it not that the time gap between John Blanke's first named appearance in the Chamber Books and Katherine's journey is substantial: Katherine travelled north in 1501, whereas John Blanke first appears in the court records in a payment of wages in 1507. John Blanke has offered Tudor scholarship a very clear indication of Black presence in the courtly context, and has, through the visualization of the musician in the Westminster Tournament Roll, as well as the description 'blacke Trumpet', opened the eyes of many to the presence of persons of colour working for the Tudor kings in a position of honour and prestige.[149] Alonso de Valdenebro, unlike John Blanke, could not be found in the English records, but we now know him to have been there, hidden behind the vague reference to 'the princesse trumpett*es*'.[150] The final remarks of this chapter address the methodological implications of this

---

[146] For the letter: *CSPS* vol. 1, #287. For the list, signed by secretary Almazan: *CSPS* vol. 1, #288.

[147] Thomas More's letter will be further addressed in Chapter 4.

[148] Habib, *Black Lives*, 39: 'he was very likely a surviving member of the Spanish princess's entourage'. Habib based his claim on K.J.P. Lowe, 'The Stereotyping of Black Africans', 39. Some scholars take a less certain tone and allow for the *possibility* that John Blanke was part of Katherine of Aragon's retinue, e.g.,: Knighton, 'Instruments, Instrumental Music and Instrumentalists', 116.

[149] *The Chamber Books of Henry VII and Henry VIII, 1485–1521*, ed. M.M. Condon, S.P. Harper and L. Liddy, and S. Cunningham and J. Ross, TNA, E36/214, f. 109r. https://www.dhi.ac.uk/chamber-books/folio/E36_214_fo_109r.xml.

[150] *The Chamber Books of Henry VII and Henry VIII, 1485–1521*, ed. M.M. Condon, S.P. Harper and L. Liddy, and S. Cunningham and J. Ross, TNA, E101/415/3, f. 74v. https://www.dhi.ac.uk/chamber-books/folio/E101_415_3_fo_074v.xml.

research, and what it tells us about using the Tudor Chamber Book records to study Black presence at court.

Conclusion: methodological implications

Reading the English records alongside sources written in Spanish and French enables a better understanding of the English scribe's way of recording. The scribe appears to have had some specific expectations, such as those evidenced by his use of the word 'Spanish' to refer to musicians patronized by Ferdinand of Aragon, so that 'Spanish' for him did not mean of Aragon *and* Castile. This demonstrates a bias in which queens regnant are not part of expectations held by the account taker. Knowing and understanding this bias has facilitated an understanding of why the trumpet player John de Cecil was not to be found in Isabella of Castile's household or the payment records that list the four trumpet players who had been sent to England with the princess. Indeed, it turned out that John de Cecil was to be looked for in the context of Ferdinand's personal musicians.

Furthermore, the use of Spanish source material has uniquely demonstrated the presence of a trumpet player and a drummer at sea with Katherine of Aragon, and has revealed that family relations were a foundational aspect of the loyalty to be expected from court servants. Isabella and Ferdinand were appreciative employers who rewarded good service, and who can be seen to have been aware of the great personal events in their staff members' lives, as illustrated by the financial contribution to the drummer Juan de Dueñas's daughter. The Spanish source material also enables us to place a heraldic instrumentalist of colour in Katherine's train, helping us to reconsider assumptions previously held about her members of staff and their social statuses. Furthermore, this places a trumpet player of colour at the court of Henry VII, at least for the duration of the wedding event, roughly six years before the first appearance of John Blanke.

Finally, the evidence in this chapter has clear methodological implications. In previous research, the Black presence in Tudor England has sometimes unwittingly been undermined. Peter Fryer has, for example, written about John Blanke: 'around the same time as that group of Africans reached Edinburgh, a *solitary* Black musician was living in

London, employed by Henry VII and his successor'[151] (emphasis mine). Similarly, referring to Black presence as a 'phenomenon' throughout his *Black Lives in the English Archives*, Imtiaz Habib has made choices in his interpretation of sources to, in his words 'compensate for the over-conservative, mutually reinforcing, multilayered assumptions of traditional early modern history that have made Black people in Tudor and Stuart England absent by default'.[152] Both Fryer and Habib have assumed Black presence in England to have been smaller than has since been revealed, among others by Miranda Kaufmann and Onyeka Nubia.[153]

Onyeka Nubia has been a leading scholar in many aspects of Black presence studies in Tudor England, but two of his methodological findings stand out: first of all, he suggests that 'the reason why Africans appear more frequently in parish records than on the subsidy rolls is not just because of the inefficiency of the latter, but because many Africans were not considered as foreign in Tudor England'.[154] Secondly, he proposes that 'one of the reasons why references to Africans do not appear constantly in contemporary narratives was because the presence of Africans in England was not as remarkable as suggested by those historians who offer the post-colonial perspective'.[155] Indeed, if Africans or persons of African descent were not seen as 'foreign' or 'remarkable' by record takers, this can account for the relative invisibility of Black Africans in records in which they are not given an 'ethnic marker'. I acknowledge and underscore these important points, and here take this suggestion one step further.

The current chapter has demonstrated that when documentary evidence in the English Chamber Books refers to musicians *as a group* (e.g., 'Spanish trumpets'), this does not specify *any* individual characteristics of the musicians within these groups apart from the general description used to describe the totality of the group members as a

---

[151] Fryer, *Staying Power*, 4.

[152] Habib, *Black Lives*, 17.

[153] Onyeka Nubia, *Blackamoores: Africans in Tudor England, their Presence, Status and Origins* (Narrative Eye, 2013). See also Miranda Kaufmann, *Africans in Britain, 1500–1640* (Unpublished doctoral thesis, University of Oxford, Christ Church, 2011).

[154] Onyeka Nubia, *Blackamoores: Critical Assessment of PhD thesis* (University of East Anglia, 2016), 49.

[155] Onyeka Nubia, *Blackamoores: Critical Assessment*, 49.

single unit. This selective notetaking can be frustrating for historians, such as when one has to rely on an accompanying Francophone Burgundian source to find out that one of Ferdinand's trumpet players present at Arthur and Katherine's wedding, was in fact a drummer. The fact that record takers were as disinterested in offering references to ethnicity or marking the presence of African persons as they were to offer other information, such as for example whether musicians were patronized by the house of Castile or Aragon, further proves Onyeka's points, as do the broader findings discussed in this chapter. In short, as this chapter has shown, placing the English and Spanish evidence side by side reveals that some Africans or persons of African descent had their presence hidden in references to groups of people, obfuscating their individual presence. This urges us to allow for the possibility that this evidence is only the tip of an evidential iceberg, and that other persons of African descent will be found to have visited the English court, contributing to its culture in the early Tudor period.

Given that my case study solely pertained to Katherine's musicians, a wider, systematic study of her entire staff might further illuminate that for which I have offered the groundwork here. To understand fully Katherine of Aragon's first encounters with, and impact on, Tudor court life, a cross-language, transnational, cross-geographical, and interdisciplinary approach is needed, prioritizing primary source material.

Deathbed Foolery

Introduction

On 9 January 1536, Imperial Ambassador Eustace Chapuys informed the Habsburg Emperor Charles V that his aunt, Katherine
of Aragon, had passed away 'on Friday, the day after Epiphany'.[1] The
dispatch was written with the retrospective knowledge of the sickbed
turning out to be a deathbed, and relates Chapuys's visit to Kimbolton
Castle, and his final moments in Katherine's company, with a regretful
undertone of his having left her side too soon:

> . . . perceiving that the Queen began little by little to recover her sleep
> and to get rest,—that her stomach retained food, and that she was evi-
> dently getting much better,—she herself was of opinion, as well as her
> physician, who now considered her out of danger, that I ought at once
> to return home, not only in order not to abuse the permission granted
> to me by the King, but also to ask for a better residence for her, as
> promised at my departure from London. I took, therefore, leave of the
> Queen on Tuesday evening; she being then, to all appearance, happy

*Chapter 2 of this book originally appeared as 'Katherine of Aragon's Deathbed: Why
Chapuys Brought a Fool', *Early Theatre* 24:1 (2021), 63–87. https://doi.org/10.12745/et.24.
1.4357. I am grateful to the editors of *Early Theatre* for their permission to reprint this
work.
[1] *CSPS* vol. 5.2, #3 (9 January 1536).

Intercultural Explorations and the Court of Henry VIII. Nadia T. van Pelt, Oxford University Press.
© Nadia T. van Pelt (2024). DOI: 10.1093/oso/9780192863447.003.0002

and contented, so much so that on the very evening of my departure I saw her smile two or three times, and half an hour after I had left she would still joke with one of my suite, rather inclined to a jest, who had casually remained behind.[2]

The English translation of Chapuys's letter in the *Calendar of State Papers: Spain*, is rather vague in its description of the person exchanging jokes with Katherine of Aragon. The *Calendar*'s editor, Pascual de Gayangos, however, offers a footnote in which he quotes directly from the original manuscript to show that Chapuys described this person as *'ung de mes gens, que fait du playsant'.*[3] 'Playsant' was another word for 'fool', and, as Tatjana Silec reminds the reader, this word for fool can be understood as a synonym for those referred to, in French, as *artificielle* or, in English, 'counterfeit fools'.[4] Literally then, Chapuys referred to 'one of his people, who *played* the fool' (emphasis mine). In the footnote, de Gayangos embellishes the translation a little by noting that Chapuys brought along in his retinue 'a servant . . . who played or attempted to play the part of a professional jester or fool'.[5] His choice of words denotes the difficulty of determining what kind of fool Chapuys refers to; the problem with the word 'professional' is that it assumes a level of permanence that the original French does not stipulate: after all, one could take on the role of *artificielle* or *plaisant*, temporarily or on a particular occasion, without necessarily having to be a 'professional jester'. By suggesting that the fool 'played or attempted to play the part', de Gayangos sought to nuance this problem, leaving the specifics of the foolery and its performer open to interpretation.

The presence of a fool at Katherine's deathbed was not unusual. Fools and jesters were a regular sight at the Tudor court, and beyond that,

---

[2] *CSPS* vol. 5.2, #3.

[3] *CSPS* vol. 5.2, #3, footnote 8.

[4] Tatjana Silec, 'Le Fou du Roi: Un Hors-la-Loi d'un Genre Particulier', *Camenulae* 2 (2008), 1–11, (p. 1): *'En effet il y a toujours eu deux variétés de bouffon: celle dite «naturelle» (natural fool en anglais, ou fol naïs en ancien français) . . . et celle dite «artificielle», l'expression la plus souvent employée en anglais étant «counterfeit fool», tandis qu'en français on lui préfère parfois à la Renaissance l'expression plus vague de «plaisant», inspirée de l'italien'.* ['In effect, there have always been two varieties of fool: those refered to as "natural" ("natural fool" in English, or *fol naïs* in old French) . . . and those referred to as "artificial", the expression most often used in English was "counterfeit fool", while in French during the Renaissance the vaguer expression *"plaisant"* was sometimes preferred, inspired by the Italian.']

[5] *CSPS* vol. 5.2, #3.

used to bring cheer and solace to the royal and noble sick across Europe. Within the context of this widely spread custom, it makes sense that legends could arise such as King Martin of Aragon (1356–1410) laughing himself to death when his jester Borra made rather too successful a joke at his sickbed.[6] While the general circumstances of Katherine of Aragon's final hours have been addressed in multiple studies, the significance of the fool in attendance has remarkably invited relatively little attention.[7] This is all the more surprising because the question of Chapuys's fool and the kind of entertainment he provided at Katherine of Aragon's deathbed sits at the heart of contemporary attitudes to fooling and what we know—or think we know—about court and household fools. It evokes questions regarding the expectations people had of (different type of) fools; what fools were assumed to be capable of; the kind of amusements or forms of entertainment they were expected to bring; the licence—social or political—that fools enjoyed to express themselves; but also how they were perceived to be related to their patrons, as demonstrated by fools' reception in their patrons' absence. Could a fool 'stand in' for a patron or use their comic license to make political or otherwise perilous statements on their patron's behalf? This chapter places Chapuys's final moments with Katherine in the context of fool-keeping at the Tudor and Spanish courts, and Katherine's patronage of entertainers. I also view Chapuys's visit in January 1536 in relation to an earlier attempted visit in July 1534, described in the Spanish *Chronicle of King Henry VIII*, for which Chapuys's permission had been revoked last-minute. The journey was continued by a large part of his retinue, including a fool.[8] That the English courtiers suspected this fool to

---

[6] Beatrice K. Otto, *Fools are Everywhere: The Court Jester Around the World* (Chicago: University of Chicago Press, 2001), 94; Paul N. Morris, 'Patronage and Piety: Montserrat and the Royal House of Medieval Catalonia-Aragon', *Mirator* (2000), 1–15, (8).

[7] Martin A. Sharp Hume and Garrett Mattingly only refer to the fool at Katherine's deathbed to establish the likelihood of him having been the same fool as the one in the anonymous *Chronicle of King Henry VIII: Being a Contemporary Record of Some of the Principal Events in the Reigns Henry VIII and Edward VI. Written in Spanish by an unknown hand*, ed. and trans. Martin A. Sharp Hume (London: George Bell and Sons, 1889), 50; Garrett Mattingly, *Catherine of Aragon* (London: Jonathan Cape, 1963), 307. Chapuys's earlier attempt to visit Kimbolton received brief scholarly attention in Antonia Fraser, *The Six Wives of Henry VIII* (London: Weidenfeld & Nicolson, 1992), 222–3; and Giles Tremlett, *Catherine of Aragon: Henry's Spanish Queen* (London: Faber and Faber, 2010), 405.

[8] Chapuys also refers to this occasion in a letter to Charles V, but he does not explicitly mention the fool. *CSPS* vol. 5.1, #75 (27 July 1534).

function as an intelligencer gathering information for the ambassador or delivering messages to Katherine of Aragon can be understood in the context of royal fools and entertainers, when travelling, gathering information to further their royal masters' interests or to advance their own situations of interests. Opportunities for this type of intelligencing can be found throughout the Records of Early English Drama (REED), for example, when Henry VIII's jester appeared in Ludlow in 1546–47.[9] Edward Tudor's (1537–53) fool was recorded to have been in Southampton in 1550–51,[10] and in Gloucester in 1552–53 money was 'likewise gevyn in reward to a geister of the kynge*s* maiesties & an other Co*m*myng w*ith* hym by the Co*m*maundement of maist*er* maire'.[11] Similarly, a jester in the service of Queen Mary (1516–58) visited Lydd in 1554–55,[12] and New Romney in 1555–56.[13] One or more of her jesters, as well as her husband's, were present in Canterbury in 1554–55 ('the kyng & the quenys Iesters'),[14] and also in Faversham in the same year.[15] In 1562, 'lockye the quen*es* mayiesti*es* Iester' was seen (and rewarded) in Newcastle.[16] Royal servants, including fools and jesters, could keep their eyes and ears open to news of different sorts; from this follows that, given the right jester, royals, courtiers, and ambassadors clearly benefitted from bringing their entertainers with them, obvious comic value aside.

The final part of this chapter reflects on the symbolic value of fools. I argue that aside from bringing fun, linguistic and political comfort, and companionship for the dying Katherine, the fool's presence may have expressed a symbolic value for Chapuys, who used his presence to assert Katherine's regal status as unchanged in the view of the Roman Catholic church, the emperor, and Catholic Europe, by conducting matters in a

---

[9] J. Alan B. Somerset, ed., *REED: Shropshire* (Toronto: University of Toronto Press, 1994), vol. 1, 79.

[10] Peter Greenfield and Jane Cowling, eds., REED: Hampshire (2020), Book of Fines, Southampton City Archives: SC5/3/1 (1550–51). https://ereed.library.utoronto.ca/collections/hamps/.

[11] Audrey Douglas and Peter Greenfield, eds., *REED: Cumberland/ Westmorland/ Gloucestershire* (Toronto: University of Toronto Press, 1986), vol. 1, 297.

[12] James M. Gibson, ed., *REED: Kent* (Toronto: University of Toronto Press, 2002), vol. 2, 694.

[13] Gibson, ed., *REED: Kent*, vol. 2, 779.

[14] Gibson, ed., *REED: Kent*, vol. 1, 174.

[15] Gibson, ed., *REED: Kent*, vol. 2, 545.

[16] J.J. Anderson, ed., *REED: Newcastle upon Tyne* (Toronto: University of Toronto Press, 1982), vol. 1, 31.

royal way. I suggest that the ambassador used his fool to comment on Katherine's treatment by king and court publicly through performance earlier, in 1534, and asserted Katherine's status by giving her the solace of a figure whom a queen would be expected to have in her retinue, or to whose entertainment she might be treated in the context of diplomatic visits between monarchs and their representatives.

Household foolery

I will note from the outset that the patronage of fools and jesters by members of aristocratic and royal households in Tudor England was extensive, as is evidenced by numerous household and account books, such as those found in REED. Henry VII was entertained by, among others, a 'Thomas Blackall the Kinges foule,'[17] and by a 'Mr. Martyn the King's fool', and the latter is listed as having been present at his funeral as one of the 'grooms'.[18] Henry's queen, Elizabeth of York (1466–1503) spent 'two shillings a month' on her own fool, William, for 'his board',[19] and also the royal children had access to entertainment and jests. Young Henry VIII, while still the Duke of York in 1502, already had his own fool, and his mother's privy purse expenses provide us with the fool's amusing name, 'John Goose', and mention that he was rewarded for 'bringing a Carppe to the Quene'.[20] A female fool called 'Jane' was subsequently patronized by Henry VIII's daughter when still the Princess Mary, whose privy purse expenses show that she paid for 'Jane the foole for the tyme of hir seeknes'.[21] Jane was also patronized by queens Katherine Parr and Anne Boleyn.[22] For example, Katherine Parr (1512–48) treated Jane to diverse poultry: '3 geese for Jane Foole' for which she paid 16d, as well as to 'a hen for Jane Foole' costing 6d.[23] The queen's

[17] A.F. Pollard, ed., *The Reign of Henry VII from Contemporary Sources* (3 vols; London: Longmans, Green and Co., 1913–14), vol. 2, 231.

[18] LP vol. 1, #20 (11 May 1509).

[19] N.H. Nicolas, ed., *Privy Purse Expenses of Elizabeth of York: Wardrobe Accounts of Edward IV, With a Memoir of Elizabeth of York* (London, 1830), 196.

[20] Nicolas, ed., *Privy Purse Expenses of Elizabeth of York*, 2.

[21] *PPE Mary*, 123.

[22] Susan James, 'Jane, the Queen's Fool (fl. 1535–1558)', *ODNB*, Oxford University Press, 2019. https://doi.org/10.1093/odnb/9780198614128.013.112276.

[23] *LP* vol. 19.2, #688 (30 November 1544).

reckoning of 1536 indicates that Anne Boleyn—in what were to be the final months of her life—bought '25 yds. of cadace fringe, morrey color, delivered to Skutte, her tailor, for a gown for her Grace's woman fool, and a green satin cap for her'.[24] Anne's fool also features in a negative account of her coronation, sometimes attributed to Chapuys.[25] According to this account, the fool, 'seeing the little honor they showed to her [Anne], cried out, "I think you have all scurvy heads, and dare not uncover"'.[26] The *Letters and Papers* excerpt of this account notes that the fool 'has been to Jerusalem and speaks several languages'.[27] While this story is an excerpt from 'a catalogue of papers at Brussels, now lost' that cannot be verified, the account is distinctly problematic. If the aim of the report had been to suggest that Anne was not generally respected, and the fool was cast in the role of her defender, why would its writer then suggest that the fool had not been foolish but learned and well-travelled? Would the author of the report not then allude to the idea that it was indeed wise to express agitation against those London citizens who were disrespectful of Anne? And what to make of the reference to 'Jerusalem', which implies piety and religious pilgrimage to a place at the root of Christianity, rather than for example, Rome, which in the context of Anne's coronation would not be an innocent reference to make. The description of the fool sits ambiguously in an otherwise negative account of Anne, perhaps in itself exemplary of fools' symbolic ambiguity and their use in the expression of political messages, as well as of the range of abilities ascribed to and expected of fools by contemporaries.

Descriptions of fools in REED do not always clarify whether the entertainers under patronage were professional, 'artificial' fools of the 'buffoon'-variety, or 'natural fools' who would now be considered persons with a learning disability or mental impairment.[28] In some cases

---

[24] *LP* vol. 10, #913 (19 May 1536).

[25] *LP* vol. 6, #585, footnote 3 (2 June 1533), for example.

[26] *LP* vol. 6, #585.

[27] *LP* vol. 6, #585.

[28] The distinctions between 'artificial' and 'natural' fools have been studied, in among others, Sandra Billington, *A Social History of the Fool* (Brighton: Harvester Press, 1984); Sarah Carpenter, 'Laughing at Natural Fools', *Theta* 11, Théâtre Tudor (2013), 3–22; Sarah Carpenter, 'The Places of Foolery: Robert Armin and fooling in Edinburgh', *METh* 37 (2015), 11–26; John J. McGavin, 'Close Kin to a Clean Fool: Robert Armin's Account of Jack Miller', Theta 12, Théâtre Tudor (2016), 39–56; Irina Metzler, *Fools and Idiots? Intellectual Disability in the Middle Ages* (Manchester: Manchester University Press, 2016);

we can turn to account books for clues, but these often evoke just as many questions as they are able to answer. For example, the elaborate Newcastle chamberlains' accounts, at times, but not consistently, refer to one Thomas Dodds as a 'naturall foole', and to further confusion, the other fools mentioned along with him do not receive this nomenclature although they appear to have been treated similarly.[29]

Sometimes an indication of natural foolery is given by fools having been given a 'keeper', such as we find in the records of the wardrobe preparation for the coronation of Henry VIII in 1509, listing the presence of 'Phyppe, keeper of Merten the King's fool'.[30] Unfortunately, we cannot always distinguish between a fool's 'keeper' or 'servant', as seen in the case of John Emyson, who is listed in Henry's privy purse expenses as 'sexton's man',[31] 'Emyson that Attends upon Sexton',[32] but also 'Emyson Sextons s'vnt'.[33] Sexton's reputation for having been a 'natural' fool is suggested by an account attributed to George Cavendish. According to this anecdote, 'Patch' was a gift from Cardinal Wolsey, who, in an attempt to return to the king's favour, had asked Henry Norris: 'But if ye would at this my request present the king with this poor Fool, I trust his highness would accept him well, for surely for a nobleman's pleasure he is worth a thousand pounds'.[34] One could inherit the *patronage* of a professional fool or jester, but when a fool was given as

John Southworth, *Fools and Jesters at the English Court* (Stroud: Sutton Publishing, 1998; Reprinted Stroud: History Press, 2011); and Enid Welsford, *The Fool: His Social and Literary History* (London: Faber and Faber, 1935).

[29] Anderson, ed., *REED: Newcastle*, vol. 1, 104.
[30] *LP* vol. 1, no. 82 (24 June 1509).
[31] *PPE Henry*, 193.
[32] *PPE Henry*, 120.
[33] *PPE Henry*, 138.
[34] George Cavendish, *The Life of Cardinal Wolsey*, ed. Samuel Weller Singer (London, 1827), 257. Although Singer's edition of Cavendish's *The Life of Cardinal Wolsey* shares this anecdote, the anecdote does not seem to appear in any of the following: George Cavendish, *The Negotiations of Thomas Woolsey, the Great Cardinall of England, Containing His Life and Death* (London, 1641; Wing: C1619aA), EEBO; George Cavendish, *The Negotiations of Thomas Woolsey, the Great Cardinall of England Containing his Life and Death* (London, 1650; Wing: C1619A), EEBO; George Cavendish, *The Life and Death of Thomas Woolsey, Cardinal, Once Arch Bishop of York and Lord Chancellour of England* (London, 1667; Wing: 1618), EEBO. Singer probably took the abovementioned anecdote from (any of) two manuscripts in his possession, rather than an editorial addition, as his preface criticizes the 1641 printed edition as being 'in such a garbled form as to be hardly recognized for the same work, abridgment and interpolation having been used with an unsparing hand' (xi), and details that in order to produce his 1827 edition he acquired and

a present, their position was likened to a cherished pet rather than a salaried entertainer.

Although many fools kept under patronage in England would likely have been of the 'natural' variety, their personal skill set varied greatly.[35] Robert Armin's *Foole vpon Foole, or Six Sortes of Sottes* (printed 1600) labels the fools in his book 'a flat foole, a leane foole, a merry foole, a fatt foole, a cleane foole' and 'a verry foole'.[36] Armin's book was intended as a work of comedy, designed first and foremost to entertain, and his categorization itself is compromised by the fact that he clearly tried to get a rhyme for 'merry' and so ended up with 'very', which has no real categorizing force at all. Yet Armin's attempt to categorize fools according to their 'physical characteristics' provides valuable insight into the kind of 'humour and entertainment' that they would have been expected to provide.[37] Sarah Carpenter furthermore emphasizes that a 'fascination with their features' as well as 'undignified physical mishaps' were recurring sources of entertainment.[38] For example, the 'cleane fool' Jack Miller loses most of his facial hair, including his eyebrows, when he sticks his head in the oven to help himself to pies, to the great hilarity of those watching him who found amusement in Miller's obvious discomfort and humiliation.[39] Where Miller invited laughter at his own expense, the 'natural' fool Will Somer (d. 1560), who reputedly had a great influence over the king's state of mind,[40] appears to have favoured reflecting on the oddities of others to entertain his master. Somer's ability to wittily play with words might make him sound more like a very clever artificial fool masquerading as a natural one, rather than a true 'innocent', thus perhaps showing how difficult it is to categorize fools with any degree of certainty. To exemplify this, we might look at a bon mot attributed to Somer by Thomas Wilson in *The Arte of Rhetorique* (1553) in relation to the king's

relied on two manuscripts: one 'from among the duplicates of the late Duke of Norfolk's library', and a 'more recent' manuscript (xiii).

[35] Zoe Screti, '"A Motley to the View": The Clothing of Court Fools in Tudor England', *Midlands Historical Review* 2 (2018), 2–3.

[36] Robert Armin, *Foole vpon Foole, or Six Sortes of Sottes* (London, 1600; STC (2nd edn.): 772.3), EEBO, A1r.

[37] Carpenter, 'Laughing at Natural Fools', 8.

[38] Carpenter, 'Laughing at Natural Fools', 8.

[39] Carpenter, 'Laughing at Natural Fools', 8; McGavin, 'Close Kin to a Clean Fool', 43.

[40] Carpenter, 'Laughing at Natural Fools', 15.

ever-diminishing funds. Somer purportedly told Henry: 'you haue so many Frauditours, so many Conueighers, and so many Deceiuers to get up your money, that they get all to themselues', cleverly punning on 'Auditours, Surueighours, and Receiuers'.[41] Somer's reflection on the greedy behaviour of the courtiers could inspire the king's great merriment, not only because of the clever use of words, but also because at a court where courtiers and petitioners constantly surrounded the king, several of those seeking to ask for favours or advancement would have stood in attendance with burning ears and a request frozen in their throats.

Comic license

The kind of humour that fools such as Somer could offer was brought about by a special license to speak, which, in the context of the court, was reserved for fools because of their honesty. Desiderius Erasmus in *Moriae Encomium*, better known as *The Praise of Folly* (printed 1511), explains that 'princes' ('*principes*') find themselves surrounded by courtiers who would tell a ruler what they *want* to hear rather than what they *need* to hear, and that this is further complicated by some rulers being unaccepting of the truth when offered to them by their councillors.[42] He continues:

> Sed tamen hoc ipsum mire in fatuis meis vsu venit, vt non vera modo, verum etiam aperta conuicia cum voluptate audiantur. Adeo vt idem dictum, quod si a sapientis ore profiscatur, capitale fuerat futurum, a Morione profectum, incredibilem voluptatem pariat.[43]

---

[41] Thomas Wilson, *The Arte of Rhetorike for the Vse of All Suche as are Studious of Eloquence, Sette Foorthe in Englishe, by Thomas Wilson. 1553* (London, 1584; STC (2nd edn.): 25805), EEBO, 204.

[42] Desiderius Erasmus, *Moriae Encomium* (Paris: Jocodus Badius, 1519), fol. 40r–v. I consulted the 1519 printed edition in Latin at the Librije in Zutphen, and thank Dr Jan Bedaux for his help in accessing this source. Please note that in this quote all abbreviated forms have been silently extended, to render the text more readable. I thank Dr Renske Janssen for kindly helping me with this translation into English; any remaining errors are, of course, my own. An accessible English translation can be found in: Desiderius Erasmus, *The Praise of Folly*, ed. Anthony Grafton (Princeton, NJ: Princeton University Press, 2015), 49.

[43] Erasmus, *Moriae Encomium*, fol. 40v.

[But yet this very thing comes as a surprise in my fools, that not only their truths, but also their open reproaches are heard with pleasure. This is so much the case, that the same remark, that if it proceeded from the mouth of a wise man would have been a capital offence, coming from the fool it produces an incredible pleasure].

'Feigned' or 'artificial' fools or jesters employed strategies to evoke laughter similar to those that came 'naturally' to 'innocent' fools. Yet their buffoonery and the services provided to their prince or the nobles they served, were complex, as these fools were expected to provide humour and wisdom, but at the same time, did not have the same license to act as those protected by the suggestion of innocence or limited understanding. The antics of the Spanish buffoon Antoni Tallander, nicknamed 'Mossen Borra', provide insight into this careful balance. Tallander (to whom I briefly referred to earlier as the royal jester who was allegedly held responsible for killing King Martin of Aragon with his wit)[44] continued his position at the court of Ferdinand of Antequera, King of Aragon (ca. 1379–1416). Tallander's career as a comical entertainer aside, he was also, however, 'a respected grammarian and ambassador'; a man with scholarly qualities.[45] Due to his reputation for learning, Tallander could hardly be seen to be overtly counselling the king, although he could use his wits to get across a point by causing laughter and self-reflection. A jester of this sort could be seen to resemble a 'lord of misrule' or a 'master of revels': a deviser as well as an actor or participant in the entertainments, and someone who acts the part of the 'natural' fool, while generally known as an artificial one. Alvar García de Santa María recorded an example of Tallander's foolery at the coronation banquet in honour of Ferdinand's queen consort, Eleonor Countess of Alburquerque (1374–1435), performed simultaneously with a representation of Death using a clever mechanical device that would have been the pinnacle of technology available to the court entertainers at that moment:

[44] This story smacks of the stuff of legends; after all, Martin of Aragon's death caused a major succession crisis, and any individual held responsible for the king's death would have faced execution rather than a continuation of one's career as court entertainer.

[45] Francesc Massip, 'The Cloud: A Medieval Aerial Device, Its Origins, and Its Use in Spain Today', in Clifford Davidson, ed., *The Dramatic Tradition of the Middle Ages* (New York, NY: AMS Press, 2005), 262–74 (265).

The jester was in the hall where the Queen was eating, and when Death came on the cloud . . . [The jester] showed great fear on seeing Death and shouted loudly at it not to come near him. Then the Duke of Gandía sent word to the King, who was at the window watching the Queen dine, that when Death descended and the jester began to shout, he [the Duke] would take him underneath and tell Death to throw him a rope and pull the jester up to him. And this was done. When Death came out on his cloud before the table, Mossen Borra started to shout, and the Duke carried him underneath Death who threw down a rope which they tied to the body of the said Borra, and Death wound him up. Here you would have marvelled at the things Mossen Borra did and at his wailing and at the great fear which seized him, and, whilst being pulled up, he wet himself into his underclothes, and the urine ran on to the heads of those who were below. He was quite convinced he was being carried off to Hell. The King and those who watched were greatly amused.[46]

At first sight, the record shows Tallander's humiliating display of bodily functions to be a source of humour, and the jester appears to be tricked into a situation in which the spectators could laugh at their own knowing and at the fool's unknowing, and the latter's falling into a trap set out for him, reminiscent of the hilarity evoked by the likes of poor Jack Miller and other 'natural' fools in similar plights. Yet, as Lenke Kovács explains, the jester's display of fear does not have to be interpreted as genuine, but could in fact be seen as the action of a 'wise fool', seeking to alleviate the audiences' potential shock and horror at seeing a representation of death. Kovács writes: '[the jester] portrays people's fears so graphically that he seems to hold up a mirror in which the spectators can recognize the foolishness and uselessness of their resistance towards Death.'[47] Tallander's memento mori lesson to the audience then, was

---

[46] William Tydeman, ed., *The Medieval European Stage, 500–1550* (Cambridge: Cambridge University Press, 2001), 597. © Reproduced with permission of The Licensor through PLSclear. Another useful translation can be found in: Peter Meredith and John E. Tailby, eds., *The Staging of Religious Drama in Europe in the Later Middle Ages: Texts and Documents in English Translation* (Kalamazoo, MI: Medieval Institute Publications, 1983), 94–5. See this source also for other late medieval uses of this kind of machinery in drama or performance. For the original Spanish, see: N.D. Shergold, *A History of the Spanish Stage: From Medieval Times until the End of the Seventeenth Century* (Oxford: Clarendon Press, 1967), 121.

[47] Lenke Kovács, 'Frightened or Fearless: Different Ways of Facing Death in the Sixteenth Century Majorcan Play Representacio de la Mort', in Sophie Oosterwijk and

distributed in such a way that it was not only made palatable, but even side-splittingly funny. Although we might wonder if those whose coiffures had been ruined had laughed quite as much as the king and the Duke of Gandía.

In the context of these different traditions and types of foolery, then, we can better understand the significance of the fool at Katherine of Aragon's deathbed. Ambassador Chapuys must have been confident that the fool he brought with him was either so manifestly 'innocent' or actually so sophisticated that he would not give offence to someone in Katherine's plight. They might be trusted either to act in ways which were refreshingly devoid of formality and protocol, or could be trusted to speak the truth with decorum and always with the good of the person in mind, so that solace was brought to Katherine's sickbed. But Chapuys had other agendas apart from bringing a welcome distraction to the dying. In order to reconstruct his political goals for bringing the fool, we will first turn to Katherine's enjoyment and patronage of entertainments in her earlier years as Spanish *Infanta*, princess of Wales, and queen.

Entertaining the *Infanta*

As we have seen in the previous chapter, the *Cuentas* [account books] of Queen Isabella of Castile, kept by Gonzalo de Baeza, offer a treasure trove of information about the different entertainments at the Spanish court of the *Reyes Católicos*. References to *trompetas* [trumpeters], an *atabalero* [kettle drum player], and *menestriles altos* [minstrels], some of these foreign artists, such as the Portuguese *bayladores* [dancers] who received payment in 1492,[48] give the impression of a court in which cultural expression was highly valued. Isabella also kept *locas* [fools] at her court. In 1491, alongside charity to provide food for the poor, a payment to a 'Teresa la Loca' is noted in the *Cuentas*.[49] More prominent in the account books is one 'Maria, la Loca', who is listed as a *moça de camera*,

Stefanie A. Knöll, eds., *Mixed Metaphors: The Danse Macabre in Medieval and Early Modern Europe* (Cambridge: Cambridge Scholars, 2011), 207–36 (212).

[48] *Cuentas*, vol. 1, 393.

[49] *Cuentas*, vol. 1, 397.

a non-noble servant in the queen's household. Although Maria is not consistently singled out, her nickname, 'La Loca', is the name by which she is known in de Baeza's *Cuentas*.[50] An account from 1501 refers to a specific outfit to be paid for to attire 'the maids *and* the Fool, and a girl and a boy that were in the retinue of your Highness with Violante de Albion'[51] (emphasis mine). Mentioning 'La Loca' separately from the other maids suggests that Maria may have had a special position: both part of the inner circle of the queen's trusted servants, as well as a special figure among them. A further indication of her social position can be found in the account recording Maria's being given '*paño verde*' [green cloth or wool] as well as yellow fabric, together perhaps suggestive of a traditional fool's or entertainer's costume.[52] Green cloth of this sort had in 1484 been ordered for a green skirt for 'Juanica, *esclaua*' [slave], alongside '*paño morado*' [cloth or wool in dull purple] and other new wardrobe items, totalling 2,648 maravedís.[53] Green fabric totalling 1,000 maravedís was also bought for two slaves by the names of Maria and Ynes in 1492.[54] De Baeza's accounts do not tell whether this last Maria was the Maria who converted to Christianity in 1499,[55] nor if Ynes were the same as the 'Ynes, *esclaua*' who in June 1504 was given 8,000 maravedís to buy a bed and other necessities.[56] This considerable payment indicates Ynes's importance to someone in the royal household, but if this was because she was a companion with a special status or because of other qualities, is uncertain.

Before sending their daughter, the Princess of Wales, off to England to marry Prince Arthur, Ferdinand and Isabella bargained with Henry VII about the size of Katherine's household and gave instructions to their ambassador, González de Puebla, to see to it that her attendants would obtain their salaries.[57] In an earlier dispatch, the royal couple had already told de Puebla that 'It also seems good to us that the Princess should take the majority of them with her, and the remainder she may

[50] *Cuentas*, vol. 2, 490.
[51] *Cuentas*, vol. 2, 532.
[52] *Cuentas*, vol. 2, 401.
[53] *Cuentas*, vol. 1, 67.
[54] *Cuentas*, vol. 2, 49.
[55] *Cuentas*, vol. 2, 450.
[56] *Cuentas*, vol. 2, 630.
[57] *CSPS* vol. 1, #301 (29 May 1501).

send for afterwards as the King of England may wish'.[58] The list with attendants to remain with the princess in England ranges from the highest in rank, Doña Elvira Manuel, the 'first lady of honour and first lady of the bedchamber' to the laundress, and her male staff ranged from the major domo to the lowly sweeper, and the two squires who looked after 'Doña Elvira and the ladies'.[59] The list names many of the functionaries, but also refers to individuals who are not named, such as the 'two slaves to attend on the maids of honour', and the 'servants in the rooms of the Princess'.[60]

Theresa Earenfight notes that Katherine kept 'a female dwarf who was first part of infanta María's court at Lisbon, then came to Catalina's court in Spain, and moved with her to England where she was known as the *Spanish fool*'.[61] Indeed, evidence from *La Casa de Isabel la Catolica*—the overview of offices of the queen's royal household—shows a payment made to a porter by the name of Françisco Muñoz, who in 1504 received a portion of an annual salary of 4,000 maravedís *'para mantenimiento de la enana'* ['for keeping the female dwarf'] in the household of *'la Princesa de Galez'*.[62] The *Casa* records also show that the same Muñoz went to Portugal in the 1490s, presumably with *'la enana quel tiene en su casa'*.[63] The use of *'su'* here may, at first glance, suggest that the *'enana'* lived at the porter's house (*his* house). This makes the comparison of the keeper of the *'enana'* to the keeper of the fool at the Tudor court an interesting one, especially in the discussion whether keepers of fools were servants or caretakers. After all, this suggests that the Spanish office of looking after the *'enana'* would have been quite practical: housing and, supposedly, feeding the *'enana'*. The rest of the entry, however, uses *'su'* to refer to *'la Reyna, nuestra Señora'* ['the queen, our lady'],[64] so that the word should here be understood as the second person singular form 'your', as the account keeper addressed the queen in writing. This interpretation significantly changes the meaning of the account and the

[58] *CSPS* vol. 1, #287 (3 October 1500).
[59] *CSPS* vol. 1, #288 (3 October 1500).
[60] *CSPS* vol. 1, #288 (3 October 1500).
[61] Theresa Earenfight, 'Raising Infanta Catalina de Aragón to be Catherine, Queen of England', *Anuario de Estudios Medievales* 46:1 (2016), 417–43, (427).
[62] *Casa*, 158.
[63] *Casa*, 128.
[64] *Casa*, 128.

housing arrangements of the '*enana*' who would then have lived at court in the royal household. In any case, the '*mantenimiento de la enana*' was a formal office; that the porter in the household were to be granted this job is unlikely to have been a coincidence, suggesting an important aspect of his task was protecting the '*enana*'. She was after all a woman in a court context in which the '*damas*' were also fiercely guarded by the '*guarda damas*', who controlled access to the ladies.

Unfortunately, the records do not provide the '*enana*'s name, so that when looking for her presence in the instructions given to de Puebla we can only guess whether she was one of the 'servants' or 'slaves', or one of the ladies addressed with the honorary 'doña', here perhaps used as a comic nickname. Given the position of intimacy of the *loca* and female slaves in the inner circle of Isabella's household, it seems likely that also Katherine's 'dwarf' was a highly valued companion, which may have merited her being one of the princess's retinue in the first cohort. When mooring at Plymouth Harbour in October 1501, the Princess of Wales entered her new country followed by a train that reflected her royal blood, her religious devotion, the pomp and splendour that was to underline the wealth of her family, and the traditions of her country. The presence of the female slaves reminded spectators watching Katherine's arrival of the capitulation of Islamic Granada at the hands of Katherine's parents, the *Reyes Católicos*, and thus of the strength and power of the military force supporting the young princess.

Wedding festivities

We have already briefly seen in the previous chapter that Katherine and Arthur's wedding comprised a many-day stretch of celebrations, and Garrett Mattingly observed that as part of these festivities, 'Catherine contributed the antics of the Spanish fool who performed on a high platform grotesquely dexterous feats of tumbling and balancing which kept the onlookers gasping with alternate apprehension and laughter'.[65] Mattingly did not specify the source for this claim in a footnote; instead, he generally noted that he had turned to John Leland's *Collectanea*, which records the festivities surrounding the wedding of the young

---

[65] Mattingly, *Catherine of Aragon*, 40.

Tudor prince and the new princess of Wales. It appears that Mattingly was rather free with his interpretation, however, as Leland only writes: 'Uppon the Frame and Table ascended and went up a Spanyard, the which shewed there many woondrous and delicious Points of Tumbling, Dauncing, and other Sleights'.[66] *The Receyt of the Ladie Katheryne* offers a more elaborate account of the tumbling and the skills of the 'Hispaynyard':

> First, he went upp unto the frame, and a certayn stay in his/hand, to the nombre of xlti fote, summwhat aslope, and when he cam to the hight left his stay and went uppon the cabill—sumtyme on patens, sumtyme with tenes ballys, sumtyme with 'feters of' iron, dauncyng with belles, and lepying many leapys uppon the seid cabill bothe forward and bakward. He played sumtyme with a sword and bukler. Eftson he cast himsilf sodenly from the rope and hang by the tooes, summtyme by the teethe moost marvelously, and with grettest sleighte and cunnyng that eny man cowde possibly excercise or do.[67]

Who was this Spanish tumbler? As early as 1492, Henry VII was entertained by a 'Spaynarde that pleyed the fole'.[68] John Southworth, in his influential study, presented other references that mentioned a—perhaps this—Spanish fool: 'at the end of July, the Spaniard, then named as "Dego, the Spanish fole", was supplied with a saddle, bridle and spurs to accompany Henry to Dover. On 2 October he embarked with the king for France, where a large English army was assembling to oppose the French usurpation of Brittany'.[69] Southworth continues: 'Dego's last recorded performance at court was on 11 March of the following year (1493). Among other Spanish performers rewarded by Henry in the years that followed were a 'Spaynyard that tumbled' in 1494, and, in June 1501, a 'Spaynyard that pleyd on the corde' (a rope-dancer), who pocketed the munificent sum of £10'.[70] Considering the performances of Spanish entertainers at the Tudor court predating Katherine's arrival, the Spanish tumbler mentioned by Leland to have performed at Arthur's and Katherine's wedding festivities could

[66] John Leland, *Collectanea*, editio altera (6 vols; London, 1774), vol. 5, 372.
[67] *Receyt*, 75.
[68] Pollard, ed., *The Reign of Henry VII*, vol. 2, 228.
[69] Southworth, *Fools and Jesters*, 169.
[70] Southworth, *Fools and Jesters*, 170.

possibly be the same tumbler who had previously entertained King Henry VII, instead of, as Mattingly suggested, a member of Katherine's retinue. One complicating matter is that payments made in the king's record books do not always give a straightforward idea of whose retinue a retainer belonged to, as the monarch paid expenses for members of his family. But one can, it seems, claim a tradition of Spanish funambulists who were sought to entertain the English monarch, and either royal court—English or Spanish—might have thought this an appropriate entertainer at the festivities, by whichever route he arrived there.

From genteel economies to queenly patronage

In the years following Prince Arthur's early death on 2 April 1502, Katherine did not have the means, nor the space at Durham House, to keep the whole of her original retinue, stuck as she was between Ferdinand II of Aragon, her tight-fisted father, and her father-in-law Henry VII who continued bargaining about the final payments of her dowry as well as her dower portion. Some of her more intimate companions and attendants remained,[71] but most of her earlier household returned to Spain. John de Cecil, a Spanish trumpeter whom we have already seen in the previous chapter, and who possibly played at Katherine's wedding, found himself a position at Henry VII's court.[72] In 1509, de Cecil appears in the record detailing the coronation of Henry VIII as 'the King's trumpets',[73] and, as we have seen, he is last seen in the court records in 1514.[74]

The REED volumes do not record Katherine having ever patronized jesters or fools, but they do register her patronage of minstrels on her

[71] For example, her attendants at the funeral of Henry VII. See *LP*, vol. 1, #20. See also, Theresa Earenfight, 'A Precarious Household: Catherine of Aragon in England, 1501–1504', in Theresa Earenfight, ed., *Royal and Elite Households in Medieval and Early Modern Europe: More than Just a Castle* (Leiden: Brill, 2018), 338–56.

[72] Michelle Beer, 'Practices and Performances of Queenship: Catherine of Aragon and Margaret Tudor, 1503–1533' (Unpublished doctoral thesis, University of Illinois at Urbana-Champaign, 2014), 197.

[73] *LP* vol. 1, #82 (24 June 1509).

[74] Beer, 'Practices and Performances', 198.

arrival in Plymouth in 1501,[75] as we have just learned, and, significantly, at Furnival's Inn in London when she was already widowed.[76]

James Forse suggests that in the years before her marriage to Henry VIII, Katherine patronized entertainers in order to 'advertise or assert [her] status' as a royal princess and as an influence to reckon with.[77] Forse importantly notes that 'Katherine's and Prince Henry's musicians were visiting Canterbury together in 1507', which he interprets as 'a way to link her with Henry in a year when Katherine's status and chances of marrying Prince Henry seemed especially bleak'.[78] It appears that Katherine was very much aware of the political benefits of entertainments that contributed an element of festivity and royal splendour to an entourage, and used this to her advantage.

On 11 June 1509 Henry VIII married Katherine at Greenwich, framed as, to borrow John Edward's words, 'fulfilling a deathbed command from his father'.[79] This brought an end to Spanish–English tensions about Katherine's dowry payments, and, for Katherine, signalled the beginning of a period of renewed affluence as Henry's queen, as well as increased patronage of entertainers befitting her new social position. The King's Book of Payments from 1510 records a fee paid to the 'Queen's minstrels' of 40 s,[80] and the same payment occurs in 1519, made out to 'the minstrels of the Queen's chamber', this time mentioning the musicians' names: 'Baltazar, Jaques, Evans and another'.[81] The queen's

---

[75] John M. Wasson, ed., *REED: Devon* (Toronto: University of Toronto Press, 1986), vol. 1, 215. Leland also notes that Katherine had minstrels in her entourage, as during the wedding festivities, he writes that 'she and her Ladyes called for their Minstrells'. Leland, *Collectanea*, vol. 5, 355.

[76] Alan H. Nelson and John R. Elliott, Jr, eds., *REED: Inns of Court* (Cambridge: D.S. Brewer, 2010), vol. 1, 30.

[77] James H. Forse, 'Advertising Status and Legitimacy: or, Why Did Henry VIII's Queens and Children Patronize Travelling Performers?', *ET* 16:2 (2013), 59–90 (64).

[78] Forse, 'Advertising Status', 64.

[79] John Edwards, *Mary I: England's Catholic Queen* (New Haven, CT: Yale University Press, 2011), 2.

[80] 'The King's Book of Payments, 1510', in *Letters and Papers, Foreign and Domestic, Henry VIII, Volume 2, 1515–1518*, ed. J.S. Brewer (London, 1864), 1444–9. *British History Online* http://www.british-history.ac.uk/letters-papers-hen8/vol2/pp1444-1449 [accessed 05.04.2023].

[81] 'The King's Book of Payments, 1519', in *Letters and Papers, Foreign and Domestic, Henry VIII, Volume 3, 1519–1523*, ed. J.S. Brewer (London, 1867), 1533–9. *British History Online* http://www.british-history.ac.uk/letters-papers-hen8/vol3/pp1533-1539 [accessed 05.04.2023].

minstrels are also referred to in the Winchester chamberlains' accounts in 1512–13.[82] Katherine appears as a generous host and organizer of court events, such as the elaborate revels held on Epiphany night in 'the Queen's grace in her chamber' in the second year of Henry's reign.[83] We furthermore see her in the role of honoured spectator at numerous jousts, revels, masques, and disguisings, sports, banquets, and diplomatic events, such as, for example, at the Field of Cloth of Gold (1520), where her adoring gaze was to complement the king's royal image-making. Additionally, many a musical evening of singing and dancing relied on the involvement of the queen's ladies, such as on the occasion reported by the Venetian ambassador Sebastian Giustinian, when the company, including Margaret Tudor, queen of Scots, was entertained by a well-known and celebrated musician.[84] As queen, Katherine seems to have enjoyed Henry's entertainments at his side, listening to musicians whom he paid for, watching spectacles devised in his honour, and perhaps, laughing at his fools. When on progress, Katherine appears to have had her own minstrels work together with those patronized by her husband the king, as can be seen in the example of the sheriff of Bristol's 'revised estimates of expenses incurred for others, as corrected by mayor' which list a payment 'to the Kyng and Quene is mynstrellis.'[85] Forse explains:

> Henry and Katherine were together on progresses in 1517 and 1518, and the period from about 1510 to 1525 marks a time when Katherine was being presented with her husband as almost a co-ruler. The joint appearance in provincial records of the king's and the queen's minstrels in 1517 and 1518, while the pregnant queen was on progress with her king, may be an outward manifestation of that status.[86]

[82] Greenfield and Cowling, eds., *REED: Hampshire*, Chamberlains' Accounts, HRO: W/E1/50 (1512–13), https://ereed.library.utoronto.ca/collections/hamps/.

[83] 'Revels', in *Letters and Papers, Foreign and Domestic, Henry VIII*, vol. 2, 1515–1518, ed. J.S. Brewer (London, 1864), 1490–1518. *British History Online* http://www.british-history.ac.uk/letters-papers-hen8/vol2/pp1490-1518 [accessed 05.04.2023].

[84] Sebastian Giustinian, *Four Years at the Court of Henry VIII*, ed. Rawdon Brown (2 vols; London: Smith, Elder, and Co., 1854), vol. 1, 301.

[85] Mark C. Pilkinton, ed., *REED: Bristol* (Toronto: University of Toronto Press, 1997), vol. 1, 29–30.

[86] Forse, 'Advertising Status', 64.

Shared patronage of entertainment, then, could be used to indicate marital harmony within the royal couple, and allowed Katherine to assert herself as queen of England. As the years progressed and Katherine did not give birth to any more living heirs, having given her husband 'only' the Princess Mary as legal offspring, however, Henry gradually cooled towards Katherine.[87] During the years Henry was trying to divorce Katherine, the king physically distanced himself from his consort and had her moved to increasingly less comfortable homes where she was to also relinquish part of her staff. Already at the More palace in Hertfordshire in 1531 she no longer had the entourage that she had been accustomed to in her heydays at Henry's side, and complained about her diminished position. After the Venetian ambassador visited her at the More, he reported the following: 'In the morning we saw her Majesty dine: she had some 30 maids of honour (*donzelle*) standing round the table, and about 50 who performed its service. Her Court consists of about 200 persons, but she is not so much visited as heretofore, on account of the King.'[88] Although Katherine did not live in the splendour to which she had once been accustomed, her lifestyle could hardly be described as financial hardship. Yet, this was the beginning of a gradual diminishing of status and means.

The 'princess dowager of Wales'

In May 1533, Thomas Cranmer, as archbishop of Canterbury, annulled the king's marriage to Katherine, and in July of the same year, a proclamation was issued that took Katherine's title of 'queen' from her, naming her princess dowager of Wales, and forbidding subjects from addressing her with her former title.[89] Katherine's change in status can be seen reflected in her patronage of performers; while the mayor's own

---

[87] Much has been written about the royal divorce and the events leading up to it. See J.J. Scarisbrick, *Henry VIII* (New Haven, CT: Yale University Press, 1997); G.W. Bernard, *The King's Reformation: Henry VIII and the Remaking of the English Church* (New Haven: Yale University Press, 2005), esp. 1–72; and C.S.L. Davies and John Edwards, 'Katherine [Catalina, Catherine, Katherine of Aragon] (1485–1536)', *ODNB*, Oxford University Press, 2004. https://doi.org/10.1093/ref:odnb/4891.

[88] *CSPV* vol. 4, #682.

[89] T.E. Tomlins and W.E. Taunton, eds., *Statutes of the Realm* (London, 1817), vol. 3, 484: 'And also the said Lady Katheryn owyth not to bere or have the name title Dignitie

accounts[90] and the Steward's Accounts[91] both clearly state that Katherine still patronized players who performed in Southampton in 1530–32, and the queen's players also performed in 1531 in Magdalen College, Oxford, in 1533 all performances by groups of players patronized by Katherine had been cancelled.[92] From the same year onwards, we see Queen Anne Boleyn's players and minstrels performing in various places.[93] The patronage of players was not an exclusive right of queens, as can be seen, for example, in the Lady Anne Percy's (1485–1552) patronage of a troupe called the 'Lady Mautravers' Performers' ('Mimis domine Matervers').[94] Yet, the queen's players would, by the time of the annulment, no longer be at Katherine's disposal. For Katherine, who did not accept the removal of her title, nor the king's understanding that he was not married to her, patronizing a group named anything but the queen's would have been unthinkable. In a letter to the emperor, Chapuys complains that Katherine had so far coped with the distress caused by the king's divorce matter 'imagining that as long as she retains the allowance and estate which queens generally enjoy she may consider herself as a queen, and not be dispossessed of her rank and dignity'.[95] When Henry, however, divested her of her title and the dignities normally reserved for the queen, even including her jewels and her barge, this fell heavy on her. Even more disconcerting to Katherine, however, was the loss of her marriage portion from which she had meant to pay the 'pensions and salaries' of 'her servants and domestics, besides

or style of the Quene of this Realme but hath justely lost the same; BE IT therfor enacted by auctorite of this psent parliament that the said Lady Katheryn from hensforth shall not be called reputed nor taken by the name Dignite or style of the Quene of this Realme, but shall utterly lose the same'. See also: Timothy G. Elston, 'Widow Princess or Neglected Queen? Catherine of Aragon, Henry VIII, and English Public Opinion, 1533–1536', in Carole Levin and Robert Bucholz, eds., *Queens and Power in Medieval and Early Modern England* (Lincoln, NE: University of Nebraska Press, 2009), 16–30 (16).

[90] Greenfield and Cowling, eds., *REED: Hampshire*, Book of Fines, Southampton City Archives: SC5/3/1, f67r (1530–32). https://ereed.library.utoronto.ca/collections/hamps/.: 'Item gevon to the quenys players yn reward vj s. viij d.'

[91] Greenfield and Cowling, eds., *REED: Hampshire*, Steward's Accounts, Southampton City Archives: SC5/1/37, f21v (1530–31). https://ereed.library.utoronto.ca/collections/hamps/.: 'Item to the quenes playeres v s.'

[92] Forse, 'Advertising Status', 62.

[93] Forse, 'Advertising Status', 62.

[94] Cameron Louis, ed., *REED: Sussex* (Toronto: University of Toronto Press, 2000), vol. 1, 15.

[95] *CSPS* vol. 4.2, #1123 (3 September 1533).

other people whose fidelity she has rewarded with sundry offices in her household'.[96] Having no way to pay for their services, Katherine would have been honour-bound to let go of most of what was left of her trusted entourage.

'Like the entrance of a prince'

We can thus interpret Chapuys's first attempt to visit Katherine at Kimbolton, in July 1534, in this light. On this occasion, Chapuys brought a large entourage in the form of a train of Spanish merchants and 'nearly a hundred' horses, and 'minstrels and trumpeters', so that 'when they rode into the places on the road it was like the entrance of a prince'.[97] Henry VIII, no doubt fearful of the visual impact this procession would make—not only on the former queen and her household, but also on the subjects spectating along the route—had a messenger intercept the visitors while they were on their way, prohibiting the ambassador from speaking with Katherine. As a result, thirty of the horsemen continued to Kimbolton, but without Chapuys. The horsemen, so the *Chronicle* says, 'took with them a very funny young fellow who had been brought by the ambassador, and who was dressed as a fool, and had a padlock dangling from his hood'.[98] The report significantly does not say that they brought a *fool*, but rather a man who was *dressed* as one. He was clearly fashioned to make apparent his jesting *role*, even from a distance, but that did not exclude the possibility that he could have also acted as a political messenger or a spy. But what sort of fool was he? As Katherine's ladies presented the visitors with an elaborate breakfast, the fool did not partake in this meal, but made a song and dance about suffering from toothache:

> ... so he clapped his hands to one of his cheeks and began to cry, and went to the place where the barber was, and made signs that he had the toothache. The barber out of pity for him made him sit in a chair and put his finger in his mouth, and the fool began to clench his teeth and scream out, and made the poor barber scream out too with pain

[96] *CSPS* vol. 4.2, #1123.
[97] Hume, ed., *Chronicle*, 47.
[98] Hume, ed., *Chronicle*, 47.

of the bitten finger, so that the noise they both made brought all the ladies and gentlemen to them, and they mightily enjoyed the joke.[99]

Where the fool's act might first remind us of the Jack Miller-type joke in which the fool draws attention to his own physicality and the limitations of the body, as well as giving his spectators the fun of his bodily unease and pain, the joke quickly turned against the barber, who was tricked into believing the fool, and thus himself 'fooled'. That is, unless the barber was part of a 'managed' performance, and cooperated in a preorganized joke. In either case the fool showed himself capable of a cunning trick of 'making a scene' on his 'victim', and he demonstrated that he was aware of the powers of attracting spectatorship. After all, the ladies and gentlemen watching the 'spectacle' had arrived to the scene attracted by the fool's fake crying, assuming to be about to watch a performance in which the fool debases himself, only to find out that the joke was to be made much better when the fool turned out to be a 'clever' fool.

The fool's ability to attract an audience and turn his visibility to advantage was not only used to cause hilarity, but also took on a political form. The *Chronicle* reports that on his arrival Chapuys's fool artfully commented on Katherine's imprisonment by overtly attempting to swim the moat surrounding Kimbolton Castle to reach Katherine and her ladies. This action brought comic attention to a protection mechanism that was of course an actual barrier against unwanted visitors, as well as a means to keep the former queen from fleeing from the castle in which she was perhaps not officially kept prisoner,[100] but where in practice, she was very much detained. The fool is said to have made a show of fearing to be drowned, and was pulled out by 'two or three of the gentlemen on horseback'.[101] The fool then removed the padlock from his hood and 'threw it at the windows', shouting in Spanish: 'Take this, and the next time I will bring the key.'[102]

The *Chronicle* notes that the padlock was confiscated by Henry's servants, who suspected that it carried a secret message to Katherine.

[99] Hume, ed., *Chronicle*, 48.
[100] Although Chapuys does interpret her to be Henry's prisoner in his letter to the emperor. *CSPS* vol. 5.1, #75 (27 July 1534).
[101] Hume, ed., *Chronicle*, 48.
[102] Hume, ed., *Chronicle*, 48.

The thought that they entertained the possibility that the fool might actually be a secret agent is interesting as a comment on current thoughts about fools' functions and capacities. Contrary to their expectations, however, Henry's servants found that the lock did not contain a letter. Indeed, the message was more likely to have been the fool's performance itself. Criticizing the former queen's imprisonment through burlesquing his desire to visit her no doubt drew attention to his patron's inability to visit due to the king's orders. Furthermore, conveying the message in Spanish rather than English was significant, not only because it gave Katherine the pleasure of hearing her own language spoken by people who were, both through their background, and by inclination, on her side, and indeed made a great show of it, but also because it excluded the English people present at Kimbolton who could not understand what the fool said, but only heard him shout something incomprehensible while throwing an unknown missile (which later turned out to be the padlock) at the windows. The fool's action can be seen to have created an 'us' and 'them' and drew Katherine—who had tried so hard to be an English princess and queen, but who had been let down by her husband the king—in with Chapuys's Spanish train of people who technically were not the king's subjects, and reminded her of the culture and language of her youth when she had been the *Infanta* Catalina.

The English were clearly suspicious of the Spanish fool considering his apt political commentary through play and his hurling of the mysterious padlock. The thought of him smuggling something in the manner of a spy or a foreign threat was not far off the reality of the situation, and indeed, not unique, as later examples of suspicions directed at foreign fools show. For example, when in 1546 Henry Howard, the earl of Surrey, was suspected of treason against King Henry and Prince Edward, evidence was sought both in the earl's living above his station such as in the bearing a coat of arms which was too regal ('My lord of Surrey's pryde and his gowne of gold. Departure of the Kinges apparel'[103]) but also in the keeping of 'one Pasquil an Italian as a jester, but more

---

[103] *LP* vol. 21.2, #555 (15 December 1546).

likely a Spy, and so reputed.'[104] Similar suspicions can be found in a later letter by the earl of Salisbury, who in 1605 wrote to Sir John Ogle to inform him of a potential gathering of intelligence. He wrote, 'I know that wolves do often walk under sheep's clothing, and how usual it is for buffoons to be used as spies', before hurryingly disclaiming that he held it 'a weakness in wise men to believe that all sheep are wolves'. Yet his message urges Sir John to watch out for: 'a Spanish jester, in whom the King and Queen of Spain take great delight, the rather because he is of such a humour of ranging abroad as he becomes delightful at his return to those that hear his foolish discourses of his adventures'.[105] Assuming that the jester would 'hereafter . . . talk of his usage', Sir John Ogle was advised to see to his 'lodging and diet' and 'not to bring him within shot or danger' so that the jester could be back on his way to Spain as soon as possible.[106] The English, and also likely the Spanish, would have assumed Chapuys's fool was keeping his eyes and ears open to report back to Chapuys, aside from teasing the barber, entertaining the ladies, taking a dive in the moat, and brightening Katherine's spirits by conveying an implicit political message.

'In plain view of "Cromwell's spies"'

Besides the advantages of an extra pair of eyes for intelligence-gathering, and his using play as political commentary that would have both entertained and brought solace to Katherine, the fool in Chapuys's retinue also had a ceremonial function. When in December 1535 the ambassador learned that Katherine's health had deteriorated, he rushed to Kimbolton, 'followed by a numerous suite of my own servants and friends'.[107] At such short notice, however, he could hardly have gathered all the Spanish merchants in London as he had earlier in the year,

[104] Edward, Lord Herbert of Cherbury, *The Life and Raigne of King Henry the Eight* (London, 1649), 564. Cf; Susan Brigden, 'Henry Howard, Earl of Surrey, and the "Conjured League"', *HJ* 37:3 (1994), 507–37, (532).
[105] 'Cecil Papers: September 1605, 16–30', in *Calendar of the Cecil Papers in Hatfield House*: Volume 17, 1605, ed. M.S. Giuseppi (London, 1938), 423–44. *British History Online* http://www.british-history.ac.uk/cal-cecil-papers/vol17/pp423-444 [accessed 05.04.2023].
[106] Giuseppi, ed., 'Cecil Papers: September 1605', 423–44.
[107] *CSPS* vol. 5.2, #3.

and there was no time for an elaborate procession with pomp and splendour. Chapuys then, did not have the opportunity to make the 'entrance of a prince' as he had on the earlier occasion, had he been permitted to reach Kimbolton.[108] Yet despite the limitations of his entourage, he attempted to conduct the visit in as royal a manner as possible. In his letter to Charles V, Chapuys reports that after formally greeting Katherine and kissing her hand, he was thanked for his services rendered over the years, and, so he claims, for visiting her during her final hours. Chapuys describes their ceremonial meeting as witnessed by 'a friend of Cromwell's whom that secretary had sent to accompany me, or rather to act as a spy on my movements and report what I might say or do during my visit', 'the principal officers of her household, such as her own chamberlain', and 'many others', all of whom he did not trust.[109] It was of paramount importance to Chapuys that these 'spies of Cromwell's' witnessed his actions, and the manner of his conduct, so that when they reported back to their master, they would be likely to report something that Chapuys wanted them to see and remember. The ceremonial display of strong affection between the representative of Charles V and the former queen, for example, would have been duly noted, and even Katherine's supposed claim recorded by Chapuys in his letter, that 'if it should please God to take her to Himself, it would at least be a consolation to die as it were in my arms, and not all alone like a beast',[110] was far from innocent.

The ceremonial part of the visit aside, Katherine and Chapuys also had long, private conversations during which they discussed matters both personal and political.[111] Unfortunately, what was exchanged between Katherine and the fool has not been recorded. We only know that Katherine 'laughed' ('*rire deus ou troys fois*') and that it was her wish to relax with ('*soy recreer avec*') the fool, suggesting a situation in which the fool was a distributor of fun rather than an object of ridicule. If this fool was the same as the fool who had visited Kimbolton earlier, as Mattingly and Hume have suggested,[112] the likelihood is high that the fool would have again comforted the former queen with the

---

[108] Hume, ed., *Chronicle*, 47.
[109] *CSPS* vol. 5.2, #3.
[110] *CSPS* vol. 5.2, #3.
[111] *CSPS* vol. 5.2, #3.
[112] Hume, ed., *Chronicle*, 50; Mattingly, *Catherine of Aragon*, 307.

language of her childhood, the pleasure of witticisms and fun antics, and political remarks dressed as play. Importantly, if this fool was the same jester who had delighted Katherine at an earlier time, then he was likely again 'dressed as a fool',[113] making his role apparent to anyone watching Chapuys's retinue enter Kimbolton Castle. Clearly marked as a figure of entertainment, the fool's presence placed extra emphasis on Chapuys's status as a representative of the emperor, and reminded spectators watching his arrival that this was not the visit of a courtier to a dowager princess, who could be expected to live away from the splendour and bustle of worldly entertainment, but that of an ambassador paying homage to a queen.

Similar diplomatic use of entertainment can also be found in Henry VIII's privy purse expenses, which offer insights into the honours that monarchs bestowed on one another in the form of entertainment, while also underlining their status and evidencing good taste. For example, when in 1532 in Calais Henry consolidated his friendship with the king of France, the king of Navarre, and the cardinal of Lorrain, the different parties treated the other leaders to entertainments while the entertained parties rewarded the amusement-providing servants. Thus we see that Henry paid for 'doubeletts for the garde to wrestle in bifore the king and the frenche king', suggesting an entertainment sponsored by himself, and that he showed gratitude to entertainments received when he 'paied to the frenche kings Jester in Rewarde ix. li. vj s. viij d.',[114] and 20 crowns to the 'singers of the Cardynalls de larena'.[115] The reciprocity in offering entertainment and the largesse of the steep rewards are suggestive of the equally honorary nature of providing amusement to the other leaders and taking the role of the entertained party. Similarly, by bringing his fool for Katherine's entertainment, Chapuys treated her just as the French king had Henry VIII in 1532: showing respect while emphasizing that it was in his gift to provide such diversion. But just as the camaraderie between Francis I and Henry VIII placed a superficial layer of 'fun' over what was clearly a politically driven encounter, the outward appearances of Chapuys's visit to Katherine, performed in plain view of 'Cromwell's spies', simultaneously concealed and revealed

---

[113] Hume, ed., *Chronicle*, 47.
[114] *PPE Henry*, 269.
[115] *PPE Henry*, 269.

a clear political message. Chapuys pointedly left room for interpreters to see a politically innocent act during which an old friend treated a dying lady to foolery, while displaying to those who could, or permitted themselves to see the symbolic ritual and what is now understood as cultural diplomatic conduct with which a statesperson or their representative would dignify royalty. Thus, while at Kimbolton in 1534 the fool's actions themselves could be seen as an outwardly made political comment, in January 1536, the fool's actions were likely mostly 'just' fun and, if political, made for Katherine's benefit. Chapuys's actions, however, in providing the fool's entertainment, can be seen as a separate layer of action, using the visit to express a political statement that undermined Henry's view on the divorce, by implying that not only Chapuys considered Katherine to still be queen of England, but that Charles V, and with him, the rest of Catholic Europe, did not, and would never, accept Katherine's change of status; not during her lifetime, nor afterwards.

| 3 |

Food for Thought

Introduction

Throughout the previous two chapters, off-hand references to feasting or banquets have been made when this formed a context for
performance. We have seen feasting mentioned in relation to music, for
example when banqueting formed part of a range of celebrative or ceremonial festivities. Musical performance could equally serve as a support
act for other forms of entertainment, such as drama, or as entertainment in its own right.[1] Music was also used in a ceremonial capacity
within the context of the banquet, signalling, for example, the entrance
of guests or dishes. An example of the latter can be inferred from a letter
from Imperial ambassador François van der Delft to Charles V written
on 31 January 1547. The ambassador writes that he 'learnt from a very
confidential source that the King [Henry VIII], whom may God receive
in His Grace, had departed this life, although not the slightest signs of
such a thing were to be seen at Court'.[2] He illustrates this by noting that

---

[1] Edmund A. Bowles gives a helpful overview of music as banquet entertainment at
various courts: Edmund A. Bowles, 'Musical Instruments at the Medieval Banquet', *RbM*
12: 1/4 (1958), 41–51.
[2] *CSPS* vol. 9, 1–14 (31 January 1547), *British History Online*. http://www.british-
history.ac.uk/cal-state-papers/spain/vol9/pp1–14. [accessed 22.03.2023].

Intercultural Explorations and the Court of Henry VIII. Nadia T. van Pelt, Oxford University Press.
© Nadia T. van Pelt (2024). DOI: 10.1093/oso/9780192863447.003.0003

'even the usual ceremony of bearing in the royal dishes to the sound of trumpets was continued without interruption.'[3]

We have also seen enactments of folly performed under the auspices of the ceremonial meal. For example, Antoni Tallander's supposed ruining of dishes and hairdos at the coronation banquet for Eleonor of Alburquerque gives an idea of one kind of entertainment to which persons sitting through a feast would have been treated. However, the previous chapter specifically looked at Tallander's antics through the lens of comic licence, and how this softened, or sweetened, a deeply serious message. I have not yet emphasized that the fool's contribution to the performance of a state-of-the-art mechanized spectacle, in which a machine presented spectators with the illusion of a cloud descending from the skies, sat in a wider tradition of using *automata* or mechanical devices in *entremets* that were staged during royal banquets. Burlesquing the human body paired with displaying technological advancement can also be seen to have featured in the banquet celebrating the union of Charles the Bold and Margaret of York in 1468. On this occasion a 'Madame de Beaugrant' described as '*la naine*' [the 'dwarf'] was placed on top of the table and given as a 'gift' to the young bride, but only after '*la naine*', dressed as a shepherdess, had made a spectacular entry into the room riding an *automata* representing a golden lion, which could open and close its mouth and sing a song.[4] But *automata* were not exclusively used to complement foolery, nor was this the only kind of entertainment provided during the ceremonial meal.

The current chapter will show that by acknowledging the royal banquet as solely a *context for* performance, as this book has done so far, one misses out on an important aspect of court culture. The ceremonial meal in the early European courts was *itself* a type of performance, one that brought together different forms of art, technology, ritual, and spectacle, blurring them, and using different kinds of cultural

---

[3] *CSPS* vol. 9, 1–14 (31 January 1547). This custom of announcing dishes or transferring other messages related to the meal through the sound of trumpets occurred in other geographical and linguistic areas. Günther Schiedlausky, *Essen und Trinken: Tafelsitten bis zum Ausgang des Mittelalters* (München: Prestel Verlag, 1956), 22: '*Trompetensignale riefen die Gäste zum Handwaschen*' [The sounding of trumpets called the guests to wash their hands].

[4] Johan Huizinga, *Herfsttij der Middeleeuwen*, ed. Anton van der Lem (Leiden: Olympus, 2004; 1st edn. 1919), 40.

expression as part of, or in support of, another. The meal as performance type complemented various different celebrative occasions, such as weddings, the birth of a royal child, or ritual events such as coronations and funerals, but also proved to be a welcome addition to jousts and, among other events, entertainments hosted for foreign delegates and noble or royal guests of honour. The current chapter addresses a total performance experience that although sometimes understood as peripheral, actually sat at the heart of court ritual, celebration, and spectacle. The first part of this chapter is therefore methodological, and seeks to highlight the potential of the study of the banquet in cultural history, showing how the multimedia event that was the banquet could yield information answering a diversity of questions. Needless to say, my case study necessarily relies on the foundational interdisciplinary groundwork that has been done under the umbrella of food history, and recent developments in one of its branches that shares interests with the studies of 'scriptedness', performance, and spectatorship.

As a case study, this chapter presents Henry VIII's opportunities to host Charles V on what he [Henry] considered his own territory, both in England and across the Channel. It addresses the emperor's visits to Canterbury and Calais in respectively May and July 1520 as described by the Venetian Marino Sanuto in his *Diaries*, as well as the 1522 London visit as referred to in the *Rutland Papers*, among other sources. We will see that Henry used food and ceremonies involving food in diplomatic encounters and strategically employed them to cement alliances. The ritual meal, therefore, can be studied as a core instrument of diplomacy, touching on questions of ceremony, precedence, reciprocity, hospitality, and trust.

Part 1: The fruits of interdisciplinarity

Food history and the scriptedness of the banquet

The study of food and eating in the Middle Ages and early modern period has in the last few decades taken an interdisciplinary route that could stand as a methodological example to other fields of research. Touching on multiple aspects of food and consumption behaviours, rituals, and ceremony, studies in this field reveal the valuable fruits of bringing together wide-ranging expertise from historians, archae-ologists, nutritionists, art historians, political scientists, economists, sociologists and anthropologists in publications such as the journal *Food & History* (2003–22) and in multidisciplinary collaborations cul-minating in a number of edited collections such as, *At the Table* (2007) edited by Timothy J. Tomasik and Juliann M. Vitullo; *Food in Medieval England* (2006), edited by C.M. Woolgar, D. Serjeantson, and T. Wal-dron; and *A Cultural History of Food in the Renaissance* (2012), edited by Ken Albala.[5] Studies in this broad and rapidly developing field have taken multiple approaches and source types, engaging with objects and material cultural evidence,[6] written documentation such as cook-ery books, books of ceremony, financial accounts,[7] religious tracts,[8] legislative documents (for example, regarding sumptuary laws[9]), trial records,[10] dietaries,[11] and have also studied sites and buildings,[12] human

---

[5] *Food & History*, the European Institute for the History and Culture of Food, Université de Tours (IEHCA, at: http://iehca.eu/en/publications/food-history); C.M. Woolgar, D. Serjeantson, and T. Waldron, eds., *Food in Medieval England: Diet and Nutri-tion* (Oxford: Oxford University Press, 2006). For an overview of this expanding field of study, see C.M. Woolgar, 'Food and the Middle Ages', *JMH* 36 (2010), 1–19; Timothy J. Tomasik and Juliann M. Vitullo, eds., *At the Table: Metaphorical and Material Cultures of Food in Medieval and Early Modern Europe* (Turnhout: Brepols, 2007); Ken Albala, ed., *A Cultural History of Food in the Renaissance* (London: Berg, 2012).

[6] See for example Kirstin Kennedy, 'Sharing and Status: the Design and Function of a Sixteenth-Century Spanish Spice Stand in the Victoria and Albert Museum', *RS* 24:1 (2010), 142–55; Valerie Taylor, 'Banquet Plate and Renaissance Culture: A Day in the Life', *RS* 19:5 (2005), 621–33; Victoria Yeoman, 'Speaking Plates: Text, Performance, and Banqueting Trenchers in Early Modern Europe', *RS* 31:5 (2017), 755–79.

[7] Carl I. Hammer, 'A Hearty Meal? The Prison Diets of Cranmer and Latimer', *SCJ* 30:3 (1999), 653–80.

[8] A useful example of how scholars can use dietaries and religious tracts to obtain a better sense of the relationship between religion and food consumption, is found in Eleanor Barnett, 'Reforming Food and Eating in Protestant England, c. 1560–c. 1640', *HJ* 63:3 (2020), 507–27.

[9] David Gentilcore, *Food and Health in Early Modern Europe: Diet, Medicine, and Society, 1450–1800* (London: Bloomsbury Academic, 2016), 49–50.

[10] On food and the Inquisition: Christopher Kissane, *Food, Religion and Communities in Early Modern Europe* (London: Bloomsbury Academic, 2017), esp. chapters 1 and 2.

[11] For example, Paul S. Lloyd, 'Dietary Advice and Fruit-Eating in Late Tudor and Early Stuart England', *Journal of the History of Medicine and Allied Sciences* 67:4 (2012), 553–86.

[12] Simon Thurley, 'The Sixteenth-Century Kitchens at Hampton Court', *Journal of the British Archaeological Association* 143:1 (1990), 1–28.

and animal remains that provide insight into nutrition-intake,[13] and have turned to zoology and ornithology,[14] as well as to literary references,[15] and pictorial representations of food or consumption represented in visual arts.[16] These findings put together add an invaluable dimension to research in history, and bring to life any period under investigation. Leading studies in late medieval and early modern food history that address the banquet as a special culinary occasion, and have shaped the field include Michel Jeanneret's *Des Mets et Des Mots* (1987), translated as *A Feast of Words* (1991), Ken Albala's *The Banquet: Dining in the Great Courts of Late Renaissance Europe* (2007), and more recently, Massimo Montanari's *Gusti del Medioevo: I prodotti, la cucina, la tavola* (2012), translated as *Medieval Tastes: Food, Cooking, and the Table* (2015), and Christina Normore's *A Feast for the Eyes: Art, Performance & the Late Medieval Banquet* (2015).[17]

Within this discourse, various scholars have referred to either the theatre-like qualities or the scriptedness of the banquet.[18] These observations sit within a larger question of what constitutes performance, as

[13] C.M. Woolgar, D. Serjeantson, and T. Waldron, eds., 'Conclusion', *Food in Medieval England: Diet and Nutrition* (Oxford: Oxford University Press, 2006), 267–80 (278).

[14] W.R.P. Bourne, 'The Birds and Animals Consumed when Henry VIII Entertained the King of France and the Count of Flanders at Calais in 1532', *Archives of Natural History* 10:2 (1981), 331–3.

[15] Addressing an earlier time period: Joanna Bellis, 'The dregs of trembling, the draught of salvation: the dual symbolism of the cup in medieval literature', *JMH* 37:1 (2011), 47–61; Aisling Byrne, 'Arthur's refusal to eat: ritual and control in the romance feast', *JMH* 37:1 (2011), 62–74.

[16] Phyllis Pray Bober, *Art, Culture, and Cuisine: Ancient and Medieval Gastronomy* (Chicago, IL: University of Chicago Press, 1999).

[17] Michel Jeanneret, *A Feast of Words: Banquets and Table Talk in the Renaissance*, trans. Jeremy Whiteley and Emma Hughes (Cambridge: Polity Press, 1991); Ken Albala, *The Banquet: Dining in the Great Courts of Late Renaissance Europe* (Urbana and Chicago, IL: University of Illinois Press, 2007); Massimo Montanari, *Medieval Tastes: Food, Cooking, and the Table*, trans. Beth Archer Brombert (New York, NY: Columbia University Press, 2015); Normore, *Feast*.

[18] Jeanneret, *A Feast of Words*, 54; Albala, *The Banquet*, 4; L.B. Ross, 'Beyond Eating: Political and Personal Significance of the Entremets at the Banquets of the Burgundian Court', in Timothy J. Tomasik and Juliann M. Vitullo, eds., *At the Table: Metaphorical and Material Cultures of Food in Medieval and Early Modern Europe* (Turnhout: Brepols, 2007), 145–66 (163). Ross in his statement follows up on the work of Peter Arnade, *Realms of Ritual: Burgundian Ceremony and Civic Life in Late Medieval Ghent* (Ithaca, NY: Cornell University Press, 1996), 18; See also, Eric R. Dursteler, 'Food and Politics', *A Cultural History of Food in the Renaissance*, ed. Ken Albala (London and New York: Berg, 2012), 83–100 (95).

well as scholarship's difficulty in describing a type of performance that can neither be exclusively classified quite as 'ceremony' nor as 'spectacle',[19] but comprises elements of both, and can contribute to either. Banquets can be, or contribute to, festive events; they can also be, or contribute to, solemn events. They can be enlivened with, as we have seen in the above, all manner of fun and playfulness, but they themselves do not have to have been playful *per se*. This does not hamper our

---

[19] Helen Watanabe-O'Kelly makes a helpful distinction between the categories 'ceremony' and 'spectacle' in her chapter, Watanabe-O'Kelly, 'Early Modern European Festivals – Politics and Performance, Event and Record', in J.R. Mulryne and Elizabeth Goldring, eds., *Court Festivals of the European Renaissance: Art, Politics and Performance* (Aldershot: Ashgate, 2002), 15–25 (15–16); as well as in Helen Watanabe-O'Kelly, 'The Early Modern Festival Book: Function and Form', in J.R. Mulryne, Helen Watanabe-O'Kelly, Margaret Shewring, eds., *Europa Triumphans: Court and Civic Festivals in Early Modern Europe, Volume 1* (Aldershot, Hampshire: Ashgate, 2004), 3–17 (5–6). Furthermore, a useful introduction to 'ceremony' is offered in the sections on 'ritual' in Charlotte Backerra and Peter Edwards, 'Introduction: Rank and Ritual in the Early Modern Court', *The Court Historian* 26:1 (2021), 1–10. Crucial works on spectacle, ceremony and ritual include: Marie-Claude Canova-Green, Jean Andrews, Marie-France Wagner, eds., *Writing Royal Entries in Early Modern Europe* (Turnhout: Brepols, 2013); Fernando Checa Cremades and Laura Fernández-González, eds., *Festival Culture in the World of the Spanish Habsburgs* (London: Routledge, 2016); Rita Costa Gomes, *The Making of a Court Society: Kings and Nobles in Late Medieval Portugal* (Cambridge: Cambridge University Press, 2003), esp. Chapter 5, 357–421; Mary Tiffany Ferer, *Music and Ceremony at the Court of Charles V* (Woodbridge: The Boydell Press, 2012); Jean Jacquot, ed., *Les Fêtes de la Renaissance* (Paris: Éditions du Centre National de la Recherche, Scientifique, 1956); Barbara Hanawalt and Kathryn Reyerson, eds., *City and Spectacle in Medieval Europe* (Minneapolis, MN: University of Minnesota Press, 1994); Anna Kalinowska and Jonathan Spangler, with Pawl Tyszka, eds., *Power and Ceremony in European History: Rituals, Practices and Representative Bodies since the Late Middle Ages* (London: Bloomsbury, 2021); Gordon Kipling, *Enter the King: Theatre, Liturgy, and Ritual in the Medieval Civic Triumph* (Oxford: Clarendon Press, 1998); Geoffrey Koziol, *Begging Pardon and Favor: Ritual and Political Order in Early Medieval France* (Ithaca, NY: Cornell University Press, 1992); Edward Muir, *Ritual in Early Modern Europe*, 2nd edn. (Cambridge: Cambridge University Press, 2005); J.R. Mulryne, Maria Ines Aliverti, and Anna Maria Testaverde, eds., *Ceremonial Entries in Early Modern Europe: The Iconography of Power* (London: Routledge, 2015); Roy Strong, *Art and Power: Renaissance Festivals, 1450–1650* (Woodbridge: The Boydell Press, 1984); and Jennifer Loach, 'The Function of Ceremonial in the Reign of Henry VIII', *P&P* 142 (1994), 43–68. See also the excellent Kaya Şahin, 'Staging an Empire: An Ottoman Circumcision Ceremony as Cultural Performance', *American Historical Review* 123:2 (2018), 463–92. For works on coronations, readers are referred to, a.o, Jaume Aurell, *Medieval Self-Coronations* (Cambridge: Cambridge University Press, 2020); János M. Bak, ed., *Coronations: Medieval and Early Modern Monarchic Ritual* (Berkeley, CA: University of California Press, 1990); Alice Hunt, *The Drama of Coronation: Medieval Ceremony in Early Modern England* (Cambridge: Cambridge University Press, 2008).

understanding banquets as performances. Janette Dillon in *The Language of Space in Court Performance* (2010), convincingly argues that 'real-life events' such as, for example, executions, that cannot be conceived as playful, and of which it is only logical that 'key participants are by definition deeply unwilling to take part in such events',[20] can be seen as examples of performance on the basis that 'even the most unwilling players . . . may understand themselves to *be* players at key ceremonial events, whether they like it or not'.[21] Furthermore, Dillon observes that events such as executions share with other performances as they have been traditionally understood, 'spaces carefully dressed and prepared like theatre sets; bodies moving in scripted and choreographed motions within such specially prepared spaces; scripted speech and gesture; formal structures with beginnings and endings; and formal or conventional arrangements of spectators'.[22] These elements referred to by Dillon as 'the trappings of performance',[23] have been identified by Ken Albala as key aspects of ceremonial dining:

> Any meal, past or present . . . contains a script. It might be said that every participant in the eating event is equally an actor. Sometimes the roles are rigidly cast, particularly in the case of formal aristocratic dining but the parts can also be improvised and negotiated in the course of a meal. In this respect, a meal is a form of theatre. In the case of the banquets described here, this is literally the case, replete with an audience, stage sets, props, and interludes.[24]

Eric R. Dursteler has likewise read the banquet as a form of theatre, and has simultaneously underscored its political nature. He has observed that,

> Through the 'pomp and magnificence' of the meal—its setting, the number of courses, the diversity and complexity of the foods—a ruler, an official, or indeed a state, communicated a clear message of political propaganda. The intent was to display 'wealth and power', convey

[20] Janette Dillon, *The Language of Space in Court Performance, 1400–1625* (Cambridge: Cambridge University Press, 2010), 13 and 11.

[21] Dillon, *The Language of Space*, 11.

[22] Dillon, *The Language of Space*, 13.

[23] Dillon, *The Language of Space*, 13.

[24] Albala, *The Banquet*, 4.

a sense of political 'stability, order, and hierarchy', legitimate power, and enhance reputation.[25]

This could take various forms as case studies in food and ritual history have shown. For example, at times of political unrest ceremonial meals could be used 'to bolster [a ruler's] waning authority'.[26] Michel Jeanneret has studied the Valois court after the death of Henri II when Catherine de' Medici served as regent. He observed that ceremony and festivity of all sorts including the ceremonial meal, employed a number of complementing strategies, offering a 'dramatic celebration of power', and a 'display of wealth', as well as 'reinforc[ing] . . . hierarchy by ceremonial rules'.[27] The latter aspect is especially fascinating when looking at the banquet as a 'scripted' performance. Various powers (or from the Valois perspective, we might call these sources of disorder or unrest) when placed at the banqueting table were not only impressed (or intimidated) by the splendour and the implications of what riches could do if it came to a conflict; Jeanneret observed they were also 'subject to the laws of etiquette'.[28] This meant that they had to go through the motions of the banquet and through these actions had to take on a role of subservience. This outward presentation of participation following the established hierarchy was interpreted by Jeanneret as 'feign[ed] submission to the authority of the crown', and did not mean that participation in this ritual actually transformed the participants; Under such outward demonstrations of 'precarious conviviality', Jeanneret warns, 'civil war' could already be brewing.[29]

The performance of etiquette could, in other contexts, also be used to inspire and give a sense of security to a ruler's subjects. The most striking example, perhaps, can be found in the court of the Burgundian duke Charles the Bold whose partaking in ceremonial meals was minutely described by his courtier and chronicler Olivier de la Marche. His accounts of the duke at table give the impression that this ritual custom was, in Peter Arnade's words, 'one of the court's most cultic affairs'.[30]

[25] Dursteler, 'Food and Politics', 95.
[26] Jeanneret, *A Feast of Words*, 54.
[27] Jeanneret, *A Feast of Words*, 54.
[28] Jeanneret, *A Feast of Words*, 54.
[29] Jeanneret, *A Feast of Words*, 54.
[30] Arnade, *Realms of Ritual*, 16.

The accounts share every detail of every movement made by the duke and his servants, including 'the order of presentation, the covering and uncovering of the dishes (along with poison testing), and the ceremonial kissing of dishes and implements as they are passed on from servant to servant'.[31] Arnade reads these recordings as 'less a compendium of manners than a liturgical handbook, replete with descriptions of genuflecting courtiers and Eucharistic metaphors that vaunt the essential religious nature of serving the prince his meal'.[32] Watching the duke eat meant watching a performance of rulership. Arnade observes, 'because the duke ate with courtiers present, under constant scrutiny, he was a mirror of virtue for all. This medieval metaphor might strike us as shopworn, but it captures well how the duke served as the brilliant centre of a system of etiquette'.[33] Christina Normore's important work has, more recently, added to the field's understanding of watching or spectating within the banqueting space, which helps understand the performative act of being present at a banquet for those participants who—at first sight—did not appear to have an obvious role. Normore notes, 'Just as tapestries and other furnishings helped make the generic late medieval hall into a place of fantasy, so too the walls lined with audience members helped create a world set apart. Within the space, viewing was nevertheless highly active, attention solicited and broken by the wide range of people and things to see'.[34] As studies in this field show, looking at food and banqueting through the lenses of 'scriptedness', 'performance', 'participants', and 'spectatorship' means that one at times rubs shoulders with the fields of drama and theatrical performance, reminding us that ritual food consumption in the courtly context shares some of its core qualities with other ritual, ceremonial, and festive acts. A defining feature of the banquet, compared to the other court events, of course, was the consumption of sumptuous foods, although these were themselves also strikingly more performative than today's readers may expect. In what follows I address the concept of the *entremets*, a key to exemplifying the multifaceted event-type that was the banquet.

---

[31] Arnade, *Realms of Ritual*, 16.
[32] Arnade, *Realms of Ritual*, 16.
[33] Arnade, *Realms of Ritual*, 17.
[34] Normore, *Feast*, 57.

'Between dishes'

In French, literally, 'between dishes', the word *entremets* has invited a variety of definitions, but I here follow L.B. Ross's broad definition that 'encompasses both culinary and theatrical meanings'.[35] Ross understands the term to refer to 'elaborate and often mechanical centrepieces', as well as 'live shows consisting both of circus acts and pantomimes, the latter often specifically referred to as *mystères*, performed at various phases of banquets'.[36] Within the English tradition, for '*mystères*' one may also read 'pageants' or 'interludes'.[37] Along the same lines, this chapter acknowledges and follows Normore's understanding of the banquet as well as the *entremets* as 'a combination of visual, performing and culinary arts',[38] in which 'fluidity' is manifested through that which demonstrates to be essential qualities of the feast: an 'inventive blend of media and collaborative production' that 'blurred the boundaries between spectator and spectacle, creator and audience'.[39] Yet while this chapter understands that the idea of a multimedia event is that everything happens at once or at least conjointly within the space of the same event, and that distinguishing between types of *entremets* may not be representative of what actually took place, it should be noted that two types of *entremets* are sometimes presented as distinct categories: *les entremets culinaires*, which in English are sometimes referred to as 'subtleties' (or sotelties) made for consumption, not unlike those Claire Sponsler notes were served and eaten 'at Windsor in May of 1416, during the visit of Emperor Sigismund',[40] and *les entremets de paintrerie*,

---

[35] Ross, 'Beyond Eating', 147.

[36] Ross, 'Beyond Eating', 147.

[37] Denise E. Cole, 'Edible performance: feasting and festivity in early Tudor entertainment', in Sally Banes and Andre Lepecki, eds., *The Senses in Performance* (London: Routledge, 2012), 101–13; Roberta Mullini, '*Fulgens and Lucres*: A Mirror held up to Stage and Society', *European Medieval Drama* 1 (1997), 203–18 (203).

[38] Normore, *Feast*, 6, and 21.

[39] Normore, *Feast*. The word 'fluidity' occurs in Normore's work at different points, e.g., at 22. For the definition quoted here see 3.

[40] Claire Sponsler, ed., 'Soteltes at the Coronation Banquet of Henry VI', in *John Lydgate: Mummings and Entertainments* (Kalamazoo, Michigan: Medieval Institute Publications, 2010), Explanatory Notes; Headnote. Citations from this source are reproduced with permission.

to which David Sutton refers as 'architectural . . . huge constructions of wood, metal, and cloth'.[41]

But when making this distinction, immediately the issue arises that *Les entremets culinaires* sound more straightforward and easier to categorize than they would have been in practice. Cookery books often refer to *entremets* or subtleties, and their being included in lists of foods consumed presented at the end of a course would, at face value, make them appear as *entremets culinaires*. For example, the *Boke of Kokery* (c. 1430) preserved in British Library Harley MS 279 mentions a 'sotelty' as one of the dishes presented at the coronation banquet of Henry IV in 1399.[42] Similarly, a culinary treatise roll called *Forme of Cury* (c. 1420)[43] compiled by 'the chef Maister Cokes of kyng Richard the Se[cu]nde' opens with the promise to teach readers the preparation of 'commune potages and commune mettis for howshold as þey shold be made craftly and holsomly' as well as 'for to make curious potages & *meetes and sotiltees* for alle manere of states both h[y]e and lowe' (emphasis added).[44] The grouping of 'meetes and sotiltees' could suggest that preparing the 'sotiltees' was a craft to be understood as a type of cooking.

However, Anne Brannen has observed that source types referring to subtleties, such as extant menus, are often extremely vague, leading her to question the materials of which subtleties were made ('Wood? Paper? Marzipan?') and how these objects were utilized after the banquet ('Are they displayed in the hall? Thrown away? Eaten? (in the case of the marzipan)?'[45] The Records of Early English Drama reveal that subtleties were at times painted, which would likely render them (partly) inedible. See for example the Coventry Cappers' Records of 1525:

[41] David C. Sutton, 'Four and Twenty Blackbirds Baked in a Pie: A History of Surprise Stuffings', in Mark McWilliams, ed., *Wrapped and Stuffed Foods: Proceedings of the Oxford Symposium on Food and Cookery 2012* (Totness, Devon: Prospect Books, 2013), 285–94 (290).

[42] The British Library, Harley MS 279, *Boke of Kokery*. The British Library website has digitized the page showing the foods eaten at the coronation banquet for Henry IV. Refer to 'Image no. 3'. https://www.bl.uk/collection-items/potage-dyvers.

[43] 'Cury' translates as 'cookery', and is not to be confused with the tasty dish with a (usually) spicy sauce that we now often eat with rice.

[44] The British Library, Add MS 5016. *Forme of Cury*. http://www.bl.uk/manuscripts/FullDisplay.aspx?ref=Add_MS_5016. A transcription of the first paragraph of the roll is found in the manuscript content description.

[45] Anne Brannen, 'Intricate Subtleties: Entertainment at Bishop Morton's Installation Feast', *REED Newsletter* 22:2 (1997), 2–11 (2–3).

Item p*ai*d the syngers on candelmase daye	xx d
Item p*ai*d for sutteltes	ij s v d
Item p*ai*d to the players	iij s iiij d
Item p*ai*d for payntyng the soteltes	xij d.[46]

Partial painting of a subtlety would not necessarily have turned the whole construction into a non-food item. In fact, some food types were typically understood to be only partly edible. I here cite Sutton again who notes that, for example, 'pastry and pies were regarded as containers, to be discarded once their contents had been enjoyed'.[47] And here, in the example from the Records of Early English Drama, we see manifested the combination of 'visual, performing and culinary arts',[48] that Normore has alerted us to. Indeed, the Cappers' Records mentioning of 'players' in such close proximity to the payments for the subtleties themselves as well as to the painting of those subtleties suggests that the construction had, in the very least, a performative *aspect*.

This may sound rather abstract, so I will briefly turn to an example that provides more detail than the Cappers' Records. During the coronation banquet of Henry VI in 1429, table guests were served three elaborate courses, each of which concluded with a subtlety. On this occasion 'miniature pageants made of confectionary' befitting the context of the celebration at hand, shared a symbolic message that sought to justify Lancastrian rulership of England and France.[49] Luxury foods were served, such as 'borehedes in castelles of earmed [boars heads in castles made of pastry] with golde', where food and decorative art met in a dish, but also 'Beef', 'Moton', 'Signet' [swan], 'Capon stued Heron', 'Grete pike', 'A redde lech with lions corven theryn of white', 'Custade

[46] R.W. Ingram, ed., *REED: Coventry* (Toronto: University of Toronto Press, 1981), 123. This example is also referred to in Brannen, 'Intricate Subtleties', 9, footnote 3.
[47] Sutton, 'Four and Twenty Blackbirds', 288.
[48] Normore, *Feast*, 6.
[49] Sponsler, ed., 'Soteltes', Explanatory Notes. For a detailed discussion: Robert Epstein, 'Eating their Words: Food and Text in the Coronation Banquet of Henry VI', *Journal of Medieval and Early Modern Studies* 36:2 (2006), 355–77. In what follows, I cite the 'author post print' edition of this article, available at the Repository of Fairfield University: Robert Epstein, 'Eating their Words: Food and Text in the Coronation Banquet of Henry VI' (2006), *English Faculty Publications*, 123:

https://digitalcommons.fairfield.edu/english-facultypubs/123. Further page numbers cited from this text are thus from the 'author post print' edition.

Rooial with a leparde of golde sittyng theryn' [pastry dish], and a 'Fritour like a sonne with a flour de lice therynne'.[50] The guests were clearly invited to admire the dishes and to eat those parts of them that were meant for consumption. But what of the subtlety? At the end of the first course, a construction was presented showing 'Seint Edward [King Edward the Confessor] and Seint Lowes [King Louis IX of France] armed in cote armours bryngyng yn bitwene hem the Kyng in his cote armour'.[51] The confectionary pageant was accompanied with verse written by John Lydgate, which explained the guests what they were seeing in the confectionary and helpfully pointed out emblems used in the display of the other foods.[52] For example, in the verse for the first course Lydgate refers to Henry VI as 'Enheretour [inheritor] of the floure de lice',[53] which neatly corresponded to one of the dishes served in this course, sporting this very emblem: 'Fritour like a sonne with a flour de lice therynne'.[54] The enjoyment of Lydate's descriptions read out to the banqueters would have constituted a performative element consolidating the culinary art form, and bridging worlds of cook, host, and banqueter by underscoring the meanings underlying the representation of the food, but also by making the enjoyment of food something auditory as well as sensory.

Let us now look at the other 'category' of entremets: *Les entremets de paintrerie*, which are perhaps best defined by their primary building materials (of the non-edible variety), but could also be recognized by their scale and level of extravagance. A Burgundian example from 17 February 1454, a banquet known as The Feast of the Pheasant, was staged to gather support for a crusade to Constantinople. Chroniclers Matthieu d'Escouchy and Olivier de la Marche left to posterity an impression of this over-the-top entertainment, which can be

[50] Sponsler, ed., 'Soteltes'.
[51] Sponsler, ed., 'Soteltes'.
[52] Lancashire writes that Lydgates verses, 'would probably also have been recited aloud so that everyone in the hall could hear them'. Anne Lancashire, *London Civic Theatre: City Drama and Pageantry from Roman Times to 1558* (Cambridge: Cambridge University Press, 2002), 125. Cf; Sponsler, ed., 'Solteltes'.
[53] Sponsler, ed., 'Soteltes', l. 5.
[54] Sponsler, ed., 'Soteltes'. As Epstein remarks, 'dishes bear or represent heraldic emblems and patterns, showing that the ostentation of the feast extended to the food's presentation, and furthermore that the food was thoroughly integrated into the symbolism of the spectacular occasion'. Epstein, 'Eating their Words', 13.

exemplified by the 'enormous pie' filled with between 24 and 28 musicians, who played secular music composed by Gilles Binchois,[55] or by the construction of a whale that was brought into the banqueting area, which, when opening its mouth, gave the audience a good view of two singing mermaids ('*sirénes*'), and presented twelve mermen ('*chevaliers de mer*'), after which dancing and mock-combat was enjoyed.[56] As the accounts by d'Escouchy and de la Marche show, these examples only reveal the tip of the iceberg of the amount of spectacle, grandeur, and fun that was sampled during this feast. And, as Normore has observed, The Feast of the Pheasant utilized the combination of 'moving and still, object and performance, people and things',[57] in crossovers between art and food such as in, for example, a 'hippocras-spouting female ymage'.[58] The interchangeable aspects of the different manifestations of the *entremets* at The Feast of the Pheasant thus blur the lines between the '*entremets de paintrerie*' and the culinary variety of *entremets*.

Sometimes too a source presents a description of the *entremets* in such a way that leaves open to interpretation what media forms would have been employed to realize the performance. To illustrate, a sample menu in *The Boke of Nurture*—written by John Russell who was usher to the Duke of Gloucester—providing inspiration for a good fish dinner, rounds off the first course of the meal with a description of a subtlety that could be interpreted to have been presented in different ways:

> a semely sotelte folowynge evyñ þere.
> A galaunt yonge mañ, a wanton wight,
> pypynge & syngynge / lovynge & lyght,
> Standynge oñ a clowd, Sanguineus he hight,
> þe begynnynge of þe sesoñ þat cleped is ver.[59]

[55] Sutton, 'Four and Twenty Blackbirds', 291. See also, for example, Arjo Vanderjagt, 'The Princely Culture of the Valois Dukes of Burgundy', in M. Gosman, A. MacDonald, and A. Vanderjagt, eds., *Princes and Princely Culture, 1450–1650*, vol. 1 (Leiden: Brill, 2003), 51–79 (60).

[56] Olivier de la Marche, *Collection Complète des Mémoires Relatifs a l'Histoire de France: Olivier de la Marche*, vol. 2 (Paris, 1825), 388. Available at Gallica, BnF: ark:/12,148/bpt6k363643. A detailed account of The Feast of the Pheasant, and reference to the pageant with the whale is found in Ross, 'Beyond Eating', 153 onwards.

[57] Normore, *Feast*, 21.

[58] Normore, *Feast*, 35.

[59] John Russell, *The Boke of Nurture Folowyng Englondis Gise . . . Edited from the Harleian MS. 4011 in the British Museum*, in Frederick J. Furnivall, ed., *Early English Meals*

The first possibility is that Russell refers to a construction such as in the example of Henry VI's coronation banquet, with someone standing beside it 'piping and singing', just as Lydgate's verses would have been read out, not by the construction or group of statues, but by a person present in the room. It is also possible that Russell's subtlety could present an *automaton* like the construction of the singing lion with its moving jaws that was displayed at the wedding of Charles the Bold and Margaret of York. Or perhaps, the example refers to a real young man entering the room 'on a cloud', a mechanical achievement not unlike the performance that Antoni Tallander (whom we saw in Chapter 2) participated in. It is likely that it was all the same to Russell, who perhaps did not see the need to specify which approach to take to visualize the subtlety. It appears that organizers of such events, so Laura Weigert observes, 'considered the boundaries between different representational forms to be fluid'.[60] That is to say that within the context of the interlude, Weigert notes, 'human, sculpted, woven, or painted figures were seen within a similar set of circumstances'.[61] She continues, 'Bodies of human beings and those fabricated from other materials could potentially create the same scenario, or, alternatively, figures of different materials were incorporated together on a single platform or a sequence of automata and effigies, with sculpture and other [three- or][62] two-dimensional images, and with human beings'.[63] In other words, the mermaids during The Feast of the Pheasant evoked a kind of representation and told a story that could equally have been achieved by human performers or by a mechanical piece like an *automaton* representing a mermaid, or indeed, by a confectionary in the shape of a mermaid, each alternative accompanied by a performative aspect that brought the show to 'life' for the spectators watching. The staged combat following the singing in this instance suggests that the *sirénes* and *chevaliers de mer* were human actors, but given that the mermaids

---

and Manners, EETS, o.s. 32 (London: Oxford University Press, 1931; reprint of 1868 edn.), 51, ll. 726–30.

[60] Weigert, *French Visual Culture*, 61.

[61] Weigert, *French Visual Culture*, 61.

[62] The insertion 'three or' is my own, offered to reflect Weigert's work beyond this quote, in which she refers to the alternative use in certain performances of a 'human body or to an image in two or three dimensions'. Weigert, *French Visual Culture*, 61.

[63] Weigert, *French Visual Culture*, 61.

likely had not joined the fighting, the option remains that the mermen were human representations, whereas the mermaids may have been mechanical constructions.

A broad and fluid understanding of *entremets* suggests, to cite Bridget Ann Henisch, that 'a feast was the sum of many parts, and its aim was to satisfy many senses'.[64] Indeed, where the *entremets* combined several aspects of enjoyment, outside these particular moments within the banquet, the total experience of the banquet comprised tasting delicious foods prepared in dishes with strong visual appeal, while sitting in a beautiful banqueting environment hung with tapestries and heraldic decorations, and being treated to—either as part of an *entremets* or presented individually—music, play, folly, technological innovation, splendour, and general extravagance. But we should also not forget the art of hospitality such as expressed by good carving at the table, which Henish has referred to as 'a spectator sport, in which the way the carver handled his tools was appraised by knowledgeable, unkindly critical eyes'.[65] And what to think of the acts of serving of foods and wines, the ritual expressions of hierarchy performed, the movements of the host and notable guests, and the multiple impressions to be had while in a carefully ritualized, and orchestrated environment, performing one's role as guest, and spectating others perform this role.[66] In other words, there would have been a lot to take in.

Oh ... behave!

Accounts of banquets in chronicle-type sources, personal eye-witness or second-hand accounts, and financial records combined can provide a good first impression of the splendour of the festivities presented in the banqueting hall to entertain guests during the meal or between

[64] Bridget Ann Henisch, *The Medieval Cook* (Woodbridge: The Boydell Press, 2009), 154.

[65] Henisch, *The Medieval Cook*, 154.

[66] Spectatorship at the banquet is discussed in Normore, *Feast*; For spectatorship in drama: John J. McGavin and Greg Walker, *Imagining Spectatorship: From the Mysteries to the Shakespearean Stage* (Oxford: Oxford University Press, 2016); For spectatorship in ritual procession: Edward Muir, 'The Eye of the Procession: Ritual Ways of Seeing in the Renaissance', in Nicholas Howe, ed., *Ceremonial Culture in Pre-Modern Europe* (Notre Dame, Indiana: University of Notre Dame Press, 2007), 129–53.

courses, as well as of the kinds of dishes served, and of the fluid entertainments such as *entremets* that could sit between food and spectacle, and could best be understood as a 'multimedia' type, to follow Normore.[67] They underscore the host's success at sponsoring and ordering a grand event. Most of the persons 'staging' the banquet, however, operated behind the scenes—carpenters, painters, quartermasters, transporters, cooks, pastry chefs, artists, and others. Servants serving at the high table, however, had a special role to play, and their conduct took place in the eyes of all, including those of the most important guests, and the hosts themselves. For the banquet to be a success, their work had to be impeccable within the ritual standards of their context. A source-type that offers insights into the expectations of good service at banquets is the instruction manual. Guide books such as *The boke of keruynge* (1508) printed by Wynkyn de Worde, provide detailed information as to how to precisely function in that capacity within the banqueting setting in the great households.[68] Earlier, I have already briefly referred to John Russell, who wrote *The Boke of Nurture*. His manual takes the didactic form of a master speaking to a pupil, and provides a window into the customs of hospitality or service in great households. The 'pupil' and the reader with him is taught whether to serve particular fruits before dinner or after supper, and learns the names of sweet wines that a high-end servant should be familiar with, the secret behind making hippocras to help the digestion of rich foods—it's very consumption at the end of a banquet itself indicative of the richness of the meal—or, for example, how to lay a table using table-cloths. But the manual also provides advice on behaviour ('be glad of cher*e* / Curteise of kne / & soft of speche, / Fayr*e* hand*es*, clene nayles / honest arrayed, y the teche [i.e., I thee teach]') (ll. 269–70) and lists bad habits to avoid ('Coughe not, ner spitte ne put your*e* fyngurs in the cuppe') (ll. 271–2). A set of 'conditions' for service in the context of the great household is furthermore listed, such as making sure that one's eyes are not watery, or to not scratch one's back or head as if infested by lice. Some of this advice is quite graphic,

---

[67] Normore uses the word 'multimedia' at various moments, e.g., see the section 'Multimedia and the Late Medieval Collaborative Process', starting at Normore, *Feast*, 37.

[68] *Here begynneth the boke of keruynge* (London, 1508; Cambridge University Library, Sel.5.19.), University of Cambridge Digital Library. https://cudl.lib.cam.ac.uk/view/PR-SEL-00005-00019/1.

such as, 'pike not youre nose / ne þat hit be droppynge with no peerlis clere, / Snyff nor snitynge hyt to lowd / lest youre souerayne hit here' (ll. 283–4). Russell also considered it ill-mannered to wear garments exposing one's 'codware', calling it 'añ vngoodly gise' (l. 305).

Just as young men in the auspices of great halls had to learn how to conduct the tasks of serving a great lord, so did fledgling courtiers need to learn how to deport themselves when performing the role of guest at a banquet. Thankfully, this could also be learned from a book to avoid *faux-passes*—or worse. Erasmus in his *Monita paedagogica* [lesson in manners] (1522), like Russell taking the form of a master speaking to a pupil, offers concrete advice. For accepting portions of food he advises modesty:

> Postremus omnium admoveto manum patina. Si quid datur lautius, recusato modesté: si instabitur, accipe, & age gratias: mox decerptà portiuncula, quod reliquum est illi reddito, aut alicui proximè accumbenti.[69]
>
> [Bring your hand to the dish after everyone else. If given something more refined [a refined dish], decline modestly: if it is pressed on you, accept it and give thanks: having taken a small portion, afterwards return what is left to him who gave it, or to someone sitting [at the table] closest to you].

Drinking too much is also frowned upon: '*Si quis praebibit hilariter, illi bene precator, sed ipse bibito modicé. Si non sitis, tamen admoveto cyathum labiis*.'[70] [If anyone cheerfully toasts you, agreeably wish him well, but drink moderately yourself. If you are not thirsty still bring the cup to your lips]. Manners and ways to socialize are also dictated, and appear to be a helpful way to navigate situations of a potentially political or socially awkward nature:

> Arride loquentibus: Ipse ne quid loquans, nisi rogatus. Si quid obsoeni dicetur, nè arride, sed compone vultum quasi non intelligas. Nè cui obtrectaro, nè cui temet anteponito, nè tua jactato, nè aliena despiciro.[71]

---

[69] In this chapter, I cite from Desiderius Erasmus, *Colloquiorum Desiderii Erasmi Roterodami familiarium opus aureum. Cum scholiis quibusdam antehac non editis ... etc.* (London, 1683), 27. I am grateful to Dr Renske Janssen for kindly helping me with the translations from *Monita paedagogica*. Any remaining errors are my own.

[70] Erasmus, *Colloquiorum*, 27.

[71] Erasmus, *Colloquiorum*, 27.

[Smile at those who speak: do not speak yourself, unless requested. If something obscene is said, do not laugh but compose your face as if you do not understand. Don't belittle anyone or place yourself above/before others, do not boast about your own things/your own affairs or express contempt for those of others].

Erasmus finally warns about outstaying one's welcome at the dinner table: '*Si videris convivium esse prolixius, precatus veniam, ac salutatis convivis, subducito te à mensa*'.[72] [If you see/notice that the banquet is running too long, beg their pardon, and with greetings to your table companions, withdraw from the table]. As banquets continue, the consumption of alcohol is likely to increase, leading to behaviour or discussions that could either become impolitic or that could in another way could harm one's reputation or good rapport with the persons one needs to impress. Erasmus indirectly warns his fictional 'pupil' to not be present at the moment when this happens.

Instruction books prescribing how to serve and carve food— primarily meat, but extending to fish, pies, and pastries—how to choose the order of dishes, place napkins, select subtleties, and conduct one- self as a good servant, as well as those advising how to accept food, eat, and hold oneself as a table guest suggest that no spontaneity was expected, or indeed desired, at the ceremonial meal. Edward Muir has observed a 'late medieval and Renaissance obsession with codifying rit- uals through the appointment of ritual managers, such as heralds and masters of ceremony, and the writing up of prescriptive texts, the Books of Ceremonies', which he argues 'testifie[d] to the anxiety created by ritual kinesis'.[73] With the latter he meant that rituals, 'were effectively improvisations on a loose script, mak[ing] it impossible to affix a single meaning to a specific ritual performance'.[74] When applied to the per- formance of the banquet with so many variables operating at the same time—the banquet having in common with ritual procession studied by Muir that the guests at the table like participants in the procession were both participant and spectator—it appears that the potential for multiple meanings created during the event was enormous. At the same time, under the auspices of ceremonial, too much would have been at

[72] Erasmus, *Colloquiorum*, 27.
[73] Muir, 'The Eye', 131.
[74] Muir, 'The Eye', 131.

stake to let meanings and 'messages' roam free. Thus with so many rules, prescriptions, habits and customs, and such a high awareness of these things in the persons involved, one may understand why studying international relations and diplomacy through the lens of food and banqueting may disclose more about the dynamics of power and prestige than do the contents of some treaties. This also reveals the incredible value that food studies, and within that, the study of the banquet, holds for other branches of history.

Having laid a rather broad foundation of understanding the banquet as an event within the context of food studies, performance and spectatorship, and having introduced some of the source types extant, I now turn to this chapter's case study which addresses the conferences between Charles V and Henry VIII during which the latter took the role of host and the emperor was given hospitality in its various forms. The records extant show the magnitude of the organizational efforts and expenses made for these visits. Helen Watanabe-O'Kelly has observed that, 'Long-lived rulers who were firmly established on the throne and not in immediate conflict with forces either inside or outside of their borders quite often had no need of full-dress public festivals'.[75] The reverse is also true, and from the evidence extant it appears that Henry was investing in his relationship with the emperor, just as his father before him once splashed out to build an alliance with Isabella of Castile and Ferdinand of Aragon. But, as the case study to follow will demonstrate, Henry may also have sought to use encounters with Charles V to consolidate his status as one of Europe's leading rulers, and to boast his connection to the emperor to other political players.

Part 2: Entertaining the Emperor

The most powerful man in Europe

The ruler we now think of as Charles V was known by different titles during his lifetime, each representing the expansion of his vast domains. Following the death of his father, Philippe 'le Beau', Charles became

[75] Watanabe-O'Kelly, 'The Early Modern Festival Book', 5.

Duke of Burgundy. Charles's mother, Juana of Castile had inherited the Castilian crown after the death of Queen Isabel, but Philippe had effectively taken the throne as King of Castile. When Philippe died, Juana remained queen in name while her father, Ferdinand of Aragon, made himself regent.[76] Posterity has come to know Juana as 'mad', but Bethany Aram has shown 'a correlation between individuals' recorded assessments of Juana and their political interests'.[77] In other words, it was convenient for Ferdinand to deem Juana unable to rule, just as it had been to Philippe, and Juana's father set her up in a household in Tordesillas where she was served by servants who were on his payroll.[78] On Ferdinand's death, Charles at age seventeen became King of Aragon and Castile, although officially the latter territory was co-ruled with Juana.[79]

12 January 1519 saw the death of the Emperor Maximilian I, causing the Habsburg territories, the so-called *Erblande*,[80] to be added to Charles's Spanish lands, and providing him with the title 'Archduke of Austria'. The succession to the Holy Roman Empire, however, was not a given and did not automatically befall the previous emperor's heir; as Robert J. Knecht clarifies, 'the empire . . . was an elective, not hereditary, dignity'.[81] And although the electors appear to have been firmly rooted in or in close contact with the German lands, they could, in theory, elect whomever they wished regardless of the contestant's nationality.[82] With this in mind Francis I of France soon found himself lobbying for the honour, perhaps mostly in order to avoid Charles's becoming the most powerful man in Europe. He wrote, 'the reason which moves me to gain the empire . . . is to prevent the said Catholic king from doing so'.[83] Naturally, he also sought to protect his hard-won Italian lands.[84] Charles eventually won, and although money may have passed hands,

[76] Manuel Fernández Alvarez, *Charles V: Elected emperor and hereditary ruler*, trans. J.A. Lalaguna (London: Thames and Hudson, 1975), 16.

[77] Bethany Aram, 'Juana 'the Mad's' Signature: The Problem of Invoking Royal Authority, 1505–1507', *SCJ* 29:2 (1998), 331–58 (333).

[78] Aram, 'Juana "the Mad's" Signature', 350.

[79] Ferer, 'Queen Juana, Empress Isabel, and Musicians at the Royal Courts of Spain', 17.

[80] Glenn Richardson, *Renaissance Monarchy: The Reigns of Henry VIII, Francis I and Charles V* (London: Arnold, 2002), 19.

[81] Robert J. Knecht, *Francis I* (Cambridge: Cambridge University Press, 1982), 71.

[82] Knecht, *Francis I*, 71.

[83] Quoted from Knecht, *Francis I*, 72.

[84] Knecht, *Francis I*, 71–2.

and favours may have been promised, Henry Cohn's study has suggested that the electors had looked at the Empire on a universal scale and decided that Charles would be the better candidate for 'the defence of the eastern frontiers against the Turks' but also to ensure 'peace and good government within the Empire'.[85]

Charles was elected 'King of the Romans' on 28 June 1519, and was crowned in Aachen cathedral in October 1520.[86] Christophe le Nègre, whom we have briefly seen in Chapter 1, may have served Charles in the capacity of bodyguard during the event.[87] Officially, in order to be called Emperor, the King of the Romans had to be crowned by the pope, but Maximilian I for reasons of strained international relations never hazarded the journey to Rome, and took on the title 'Elected Roman Emperor' in 1508.[88] Charles, however, was eventually also crowned by the pope in Bologna on 24 February 1530.[89] Charles's 1519 election seriously impacted the power balance between the European political forces. Blockmans observes that at the moment in time when Charles became King of Spain, the house of Habsburg holding Spain, the Low Countries, Naples and Sicily represented the same economic potential as France with their lands in Lombardy, and their alliances with Venice, Genua, and the pope.[90] But as soon as Charles received the *Erblande* as well as the international recognition that went with the Imperial title, the balance between the two forces tilted, leaving Francis in a position of lesser influence. The French king appears to have responded aggressively by initiating a military conflict over northern Italy. As Robert Knecht aptly summarizes the political distribution of power in Europe

[85] Henry Jacob Cohn, 'Did Bribes Induce the German Electors to Choose Charles V as Emperor in 1519?' *German History* 19:1 (2001), 1–27 (27).

[86] *Beschreibung der einreittung Auch Krönung des Großmechtigsten Fürsten vnd Römischen Könings Caroli des fünften mit sampt aller andern Fürsten vnd herrn einreitten jetz Neülich beschehen zu Ach in Niderlandt im Jar Christi. M.vc.xx.* (Mainz, 1520; BL General Reference Collection 1315.c.18), British Library 'Treasures in Full: Renaissance Festival Books'. https://www.bl.uk/treasures/festivalbooks/BookDetails.aspx?strFest=0079.

[87] Van den Boogaard, 'Christophle le More', 424.

[88] Wim Blockmans, *Keizer Karel V, 1500-1558: De Utopie van het Keizerschap* (Leuven: Van Halewyck, 2001), 49.

[89] Blockmans, *Keizer Karel V*, 264.

[90] Blockmans, *Keizer Karel V*, 60: 'Ten tijden van Karels machtsovername in Spanje lagen de krachtsverhoudingen in Europa juist in evenwicht: Frankrijk, met Lombardije en zijn bondgenoten in Venetië, Genua en de paus vertegenwoordigde een fiscal potentieel van 170 ton, Habsburg met Spanje, de Nederlanden, Napels en Sicilië precies evenveel'.

in the early 1520s, 'The peace of Christendom depended on three young rulers ... Only a blind optimist could have imagined any lasting peace between them; while paying lip service to Christian unity, none was willing to abandon any of his rights'.[91] In a nutshell, as Knecht notes, 'Henry claimed the French crown, Francis the crowns of Milan and Naples, and Charles the duchy of Burgundy. Sooner or later they were bound to clash'.[92]

Ceremony and precedence

It is within this context that we can read the diplomatic and military significance of Henry VIII for both his Habsburg and Valois neighbours in the early 1520s, and their desire to confer with the English king in 1520: Francis during what become known to history as the 'Field of Cloth of Gold',[93] and Charles just before and after this meeting in May and July of that year.[94] The Venetian diarist Marino Sanuto (1466–1536) offered an account of these diplomatic events, and detailed the ceremonial and spectacle that the rulers used—in measured steps—to show each other respect while underlining their own power. His observations regarding the etiquettes surrounding royal visits manifest themselves from the very start of the account of the visit, and zoom in, as we will see next, on aspects of the visit, and within that of the banquet, that underscore aspects of precedence and the gift of honour.

Henry and Charles had met once at Doornik [Tournai] in October 1513 when Charles had been in his early teens.[95] Therefore the conference in May 1520 was not their first ever encounter, although it was the first during which they were to meet as relative equals—that is, if Henry could have been perceived as Charles's equal in terms of wealth and power; a courtesy on Charles's part that was honorary rather than

---

[91] Robert J. Knecht, *The French Renaissance Court, 1483–1589* (New Haven: Yale University Press, 2008), 124.

[92] Knecht, *The French Renaissance Court*, 124.

[93] I have already referred to this event earlier. For more information, see Glenn Richardson, *The Field of Cloth of Gold* (New Haven, CT: Yale University Press, 2013).

[94] For the accounts from the Sanuto diaries, see: *CSPV* vol. 3, #50 (21 May–14 July 1520).

[95] Ghislaine de Boom, *De Reizen van Karel V*, trans. G. de Negris (Haarlem: Tjeenk Willink, 1960), 4.

realistic, and that relied on Henry's position as husband of Charles's maternal aunt, as well as on the unique position Henry had at that moment in European history, with Francis and Charles both trying to win him to their side.

Sanuto writes that when Charles and his retinue approached Dover on 26 May 1520, Cardinal Wolsey received the emperor on Henry's behalf, 'offering him all that England afforded, and inviting him to land there, as if it were his own territory', which he 'accepted . . . most willingly', after which Charles was brought to Dover Castle.[96] In line with tradition, 'the English warder presented the keys of the castle on behalf of his King', and in accordance with good manners, 'the Emperor refused them, saying that without keys he considered himself safe in the house of his uncle and good father, the King of England'.[97] The king shortly consolidated this welcome in person, 'having heard the news [of the emperor's arrival], rode to Dover, where he arrived in the night when the Emperor had supped and was in bed, and there they exchanged embraces and other loving compliments'.[98]

An important element of the visit was the jointly taking part in religious services, during which acts of precedence were performed and symbolic gestures of respect exchanged between the two rulers. Such social rituals were extended during the repasts served after these services, and Sanuto records the seating order, indicative of both etiquette and the host's desire to honour his guest. Seating orders are often provided in documentation recording a banquet, because it was extremely relevant information to be reported: seating order confirmed and visualized the social hierarchy and indicated who was favoured or otherwise. A further, more practical reason for this information to be recorded is that account takers watching from a distance would still have been able to record this in detail, and writers relying on second-hand accounts could easily obtain this information from people who had been present. An example of a particularly elaborate description of seating arrangements can be found in a festival book titled *Le liure et forest de messire Bernardin Rince . . . conentant et explicant briefuement lappareil, les ieux, et le festin de la Bastille* (1518) detailing the betrothal

[96] *CSPV* vol. 3, #50.

[97] *CSPV* vol. 3., #50.

[98] *CSPV* vol. 3., #50.

by proxy of Henry's daughter Mary to the French dauphin François in December 1518 for which English delegates had travelled to France.[99] It is within this custom of recording that we can also understand Santuto's interest in the acts of ceremonial precedence and places taken at table by the prominent participants in the international encounter between Henry and Charles: 'In the evening about an hour after dusk', the hall on the ground floor of the Archbishop's palace—the same building in which Charles resided—was turned into a banqueting space, 'where three tables had been prepared, two lengthwise, and one at the head of the hall'.[100] The royals entered the hall via the stairs, so Sanuto remarks, and their hands were ritually washed, so that a ceremonial visualization of precedence and hierarchy was honoured as part of the performance of the banquet:

> The Emperor and the King and Queen of England washed together by themselves. The Duke of Suffolk brought a large gold basin with a cover bearing a crown, in the centre of which was a small cup, and when this had been removed by the Duke of Buckingham, the Marquis of Brandenburg's brother, who had accompanied the Emperor, took off the cover, holding it under the basin borne by the Duke of Suffolk; whereupon the Duke of Buckingham gave the water in the cup to drink to the Duke of Suffolk, who having thus made the assay, then poured the water from his basin, which had an aperture or mouth at the side, over the hands of the Sovereigns, to whom the brother of the Count Palatine of the Rhine (he likewise being in the Emperor's train) presented the towel.[101]

After this elaborate piece of ritualized custom, 'the Emperor and the King and Queen then sat down to table'.[102] The seating arrangement was carefully balanced to avoid any of the two rulers losing face: 'the Emperor in the centre, and the King on the left, both on very stately gilt

[99] Bernardinus Rincius, *Le liure et forest de messire Bernardin Rince . . . conentant et explicant briefuement lappareil, les ieux, et le festin de la Bastille* (Paris, 1518; BL General Reference Collection DRT Digital Store 811.d.31.(1.), British Library 'Treasures in Full: Renaissance Festival Books'. https://www.bl.uk/treasures/festivalbooks/BookDetails.aspx?strFest=0004. See sig. B4 for the seating order.
[100] *CSPV* vol. 3, #50.
[101] *CSPV* vol. 3, #50.
[102] *CSPV* vol. 3, #50.

chairs; the Queen sitting on the right, but on a low chair'.[103] The reasoning behind this set-up is that the emperor sat in the place of honour. The English king as host took a modest seat on his left, leaving the privileged seat on the emperor's right to Katherine of Aragon, Charles's aunt, which underlined the English queen's status as the emperor's senior family member, displaying to all who were watching the family ties between the two royal houses. Katherine's sitting on a lower chair furthermore communicated to all present that although social deference was shown to her by both rulers, in terms of real power the queen was subordinate to her husband, but also, importantly, that she did not presume to outrank the emperor.

The handwashing ceremony was repeated for 'The right reverend Cardinal of York, Queen Germaine and the Lady Mary', who 'washed their hands together'.[104] Sanuto carefully records that theirs was a 'second gold basin', meaning that the second group did not share the vessel that the emperor, his host, and his aunt had used, and the diarist underscores that this was a lesser vessel that also had 'a cover, but without any crown'.[105] In grouping Germaine de Foix with the cardinal and Henry's sister Mary, who had been queen of France and was inconsistently referred to by Sanuto as both 'Lady' and 'Queen', it was acknowledged that Germaine, a widow like Mary, could be recognized for her previous position as queen consort, although she was not considered equal to the first group of basin-sharers. In terms of practicality, it should be noted that when Sanuto writes that the three persons 'washed their hands together' he did not mean that they did so simultaneously. Each took a turn being served with the vessel, likely in the order in which he mentions the names. To serve Mary Tudor, the vessel would have to be carried to the other end of the table, as the three users of the second vessel did not sit together. Sanuto explains the seating arrangement for this group, which makes tangible, even if it does not spell out, the awkwardness of where to place Cardinal Wolsey—with whom the emperor had had close contact, and who played a key role in furthering the alliance between England and the Empire—at a table of royals. The solution was found in sitting him next to 'Queen Germaine', who was not a royal by

[103] *CSPV* vol. 3, #50.
[104] *CSPV* vol. 3, #50.
[105] *CSPV* vol. 3, #50.

birth, and had been born a French noblewoman of the house of Foix. She sat on his right (her left), and had no one sitting on her other side. In terms of 'networking' if I can be pardoned the use of this term, the cardinal was well-placed next to Germaine, who was close to Charles, her '*petit-fils par alliance*',[106] and would have been a useful contact to be on good terms with. The other former queen, the king's sister Mary, was placed on the left of the king, their proximity appropriate due to their close family relationship. Then, Sanuto records, 'the Cardinal [sat] to the right of Queen Katharine, but there was space between them for another chair'. In other words, Wolsey was not sitting directly next to Katherine, and the empty space giving the impression that another chair could be added meant that Katherine was, symbolically speaking, only sitting next to Charles, creating the optical impression of one side of the table at which Henry and Charles were flanked by Mary and Katherine respectively, and the other side of the table, where Wolsey and Germaine de la Foix would have sat. Sanuto sums up rather blandly: 'these six [were] sitting at the table placed at the head of the hall'.[107]

Showing off largesse

It was of paramount importance for rulers to show—and for chronicle writers in their employ to record—generosity in sharing food and good wine at the table. Following the footsteps of anthropologists such as Marcel Mauss,[108] historians of food and consumption have observed that inviting someone to accept one's welcome or largesse could lead to a situation in which some form of reciprocity is expected, or indeed, necessary. We have seen an example of this towards the end of Chapter 2, in the discussion of the 1532 conference between the kings of England, France, and Navarre. During this diplomatic encounter the

---

[106] I borrow this beautiful term for the relationship between Charles and Germaine from: Pascal Gandoulphe, 'Quelques réflexions sur Germaine de Foix (1488–1536), dernière reine d'Aragon, et sa fortune historiographique', *Cahiers d'études romanes* 42 (2021), 189–209. This article gives a useful overview of Germaine's marital and political life.

[107] *CSPV* vol. 3, #50.

[108] Marcel Mauss, 'Essai sur le don. Forme et raison de l'échange dans les sociétés archaïques', *L'Année Sociologique*, 2nd series 1 (1923–24), 30–186. Cf; C.M. Woolgar, 'Gifts of Food in Late Medieval England', *JMH* 37 (2011), 6–18 (7).

rulers sponsored entertainments provided by members of their own entourages, which would be reciprocated by the other rulers in the form of financially rewarding the performers in question, as well as through offering their own servants' entertainments to treat the others in return. Perhaps underlying this need for reciprocity—which could even take the form of competitiveness (as for example typical for the interactions between Henry and Francis at the Field of Cloth of Gold) was the idea that offering hospitality functioned as an overt mechanism to underscore the giver's ability to host. As such it had everything to do with demonstrating power. Montanari, for example, writes,

> to invite people to one's own table is a sign of liberal generosity, of economic well-being, and in the final analysis, of power: an invitation is a gesture of self-affirmation and therefore all the more impressive as the number (or rank) of the people gathered around oneself increases.[109]

This would imply that the greater the number of people hosted and catered for, and the greater the splendour recorded, the greater the honour of the host. A wealth of information about what was eaten at banquets within diplomatic contexts can be found in financial accounts, confirming the ordering (and expenses) of the foods served at a particular banquet, and in the surviving documents about the planning and preparing for such events. For finding details about culinary choices then, researchers will expect to look in the same places that they consult for learning about the patronage of musicians or the dressing and keeping of fools. Unfortunately, food historians face the same disappointments as do theatre historians when consulting the attractive eye-witness accounts and records taken by persons who had heard a second-hand account. These accounts when referring to (dramatic) performances can be notably bland or vague about what was seen.[110] Similarly, such accounts of banquets do not often record what was

---

[109] Montanari, *Medieval Tastes*, 179.

[110] Think for example of a performance attended by Henry VIII and Anne Boleyn, and described by Chapuys, who does not describe the play, but zooms in on one aspect of the performance and the king's behaviour at this occurrence: '*Et print si grand plesir veant que coppoit les testes de ces eclesiastiques que pour rire a son plesir, aussi pour donner plus de cueur au peuple de continuer en telles choses il se decouvrist*' [All this gave such pleasure seeing that one cut off the heads of the ecclesiastics that to laugh as he pleased, and to give more courage to the people to continue these things, he revealed/uncovered himself']. Haus-, Hof-, und Staatsarchiv, Vienna, Staatenabteilungen, England, Berichte, Karton 7,

consumed.[111] Or at least, they do not often provide detail of the food other than commenting on the riches of meats and the abundance of the spread.

Festival books and chronicle texts, on the other hand, prioritize proceedings and the establishment of hierarchy at banquet settings. However, there are occasions where they do record the foods consumed in addition to general statements about the richness and generosity of the table. For example, a rather elaborate taste of the dishes enjoyed can be found in *The Chronicle of London*, now attributed to Robert Fabyan,[112] which recorded the menu served at the wedding feast of Margaret Tudor and the Scottish King James IV.[113] This chronicle records what was served to 'the grete party of the Barony of scotland and many noble men of thys Realm off England', and devotes a substantial amount of space to list dishes, even exceeding the space dedicated to the description of the marriage event itself.[114] To today's reader, there may be something bordering on the comical in the wording used for the dishes listed. We see a repetition of foods ('Sullen Gese *with* sawce, Powderid Gese *with* sawce') as well as the repetition of ways of preparing foods ('Perys Bakyn, Applys Bakyn, Datys Bakyn, Prunys Bakyn').[115] But the record is very serious, and the repetition of the food types followed by the ways in which it was cooked is suggestive of a richness in variety, which in itself brought honour on the host who provided his guests with this largesse, as well as on the guests who had been deemed worthy to receive it.

When a chronicle text records in detail the foods or wine served, this is often to demonstrate the greatness of the patron of the text, often the organizer of the event commemorated, or of part of this event. This can

1535. See also Nadia T. van Pelt, 'Henry VIII Decapitating Ecclesiastics on Stage?' *Notes & Queries* 62:4 (2015), 534–6.

[111] See also, Normore, *Feast*, 11.

[112] Julia Boffey, *Henry VII's London in the Great Chronicle* (Kalamazoo: TEAMS, 2019), 3.

[113] See also, Sarah Carpenter, 'Gely Wyth Tharmys of Scotland England': Word, Image and Performance at the Marriage of James IV and Margaret Tudor', in Janet Hadley Williams and J. Derrick McClure, eds., *'Freshe Fontanis': Studies in the Culture of Medieval and Early Modern Scotland* (Newcastle: Cambridge Scholars Press, 2013), 165–77.

[114] A.H. Thomas and I.D. Thornley, eds., *The Chronicle of London* (Gloucester: Alan Sutton, 1983), 324.

[115] Thomas and Thornley, eds., *The Chronicle of London*, 324.

be illustrated by a French festival book printed in 1520 that provides an account of the Field of Cloth of Gold. The book, titled *La description et ordre du camp et festiement et ioustes des trescrestiens et tres puissans roys de France et Dangleterre* opens with a woodcut of a joust, underscoring the festive elements and sports performed at the conference.[116] It also records key aspects of this conference that would also be recorded in other accounts, such as the French delegates visiting the English camp and vice versa, and the meeting between the two kings. The well-known episode during which neither Henry nor Francis dared to dine in the other's camp as a guest, afraid to be captured by a fellow ruler whom—despite all expressions of camaraderie—in the end they did not trust, was concluded with the English king dining with the French queen, and Francis banqueting with Katherine of Aragon. About this exchange of guests the French festival book sees it important to record that there was '*une grosse fontaine*' [a great fountain] erupting with '*vin blanc cleret du meilleur*' [the best white claret wine], which was free to take for all who wanted ('*estoit commun a boire a qui vouloit*') (sig. Bii): a demonstration of largesse, good taste, and impressive technology performed at a place where just before there had not even been an encampment.[117]

A curious example of a compliment on a host's generosity is found in the work of Sanuto, who when referring to the Field of Cloth of Gold remarks on the crockery used at the English camp, as well as on the copiousness of the food served (some of it in said crockery): 'Each course consisted of 50 double dishes, that is to say, with covers, all of silver gilt except those presented to the King, winch were of gold, and they went so often to the kitchen that to count the times was impossible'.[118]

> Then all over the house below, and about the courtyard, victuals were served; the abundance of food and wine being so great that the people

---

[116] *La description et ordre du camp et festiement et ioustes des trescrestiens et tres puissans roys de France et Dangleterre* (Paris, 1520), British Library 'Treasures in Full: Renaissance Festival Books'. https://www.bl.uk/treasures/festivalbooks/BookDetails.aspx?strFest=0006.

[117] Teofilo Ruiz refers to 'the open distribution of food and the ever-present fountains pouring wine that were open to all, a tradition that persisted without notable change from the late Middle Ages into the early modern period', which he contrasts to private (elite) feasting: 'the more exclusive banquets to which only the royal family and the highest nobles were invited'. Theofilo F. Ruiz, *A King Travels: Festive Traditions in Late Medieval and Early Modern Spain* (Princeton, NJ: Princeton University Press, 2012), 142.

[118] *CSPV* vol. 3, #50.

> choked themselves. In front of the first gate there was a fountain, which spouted wine during five hours for all comers.[119]

'People chok[ing] themselves' seems an intriguing way to refer to a banquet situation, and may perhaps be seen as unflattering, as the wording marks the greed of the table guests gobbling up all the food. But that would not have been in line with the source nor its aim. Sanuto's text was not so much a personal record of the type that we now imagine when we hear the word 'diary', but rather a chronicle, and not all of it formed a first-hand account of events. Robert Finlay notes, 'He gathered those facts in the chancellery of the Ducal Palace and in the streets of the city, transcribing official legislation and ambassadorial dispatches, reporting popular opinion and Rialto gossip'.[120] Sanuto often offers information about diplomatic affairs on occasions where the Venetian ambassador was also present, suggesting that he may have been one of Sanuto's important sources of information. In the case of the Field of Cloth of Gold this may also have occurred; the *Rutland Papers* reveal in the list of 'persons who attended King Henry VIII and Queen Katharine to the Field of Cloth of Gold' that the English train took with them 'the Emperors Ambassadors, xx servauntes and xxiij horses' as well as 'the Ambassadors of Venyce, xxiij servauntes xj horses'.[121] This Venetian presence would have given Sanuto details regarding the arrangements made at the English camp.

Sanuto's identity as Venetian meant that he did not write his account to serve the glory of either Henry or Francis. However, throughout the account Sanuto is respectful towards both the English and French monarchs, concluding the entry of the Field of Cloth of Gold in the following way:

> At this interview the wealth, courtesy, and valour of the two nations were manifested in the noblest mode and fashion, of which, although many striking instances might be written in detail, yet did the reality far exceed them; nor may any one suppose that what has been written is the whole, for it could not be expressed by any memory, however vivid, though aided by the readiest of pens, for the grandeur,

[119] *CSPV* vol. 3, #50.
[120] Robert Finlay, 'Politics and History in the Diary of Marino Sanuto', *RQ* 33:4 (1980), 585–98 (588).
[121] *Rutland*, 33.

address, personal beauty, manners, fashions, deeds, and words, of these two most powerful Kings, in the field, at table, in conversation, at audience, and during amusements and '*serizi*' (sic) were altogether remarkable and incredible.[122]

And the respectful tone used to reflect on the hospitality aside, Sanuto was generally not disparaging of riches flaunted and grandeur shared. It is therefore likely that the remark about the choking table guests is to be read within the spirit of enlivening the text, which can be found throughout the diary. To quote Robert Finlay again, in Sanuto's writing 'the continuity of events and institutions collapses into the quotidian, so that the beaching of a whale has a place within an account of an invasion of Italy and a joke at a wedding is inserted in a review of a doge's reign'.[123]

We see this comical streak also in Sanuto's description of the banquet of the first 1520 conference between Henry VIII and Charles V, in which he uses a remark on the general atmosphere of the banquet to justify a delicious piece of gossip that was apparently too good to resist:

> The banquet was most sumptuous, the tables being surrounded by enamoured youths (*gioveni innamorati*), who stood behind the ladies; and amongst the rest, certain Spaniards played the lovers' part so bravely that nothing could have been better (*nihil supra*). One of them, the Count of Capra, made love so heartily, that he had a fainting fit, or swooned for his mistress, and was carried out by the hands and feet until he recovered himself.[124]

To return to Henry's largesse at the Field of Cloth of Gold as an act of self-affirmation as a generous host, one may wonder, had this food been enough to literally choke on? What quantities of food were to be expected on such an occasion? A general impression of the total amounts that were expected to be consumed during the visit can be found in *Rutland Papers* in a paper titled, 'An Estymacion for the Kinges dietts and the Quenes, with other Nobles, being at Calays and Guynes for one moneth in June and Julye, Anno xij^mo Regis Henrici Octaui'.[125]

[122] *CSPV* vol. 3, #50.

[123] Finlay, 'Politics and History', 587.

[124] *CSPV* vol. 3, #50. Note that the 'Count of Capra' mentioned is Diego Fernández de Córdoba, *conde de Cabra*, whom we have already seen in Chapter 1, where he was referred to in the Anglophone records as 'the Erle . . . of Spayne'. Wasson, ed., *REED: Devon*, 215.

[125] *Rutland*, 41.

For this estimated provision, the paper records the following numbers, to which I have added bracketed translations of the number of food items given in Latin numerals for the reader's convenience:

Fyrst, in whete at xij s. the quarter, wythe costs
and charges, vij^c quarters [700 quarters]

In wynne, Frenche and Gascoyne, at cx s. the
tonne,
wythe costs and charges, cl tonne [150 tons]
In swete wynnes by estymacion, vj butts [6 butts]
In bere, at xx s. the tonne, v^c lx tonnes [540 tons]
In bieffes, at xl s. the pece, cccxl [340 pieces]
In muttons, at v s. the pece, M^1M^1cc [2200 pieces]
In veales, at v s. the pece, viij^c [800 pieces]
In hogges, at viij s. the pece, iiij (XX above)
[80 pieces]

In fyshe, salt and freshe, by estymacion	[total price is listed as 300 pounds]
In spices, by estymacion	[total price is listed as 440 pounds]
...	
In the pultrye, by estymacion, all maner sorts that can be gotten	[total price listed as 1300 pounds].[126]

To arrive at an estimation of the royals' and nobles' joint daily consumption, this month's ration can be divided by 31, revealing that, roughly speaking, they would collectively have been apportioned 22,6 quarters of wheat, 4,8 tons of French and Gascon wine, 17,4 tons of beer, 11 pieces of beef, 71 pieces of mutton, 26 pieces of veal, 2,5 hogs, aside almost £10-worth of fish, and just short of £42-worth of different kinds of 'pultrye', a broad term suggesting any kind of bird available. The size of the group partaking in this ration would have been under a hundred persons, if we rely on 'A List of Persons who Attended King Henry VIII. And Queen Katharine to the Field of Cloth of Gold, with the Number of their Servants and Horses'.[127] Given that the month's ration is 'An Estymacion'

---

[126] *Rutland*, 41.
[127] 'A List of Persons who Attended King Henry VIII. And Queen Katharine to the Field of Cloth of Gold, with the Number of their Servants and Horses' comprises in the king's service: 1 cardinal, 1 archbishop, 1 marquis, 1 duke, 10 earls, 5 bishops, 20 barons and a

and does not specify the particulars of the banquet that Sanuto refers to, it can be helpful to contextualize the Venetian diarist's statement with what we know of other banquets—albeit at other moments in time—hosted for diplomatic purposes. W.R.P. Bourne notes that on 22 and 23 September 1465 a banquet was organized to celebrate Chancellor Neville's appointment as Archbishop of York, for which 14,451 birds were planned to be cooked for the dinner table.[128] At a later date, from 20 to 24 October 1532, when feasts were shared between Henry VIII and Francis I and the King of Navarre,[129] the rulers and their trains ate their way through more than 40,000 rabbits and birds, including luxury fowl such as swans.[130] Other meats were also had, such as a total of 300 'muttons', 120 'veals', 18 'boars', 'hogs', 8 'hinds', 336 'does', and several other types of viands such as 'neats' tongues'.[131] The party also consumed, among various other things, 26,000 eggs, 200 gallons of cream, 80 gallons of milk, 400 oranges, 2,000 apples, and assorted fish, such as cod, salted salmon, 'congers, haddocks, birts, halibuts, breams, dories, basses, mullets and soles', 'herrings, whitings, rochets and plaice', but also 'fr[esh] sturgeon', and, curiously, 'porpoises or seals'.[132] The company washed it all down with '3 vats' of 'Rhenish wines', 30 tons of French wine, 20 tons of Gascon wine, and 100 tons of 'London beer and ale'.[133] The daily meat and fowl ration for the whole entourage is

person representing a baron, 3 knights of the garter, 4 'spiritual councillors', 100 knights (and squires), and the ambassadors representing the Emperor and the ambassadors of Venice. The queen was attended by: 1 earl, 3 bishops, 4 barons, 30 knights, 1 duchess, 7 countesses, 16 baronesses, 18 wives of knights, and 25 gentlewomen. The number of servants belonging to all these individuals are not counted here, but can be found in *Rutland*, 29–38. To determine who in this group would have been understood as having been part of the 'nobles', and therefore selected for partaking in the rations, I follow G.W. Bernard's definition: 'The strict definition of a nobleman was a man summoned personally to attend as a member of the House of Lords whenever the monarch called a parliament. Noblemen held titles: in order of precedence dukes, viscounts, marquesses, earls or barons'. G.W. Bernard, *Who Ruled Tudor England: Paradoxes of Power* (London: Bloomsbury, 2022), 53.

[128] Bourne, 'The Birds and Animals Consumed', 331.

[129] Bourne, 'The Birds and Animals Consumed', 331–3.

[130] Bourne, 'The Birds and Animals Consumed', 331.

[131] Marjorie Blatcher, ed., *Report on the Manuscripts of the Most Honourable The Marquess of Bath Preserved at Longleat, Volume IV: Seymour Papers, 1532–1686* (London: Her Majesty's Stationary Office, 1968), 9. Contains public sector information licensed under the Open Government Licence v3.0.

[132] Blatcher, ed., *Seymour Papers*, 9.

[133] Blatcher, ed., *Seymour Papers*, 8.

also given, amounting to '6 oxen, 8 calves, 40 sheep, 12 pigs, 3 doz. "gr" (i.e., capons gras), 8 doz. good capons, 7 swans, 20 storks, 34 pheasants, 16 doz. partridges, 4 ½ doz. herons, 16 doz. cocks, [blank] quails, 7 doz. pullets, 60 doz. larks, 20 doz. "pewns" [pigeons?], 2 doz. peacocks, 8 doz. plovers, 8 doz. teals'.[134] W.R.P. Bourne wryly notes that the overview of the consumed goods 'goes far to confirm the traditional image of Henry VIII as a glutton, and to explain why, with the appearance of sporting firearms, cranes, storks, spoonbills, and bustards have become rare birds in western Europe'.[135] Perhaps it may be more useful, however, to say that both the English banquet provisions at the Field of Cloth of Gold and the Anglo-French meeting of 1532 were textbook examples of, to use Montanari's phrase again, 'gesture[s] of self-affirmation'.[136] Henry took his role as host very seriously, and on occasions of international and diplomatic importance, was careful to display himself as open-handed, asserting his wealth, power, and—dare I say it—good taste.

'Vitailles for themperor'

In line with being a conscientious host, Henry VIII was not only open-handed during banquets, but also showed himself happy to foot the bill for the emperor and his inner party's daily culinary needs, as evidenced by records from 1520, such as the 'Payments for victuals, &c. which the Emperor's train took in Calais and the marches by the King's proclamation that no one should take any money of them'.[137] The logistics of feeding the rest of the large entourage were also carefully organized. A preparatory note advises, 'Item, that the counsail of Calaies cause sufficient prouision of wyne, floure, bief, muttons, and all other maner of

---

[134] Blatcher, ed., *Seymour Papers*, 7. Also quoted in: Bourne, 'The Birds and Animals Consumed', 331. For an idea of the size of the retinues, it should be noted that it was agreed beforehand that Henry would bring a retinue that was 'not to exceed 600 horsemen or footmen', and similarly, Francis would stay at Calais also with a retinue 'with not more than 600 men'. These numbers were carefully monitored, and the 'Ordo' setting the ground rules for the interview between Henry van Francis states that, 'The retinues of both are not to exceed 600 as before mentioned, and Norfolk and Montmorency will arrange for posting guards'. *LP* vol. 5, #1373 (October 1532).

[135] Bourne, 'The Birds and Animals Consumed', 333.

[136] Montanari, *Medieval Tastes*, 179.

[137] *LP* vol. 3, #907 (10 July 1520).

vitailes, to be put [in] sufficient arredines in the towne, for the honor-
able enterteynment of themperor and his trayne duering thair abode
ther'.[138] It should be noted here that providing enough victuals did not
mean that the *entire* entourage trailing the emperor was to be fed at
the expense of the English court. The note continues to specifiy: '. . .
at the propre expenses and charges of the said Emperor and his said
trayne'.[139] Similarly, when preparing Dover for the impactful visit, a note
was drawn up advising: 'Item, it is thought necessary that the towne of
Dover be plentuously provided and furnished with all maner vitailes
for horse and man, so that aswell the trayne of themperor and of my
said Lord Cardinall, with suche as shall attende vpon hym, may have
furnishing of vitailes *for thair money*, duering the tyme of thair abode
ther' (emphasis added).[140] It was furthermore specified that since the
emperor 'shalbe alwaies lodged in such places where the King shalbe'
it should follow that 'themperor, *with a reasonable noumber of his
famylier seruitures* attending vpon hym, of good congruence, must be at
the Kinges costes and charges' (emphasis added).[141] In terms of organization it was therefore 'thought necessary that thofficers of the Kinges
household haue the charge therof, so that euery thing may be honorably
and plentuously prouided'.[142]

Let me first give an idea of the size of the entourage to explain why
Henry thought it necessary to restrict his generosity to the emperor
and his nobles and close attendants. Jerdan noted in his edition of the
Rutland Papers that, 'the sum total of this vast retinue amounted to
2,044 persons, and 1,127 horses, but it would seem that, upon consideration, the Emperor made a reduction in those numbers'.[143] Charles
spent a large part of his reign on the road with an itinerant court,
travelling to his different territories, and his journey to England was
conducted in the same manner, even if on this occasion he was being
hosted by a fellow ruler. This meant that Charles brought with him
his *Petit Chapelle* with it almoners and other staff, as well as the most

[138] *Rutland*, 71. See also, *LP* vol. 3, #2288.
[139] *Rutland*, 71. See also, *LP* vol. 3, #2288.
[140] *Rutland*, 72.
[141] *Rutland*, 75–6.
[142] *Rutland*, 75–6.
[143] *Rutland*, 65.

important household officials, such as the '*grant chambellan*'.[144] The extent of Charles's power is made tangible by the list of '*princes and grand maystres*' present in his entourage, representing various areas in his vast empire. This intercultural party can be exemplified by, for example, the presence of the Duke of Alva, the Marquis of Branden-bourg, but also 'Le Prince doranges' and 'Le Duc de Cleves'.[145] The latter being the father of Anne of Cleves, who would marry Henry VIII in 1540. And in terms of bodies of counsel, a '*conseill de Castille*', a '*conseil daragon*', and a '*conseill de Flanders*',[146] are recorded to have represented the different parts of Charles's territories. A number of '*gentilzhommes de Espaigne*' [gentlemen from Spain] and '*gens desglise despagne*' [Spanish ecclesiastics] are also listed.[147]

In line with earlier meetings between Henry and Charles, a daily ration was planned for the 'noblemen and gentlemen', including two meals, a dinner and a supper, each comprising two specified courses:

> First course dinner: Potage, Boyled capon, Gr. Sh., Young Vele, Grene Gese, Kyde l. Lambe, Custardes, Fruttour.
>   Second course dinner: Jussel, Chykyns, Peions, Rabettes, Tarte[s].
>   First course supper: Potage, Chykyns boyled, Jegges of Motton, Capons, Kyde l. Lambe, Dowcettes.
>   Second course supper: Jely. Ipocras, Peions, Chykyns, Rabettes, Tarttes.[148]

The surviving records of the preparations by the Lord Mayor of Lon-don reveal the complexity of the logistics of making sure that this food reached the lodgings where the emperor's nobles resided. Some of these records are orders concerned with the processing of the raw food prod-ucts that would be distributed to the different lodgings, where they were to be cooked:

---

[144] *Rutland*, 61. Originally, he had planned to also bring his Grand Chapelle, with a 'grand chapellayn' and a 'premyer chappelayn' (first chaplain), sixteen singers, a master for the chapel children ('vng maystre des enfants'), eight children, three priests who could conduct high mass, an organ player, 'vng souffleur dorghanes', two clerks, and a 'fourryer' (p. 60). However, upon consideration it was decided that '"La Grande Chappelle" will remain with the fleet in Zealand'. *LP* vol. 3, #2288.

[145] *Rutland*, 61.

[146] *Rutland*, 62.

[147] *Rutland*, 62–3.

[148] Slightly modified from: *Rutland*, 96.

Item, to assign iiij bakers within the citie of London to serue the noblemen belongyng to themperor that be lodged in the canons howses of Paules and ther aboutes, and oder places within the Citie.[149]

Item, to assign iiij bochers for seruyng of oxen, shepe, calves, hogges of gresse, fleches of bacon, marybones, and such oder as shalbe called for.[150]

Item, to assigne ij fysshemoungers for prouision of lynges to be redy waterd, pykes, tenches, bremes, caluer salmon, and such oder deyntes of the fresshe water.[151]

The Lord Mayor also ordered for the appointing of 'ij fyshemoungers for prouision of see fysshe', and four 'pulters' were also taken on, as were two men responsible for preparing sauces.[152] The 'Kynges grocers' were, furthermore 'to be appouynted to serue for all maner of spices'.[153] The Lord Mayor was also not above planning what kind of kitchen equipment should be organized and transferred to every house lodging the emperor's noblemen.[154] And, leaving nothing to chance, he detailed the names of the persons who were to be responsible for 'the surveying and particular receite and delyuerynge of brede, flessh, fissh, pultry, wares, spices, sawces, and other vitailles, to the lodgynges of dyuers lords and estates belongyng to the Emperours grace'.[155]

Since Charles travelled with an itinerant household, it goes without saying that he brought his own kitchen staff on his visit to England. The 'Officiers' listed to accompany the emperor included the 'Panetrie' [bakery and pantry staff] with five officials; the 'Eschansonnerie' comprising four members of staff; the 'Cuisine de lempereur' [imperial kitchen] brought its own master cook ('vng maystre keux') and patissier ('vng patissier') as well as supportive staff, and the 'Sausserye' and 'Fruyterye' included a 'maystre des torches' so that sufficient torches and candles were to be had.[156] Three medical doctors ('medecin') were also

[149] Rutland, 83.
[150] Rutland, 84.
[151] Rutland, 84.
[152] Rutland, 84.
[153] Rutland, 84.
[154] Rutland, 84.
[155] Rutland, 85.
[156] Rutland, 63–4. Finding an official responsible for candles listed here is in line with the custom in the kitchens of the Burgundian ducal households that, as Otto Cartellieri

brought along, as were five surgeons ('*cynq cirurgiens*').[157] And so the list
continues with various offices indispensable to the emperor's comfort,
including musicians, running all the way down to the persons responsible for the imperial laundry. It is unlikely that Charles would have
lacked anything. But of course, Henry was eager to provide him with any
necessary comfort. The *Rutland Papers* show that payments were made
'to diuers personnes for prouision of vitailles for themperor', including
Rhinish wine, ale, fowls for consumption, but also for other items such
as wardrobe stuff for beds, kitchen necessities, 'diaper' (cloth for use at
the table), wax for candles, and other things.[158]

Getting it right was of paramount importance to the organizers of
the visit, who—aware that the devil was in the detail and that diplomatic success could rely on scripted social rituals—found themselves
planning and discussing how to set the stage for the ceremonial aspects
of the visit involving food and consumption. A 'memoranda' account
written up by a person responsible for some of the 1522 preparations
shows that advice was sought from someone higher up in the hierarchy regarding matters of serving the emperor. Answers to some of these
questions were written on the same document.[159] Some questions are
logistical in nature, such as: 'Item, whether ther shalbe any banque-
tyng, and in what places?', to which the other responds: 'At Grenwyche,
London, Richemount and Wynsore'. But we also see questions touching
on the implications of the 'props' needed during the banquet. Take for
example the organizer's question regarding the use of napkins: 'Item,
whether themperor and his nobles shalbe serued with his own dyaper,
or elles with the Kynges?'. We know from the payments made that 'diaper' was bought, but the fact that the organizer questioned whether the
emperor would prefer to use his own or whether the practicalities of
providing this for him would be desired, shows that these things truly
mattered. The answer given by the organizer's superior is: 'Themperor
and his court with the Kynges'. From this follows that the king's 'dyaper'
could be presented to the royal guest without anyone losing face and

observes, the '*sausserie* and the *fruiterie*... had to supply wax and tallow for the innumer-
able candles and torches'. Otto Cartellieri, *The Court of Burgundy*, trans. Malcolm Letts
(London: Routledge, 1996; 1st edn. 1929), 69.
  [157] *Rutland*, 64–5.
  [158] *Rutland*, 76–7.
  [159] In what follows, I refer to *Rutland*, 78.

without undermining any ritual custom. We see a similar question in the official's conundrum regarding the crockery used to serve food: 'Item, whether themperor shalbe served with his own siluer vessells, or elles with the Kynges?' The answer given is: 'At Dover with the Kynges'. The implication is that as soon as the emperor's own vessels had arrived, these would be used to serve him. The vessels contained crests and it is conceivable that his being served from vessels sporting his own crest rather than Henry's would have been the preferred thing to do.

Civic involvement

The persons chosen to perform organizational tasks surrounding the logistics of food and other necessary items for the emperor and his nobles were, as Jerdan has observed, 'chief members of their several companies', and we see in the list representatives of, respectively, the Drapers, Mercers, Grocers, Fishmongers, Goldsmiths, Skinners, Tailors, Haberdashers and Vintners.[160] It shows that for this great undertaking, the civic companies were relied on, included, and as such, provided with the recognition that was of paramount importance for the cooperation between crown and town when planning an event of this scale. Civic involvement in the event is also seen in the organization of the entertainments performed for the emperor. A very short record yielding information about this can be found in the *Chronicle of the Grey Friars of London*. The account taker records the places in London where the pageant entertainments took place, and provides an insight into the extent of the preparations that were to be made, such as sprucing and cleaning the relevant parts of the city that Charles was to grace with his presence, and beautifying Bridewell Palace, one of Henry's newly built city residences[161]:

> xiij°. A°. Thys yere the emperor Charles came in to Ynglond and soo to London, and there was honorabullie resevyd with many pagenttes,

---

[160] *Rutland*, 85.

[161] Archaeological research confirms the *Chronicle of the Grey Friars of London*'s description of 'Bryddewell' as 'was new made'. For example, the building of Bridewell as a royal palace between 1515 and 1523 is mentioned in Derek Gadd and Tony Dyson, 'Bridewell Palace Excavations at 9–11 Bridewell Place and 1–3 Tudor Street, City of London, 1978', *Post-Medieval Archaeology* 15:1 (1981), 1–79.

as on the brygge, in Graschestret, Ledynhalle, the condet in Cornell, at Stockes, at the gret condet in Chepe, at the standerd, the crosse new gylte, at the lyttell condet, and Powlles church dore; and soe to Bryddewell, wych was new made and gylte agenst hys comynge.[162]

Just as in the guilds' participation in and responsibilities within the chain of activity that enabled the distribution of foods to the emperor's entourage, the civic investment in making the city of London appear rich, fresh, and festive, and the staging of pageants underlines the joint efforts of the court and the city officials.

The English people's efforts to welcome Charles did not go unnoticed. Charles himself in his correspondence writes to his secretary that after meeting the 'Queen and Princess', his aunt Katherine of Aragon and cousin Mary, at Greenwich castle, 'they all entered London together, and met with a magnificent reception from a great company of knights and gentlemen, with solemn and costly pageants, to the great joy of all the people'.[163] To Charles de Poupet, Lord of La Chaulx, who had in the past worked for Philippe le Beau and now offered council to Charles, the emperor wrote that 'The joy of the people, great and small, is shown in every possible way. On the 6th entered London in great triumph, not only like brothers of one mind, but in the same attire'.[164] It can be noted here that Charles in his letter merges the experiences of being welcomed by the English civilians and his dressing in the same clothes as Henry. This dressing 'like brothers' between the rulers can be seen as a gesture of friendship. This kind of demonstration of affection can perhaps be read in a similar way as Henry's and Francis I's expressed vows to let their beards grow in anticipation of their meeting at the Field of Cloth of Gold, as a sign of their friendship.[165] Perhaps even more important was that when the emperor and the English king appeared in London, dressed alike, they outwardly demonstrated their unity to the English people, the nobles and dignitaries from overseas, as well as all the other

[162] J.G. Nichols, ed., *Chronicle of the Grey Friars of London*, Camden Society Old Series: Volume 53 (London: Camden Society, 1852), 29–53. *British History Online*. http://www.british-history.ac.uk/camden-record-soc/vol53/pp29-53 [Accessed 22.03.2023].

[163] *LP* vol. 3, #2306 (7 June 1522).

[164] *LP* vol. 3, #2309 (9 June 1522).

[165] This anecdote is much-discussed, and a good introduction to this gesture can be found in: Mark Albert Johnston, *Beard Fetish in Early Modern England: Sex, Gender, and Registers of Value* (London: Routledge, 2016), 38.

international visitors trailing the emperor's entourage. The two rulers thus expressed a powerful message that was afterwards to be widely shared. No doubt it was also partly staged for the benefit of Francis, who would hear about this through the grapevine. It is telling that as part of the spectacles organized for Charles in London, an impression of naval prowess was demonstrated on the Thames. The planning of this contribution to the emperor's welcome can be found in the *Rutland Papers*: 'Item, all such shippes as than shalbe in Thamys to be layde bitwext Grenewiche and Grauisende, in a conuenient distaunce bitwext euery ship, well garnished with stremers and banners, gunnes and ordynaunce, to shote as themperor shall passe by'.[166] We can see how this spectacle unfolded in Hall's *Chronicle*:

> After the departyng of Themperour to the lande from hys navy, the apparell of every ship then shewed, as flagges, banners, stremers and targetes, then the mighty ordinaunce of every of them brake oute by force of fyer as though the see had brente, marvelous was the noyse of the gonnes . . .[167]

'Maruelous' as the 'noyse of the gonnes' may have been, this was not an innocent display of delight at Charles's coming, nor a celebration of the nautical landscape of the Thames brightened up with flags just as the houses in London had been decorated. Indeed, in a letter written on 7 June 1522, Charles informed his secretary that an English army had crossed the Channel to accompany him on his journey, and to protect him from any potential threats from the French naval forces.[168] Therefore, it is likely that symbolically speaking, the ships 'festively' fashioned for war on the Thames formed a clever piece of image-making: to the English subjects watching the ships from land, it enhanced the sense of splendour of the occasion, and gave off a message of safety: any unrest with France was not to be worried about, as the naval forces would deal with it; to Charles and his company it would signal that Henry was a good alliance, and the emperor was almost pompously reminded of the nautical safety net that had ensured his passage across the Channel and

[166] *Rutland*, 75.

[167] Edward Hall, *The Triumphant Reigne of Kyng Henry the* VIII, ed. Charles Whibley (London: Jack, 1904), vol. 1, 188; *Rutland*, 75.

[168] *LP* vol. 3, #2306 (7 June 1522). This information is also shared in a letter from Gasparo Contarini to the Signory: *CSPV* vol. 3, #461 (22 May 1522).

of the future support that Henry would bring if they were to come to an alliance, which was the aim of the visit; to any correspondents or reporters to other rulers, it demonstrated that Henry had the means, equipment, and personnel to be ready for war.

And apparently news did travel fast, because on 11 June a letter from Margaret of Savoy to the town of Malines recorded that 'The Emperor has written to her that the king of England and those of his realm treat him as if he were their king, and Henry has defied France along with him'.[169]

Jousting with Henry

There are various sources that refer to the jousts and spectacles hosted in Charles's honour. Some do so only in passing. For example, a German-language remembrance of the event is recorded in the festival book by the title, *Wie vnd in wellicher gestalt Kay. May. von Bruck auss gen Lunden in Engeland gezogen / ankommen und Empfangen worden ist* (1522).[170] In this festival book the joust is also presented as an element of a larger event or spectacle that encompassed dancing, drinking, feasting, and jousting:

> '... mit Banckethieren / Tanzen / Stechen Thurnieren / Unnd anderm gemacht / und yederman mit essen undd Trincken Kost frey gehalten'
>
> [... with Banqueting / Dancing / jousting tournaments / and other things were done / and everyone was given free food and drink] (sig. A4r).[171]

The two-word description (if we can even call it that) of the activity is very short, but then, the book is only eight pages long, and the first page of the account is used to display a woodcut image of a portrait of Charles V, his mouth characteristically open. From the space dedicated to aspects of the visit, it appears that the German-language festival book goes through the motions of mentioning the festivities

---

[169] *LP* vol. 3, #2312 (11 June 1522).

[170] *Wie vnd in wellicher gestalt Kay. May. von Bruck auss gen Lunden in Engeland gezogen/ ankommen und Empfangen worden ist* (Augsburg, 1522; General Reference Collection DRT Digital Store C.33.e.3.), British Library 'Treasures in Full: Renaissance Festival Books'. https://www.bl.uk/treasures/festivalbooks/BookDetails.aspx?strFest=0082.

[171] Note that for reasons of clarity a free rather than a literal translation is given here.

and the host's generosity, but is not so interested in documenting the entertainments and banquets provided, much unlike what we have seen in Francophone festival books recording the Field of Cloth of Gold, and in particular, the one titled *La description et ordre du camp et festiement*, which indeed took the jousts as a starting point.[172] The obvious difference, however, between the goals of the two texts, is that the Francophone text detailed sports and splendour to which Francis I had contributed, which reflected on his wealth and generosity as a patron or commissioner as well as on his sportsmanship. The German-language text recording Charles's 1522 visit would not have been able to add splendour to Charles's status or reputation by describing the festivities that Henry had commissioned, as they of course reflected on Henry's success at being a good host, and thus on *his* kingship. It is therefore no surprise that the German festival book appears to be more interested in Charles's piety demonstrated by his visiting St Thomas's tomb (sig. A2), as well as in the expressions of pleasure at his visit displayed by the English citizens. The authorities had thought of the Emperor's comfort when they made sure that the '*gassen*' [alleys/streets] '*dadurch Kayserlich Mayestat unnd künig von Engeland haben reiten müssen* [through which [His] Imperial Majesty and the king of England had to ride], were covered with sand ('*mit sand beschit*'). They also had been attentive to making the welcome appear festive by decorating the houses with tapestries on both sides of the street through which Charles and Henry rode ('... *auf bayde seyten / die Heüser mit Tappessern Behenckt gewekt*') (sig. A3). The latter, documented in the German-language festival book, would have given readers a sense of the popularity of their ruler across the boundaries of his territories.

Another reference made, in passing, to the jousts staged for Charles can be found in a rather grumbling letter from Martin de Salinas—who was the ambassador of the *Infante* Ferdinand at the Imperial Court— written to Treasurer Salamanca, in which he complains about every single aspect of his stay: from his encounters with the native population ('travelling in England is troublesome and intercourse with the English by no means agreeable'), to the weather ('the weather was as bad as it could be'), access to food and other necessities ('Few provisions were obtainable at Dover, and the cooking was as bad as possible'), and costs

---

[172] *La description et ordre du camp.* See my Note 116.

faced by non-noble members of the emperor's train ('lodgings are bad and dear'), but he also sheds light on some of the challenges met when dealing with the transport and logistics of persons and belongings for such a large party travelling overseas ('The majority of the court officers and servants of the Emperor could not cross over to Dover that day. The Emperor remained three days at Dover, waiting for his wardrobe'), as well as travel-related inconveniences ('Although the King of England had promised to send 600 horses, the necessary number could not be obtained, and the journey to London was extremely fatiguing').[173] About the festivities he mentions 'jousts in which the King of England personally took part. They were not very splendid. Did not even go to see them'.[174] The remark evokes the question how the ambassador could have known beforehand (before he decided not to go see the jousts) that they would be 'not very splendid'? He offers a further remark about the involvement of foreign visitors, namely that 'No foreigner jousted'.[175]

When we consult 'Richard Gibson's account of preparations for a joust to be held on the 4th and 5th June' to complement de Salinas' information, it is confirmed that Henry himself participated in the joust. Gibson provides a reference to 'the King's bard and apparel' and makes provisions for 'the 9 lords who ran on the King's side'.[176] Gibson does not specify if any foreign visitors participated in the joust, but the account does contain a section detailing preparations 'For a meskeler and revels devised by Wm. Kornyche, gentleman of the Chapel' to be held on the same days as the jousts, which reveals that the participants in this masque comprised a rather international group, including some of the princes in Charles's entourage:

> The apparel was given away as follows:—On the first night, at Greenwich, to the prince of Orange, the count Vaskort, mons. Whavery and mons. Egmond,[177] long gowns of tinsel satin, pale, with double

[173] *CSPS* vol. 2, #420 (5 June 1522).
[174] *CSPS* vol. 2, #420.
[175] *CSPS* vol. 2, #420.
[176] *LP* vol. 3, #2305 (5 June 1522).
[177] 'Mons. Egmond' refers to Charles II, Duke of Guelders, also known as Charles of Egmond. As we will see in Chapter 5, he played a pivotal role in the marital agreement between the families of Anne of Cleves and Francis of Lorraine.

sleeves, with hoods of the same, velvet buskins and satin bonnets; to
master Antony Brown, a gown.[178]

For the second day, the record specifies that 'these lords' (and others) 'went into the Emperor's lodging, where all this apparel was given
them'.[179] One may guess at the narrative represented in the masque,
but a forest theme is likely to have been followed, given that the costume preparations required '22 yds. green sarsnet, at 4s., for 3 foresters'
coats and hoods', '13 yds. of fine Kendal, at 14d. a yd., for 4 hunters'
jackets', '2¾ yds. chequered Kendal, at 17d., for the keeper's hose', and—
curiously—'240 ells of canvas from the King's store, for "wodwos"
garments, covering the pageant, "and a stuffed body"'.[180] But this was
only the beginning of a range of entertainments. On Sunday 16 June, the
day that Charles and Henry drew up the articles of their new alliance
and consolidated their agreements, William Cornish staged a political
play described by Sydney Anglo as 'a crude but accurate summary of the
negotiations that had taken place during the Emperor's stay and their
expected results'.[181] The play was a farce and the object of its ridicule:
Francis I.

War horse

Our source for the contents of this play is, again, Martin de Salinas, who
mentions that 'the King gave a great banquet' but that he 'does not think
it worth the trouble to describe it'.[182] He then notes that 'After supper . . .
a French play was performed by young gentlemen. It was a farce, and in
it the King of France and his alliances were ridiculed'.[183] He summarizes
the plot:

The first actor who came on the stage declared that he was *Friendship*,
who had performed many great and noble deeds in the time of the
Romans, and afterwards. After *Friendship*, *Prudence* entered, and was

---

[178] *LP* vol. 3, #2305.

[179] *LP* vol. 3, #2305.

[180] *LP* vol. 3, #2305.

[181] Sydney Anglo, 'William Cornish in a Play, Pageants, Prison, and Politics', *The Review of English Studies* 10:40 (1959), 347–60 (358).

[182] *CSPS* vol. 2, #437 (21 June 1522).

[183] *CSPS* vol. 2, #437.

received by *Friendship* with many demonstrations of joy. *Friendship* said that he had sought him, and that both, if united, could perform very great deeds. They concluded an alliance. Whilst they were doing so, *Might* entered, and was very well received by *Friendship* and *Prudence*, who told him that they wanted no other ally than him, in order to execute their great plans. *Friendship* was to see that no disunion broke out between them; *Prudence* would counsel, and *Might* would carry out the measures.[184]

Apparently their joint ambition was to tame horses, and 'Thus, there was nothing in the world they could not do, and any horse, however wild and unruly he might be, would soon be made to obey them.'[185] Then, de Salinas notes, 'Workmen entered with anvil and hammers.'[186] He does not specify if they were there to shoe a horse, build a construction, or serve a symbolic purpose. He continues:

A man came on the stage with a great horse, very wild and ferocious. *Friendship, Prudence*, and *Might* asked him what he wanted. He answered that that horse belonged to him, but that it was so wild and untamable that he could not make any use of him. *Friendship* said to the man with the horse that he had come just to the right persons, as they knew best how to manage an unruly horse. If he would confide the horse to them, they would not only subject him, but also make him as tame and obedient as any horse in the world. They made a bridle, and bridled the horse with it.[187]

The three allegorical characters then invite the master of the horse to 'mount' him. 'First the master was afraid, but when he mounted the horse found he was quiet and obedient, although he raised his head very high.'[188] In other words, there was still a bit of resistance in the horse's demeanour. De Salinas reports, '*Friendship* said they would make him lower his head. A curb was attached to the horse, which directly lowered his head. Without being led, the horse followed his master wherever he went.'[189] The ambassador explains the meaning of the farce to Treasurer

[184] *CSPS* vol. 2, #437.
[185] *CSPS* vol. 2, #437.
[186] *CSPS* vol. 2, #437.
[187] *CSPS* vol. 2, #437.
[188] *CSPS* vol. 2, #437.
[189] *CSPS* vol. 2, #437.

Salamanca, noting: 'Thus the farce ended. The meaning of it is clear. The horse is the King of France'. He comments that, 'Whether they have bridled and tamed him he is unable to say'.[190] After this entertainment, the organizers were clever enough to offer lighter amusements in the form of dancing and feasting. De Salinas records:

> When the comedy was concluded, eight ladies came into the room in fancy dresses and danced the 'Pabana' with eight gentlemen whom they chose as partners. After them came eight gentlemen, who were disguised, and who also danced. After the dance came supper, and after supper all went to bed.[191]

The party present had been given some food for thought.

A stage for feasting: The banqueting hall at Calais

We now briefly travel back to 1520, when shortly after the Field of Cloth of Gold, Charles and Henry had a second encounter, this time at Calais. Having just discussed the confident outward self-presentation that Henry would show as host in 1522, playing in the joust to show his prowess to his guest, dressing in the same outfit as the emperor during their joint ride through London, and allowing Cornish to stage a political play that so clearly communicated the new alliance between England and the Empire against their common enemy France, we will now have to think back to a less exuberant Henry in July 1520, whose willingness to invest in meetings with Charles at Gravelines and Calais was motivated in part by the wish to establish himself, just as he had at the Field of Cloth of Gold, as one of the leading figures of Europe, on equal terms with both Francis and Charles. From the perspective of the city of Calais it can also be understood that its citizens would have been ready to put their best foot forward. Calais was in English hands, but perhaps too close for comfort to both Charles's Burgundian lands and Francis's territories, and therefore a place desperate to keep the peace and ready to curry favour with the dominant party in this political balance. As with every royal visit, sacrifices had to be made in order to ensure that the guests had a pleasant stay. The *Chronicle of*

---

[190] *CSPS* vol. 2, #437.
[191] *CSPS* vol. 2, #437.

Calais comments that housing had to be provided for the two rulers, but also for Charles's aunt, Margaret of Austria, the Duchess of Savoy (1480–1530), and for several other notables, 'wherefor all the lords and states of England were sent from theyr lodgings'.[192] Not everyone could be housed within the city gates, as exemplified by a payment of 22 s. 'To Thos. Chapman's wife, the expenses of the strangers at her house outside the gates'.[193] In other words, this was also a large-scale event, involving a great number of people. Yet the most memorable aspect of the second 1520 visit was an investment made by Henry as he built a separate banqueting house to accommodate the large visiting party while at table. I end this chapter on the Calais banqueting house, as its descriptions allow for the most detailed recording of a banquet setting for an event shared between Henry and Charles. Furthermore, the records discussing the Calais banqueting house evidence Henry's understanding of the banquet as a multifaceted event, and offer concrete evidence for the scriptedness of the banquet on this occasion.

The Chronicle of Calais commemorates that, 'ther was made a banqwetynge hows with in the town of Cales',[194] and pays significant attention to the construction of the building and its decorations, both of which represented hard labour, state-of-the-art techniques, and offered the suggestion to whoever saw the building that no expenses had been spared.[195] For example, we learn of the following artwork gracing the banqueting house as decorations to set the atmosphere of the room, and show off heritage and technical advancement:

> ... within the sayd howse was payntyd the element of starres, sonne, and mone, and clowdes, with dyvars othar things made above ovar men's heds, and there was greate images of white wykers, like grete men, and they were set hyghe above on the highest lofts and stages, and dyvars reasons written by them of the contries that they were made lyke unto, and the names of the same contries hanging by them, and many shipps under sayles, and wyndmylls goynge; and under

[192] J.G. Nichols, ed., The Chronicle of Calais in the Reigns of Henry VII and Henry VIII, to the Year 1540 (London: Camden Society, 1846), 29.

[193] *LP* vol. 3, #907 (10 July 1520).

[194] Nichols, ed., *Chronicle of Calais*, 29.

[195] Nichols, ed., *Chronicle of Calais*, 29–30.

that was set many armes of dyvars londs, and theyr reasons writen by them.[196]

The construction of the banqueting house also shows that the performance of entertainments during the banquet had been planned, and that Henry had meant to dazzle all of Charles's senses at once:

> And abowght the highe pece of tymbar that stode up right in the mydste was made stages of tymbar for organs, and othar instruments for to stand in, and men for to play upon them, and for clarks syngenge, and othar pagents for to be playede when the kyngs of England and of Romayns shuld be at theyre banqwete.[197]

Similarly, the sixteenth-century chronicle writer John Stowe ('augmented with matters Forraigne and Domestique' by his editor Edmund Howes) creates a memory of the stages built for various entertainments in his *Annales, or a General Chronicle of England*:

> ... and about the high pillar of timber in the midst was framed with diuers stages for organs, and other instruments of musicke to bee placed, with men, and children, as well to play on them, as for to set forth their musicall voices, *and* to haue made, as it were, an heauenly noise.[198]

During the planning of the event it was decreed that the 'devisyng of the pageants at the bankett is commytted to Cornyshe'.[199] William Cornishe, whom we have seen in the above as the playmaker responsible for the political play likening Francis to a horse in 1522, was in 1520 Master of the Chapel, and had in 1501 been involved in the entertainments for the wedding of Arthur Tudor and Katherine of Aragon.[200] As such he would have been a logical choice for devising pageants for an event of this scale. As for the organization of 'mummeries', the organizers decided that 'the devisyng of the mummeries is referred to the Kinges pleasure, and suche as the Kinges Grace shall appoynte for that purpose'.[201]

---

[196] Nichols, ed., *Chronicle of Calais*, 29.

[197] Nichols, ed., *Chronicle of Calais*, 29–30.

[198] John Stow, *Annales, or a General Chronicle of England*, ed. Edmund Howes (London, 1631), 512.

[199] *Rutland*, 56.

[200] Anglo, 'William Cornish in a Play', 352.

[201] *Rutland*, 57.

It had been intended by the organizers of the event that in the banqueting house, Henry, Charles, and other notables would sit and watch
the playing of music, singing, and performance of pageants as they ate,
and that their sitting at the banquet table watching these entertainments would in turn be watched by the other table guests. However, the
banquet as a whole, including the performances but also all the other
multimedia aspects comprising the banquet, was also to be watched
by spectators who did not participate in the ceremonial meal. The
Chronicle of Calais records:

> ... and with in rownde abowt by the syds were made thre loftes one
> above anothar for men and women for to stond upon, and they that
> stode behynd myght see over the hedes that stode before, it was made
> so highe behynd and lowe before ...[202]

It appears that Charles was not the only party whom the organizers of
the event wanted to impress; the spectacle that constituted the triumph
of the construction of the banqueting house in which the honoured
guest was hosted in great splendour was a statement they were eager
to make. Here is it helpful to understand that these kind of banqueting houses were not just built because it was practical to have a space
large enough to accommodate a party of a size that reflected a host's
true generosity; importantly, it was a fashionable thing to do. As can
be expected, the 'trend' was seen early in the Burgundian context. For
example, the 1468 wedding of Charles the Bold and Margaret of York
necessitated the building of a 'prefabricated wooden hall, lit by wooden
candelabra painted white and blue, and by two large, elaborate chan-
deliers', which was erected 'in the tennis court of the ducal palace'.[203]
Similarly, within the context of the Habsburg–Valois Wars (also referred
to as 'the Italian Wars') the *condottieri* Gian-Giacomo Trivulzio who
had taken Milan from Ludovico Sforza and given it to the French king
Louis XII, feasted his French patron in such a hall in 1507.[204] And in
December 1518 when Francis I received an English delegation to consolidate the Treatise of London, he entertained them at a huge banqueting

---

[202] Nichols, ed., *Chronicle of Calais*, 29.
[203] Ross, 'Beyond Eating', 158.
[204] Knecht, *The French Renaissance Court*, 72.

hall built for the purpose within the courtyard of the Bastille.[205] Henry VIII clearly sought to place his banquet within this fashion to align himself with the powerful and those of good taste, just as his father had followed Burgundian trends in *entremets* and other entertainments for the wedding of Arthur and Katherine. Unfortunately, the splendour of the banqueting house at Calais was not to last. The *Chronicle of Calais* laments,

> on the same morninge the wynd began to ryse, and at nyght blewe of all the canvas, and all the elements with the sterrs, sonn, and mone, and clowds, and the same reyne blewe out above a thowsand torches and tapers that wer ordayned for the same; and all the kyngs seets that was made with great ryches that cowlde be ordaynyd, besyds all othar things, was all dashed and lost.[206]

Sanuto—again our informant—records that the destruction of the banqueting house led to a change of sites, so that 'the banquet was served in the King's house, but confusedly, by reason of the narrow space: and also in a private manner, for there were only a few personages present, not even the ambassadors'.[207] Unfortunately, the exclusion of the spectators on the balconies and the ambassadors at the table meant that Sanuto would be unable to tell his readers what had been served at the banquet.

The waste of the prestige-project that was the fashionable banqueting hall was a disaster but is unlikely to have impeded any negotiations, and the political end results of the meeting were satisfactory. The plan was for a 'renewal of their treaties' and 'especially that of 1516'.[208] The new treaty to which Charles and Henry agreed outwardly promised far-reaching commitments between the two parties, such as a promise to 'have the same enemies and the same friends', whereby 'offence or injury to the one [was] to be repelled by the other as done to himself'.[209] And also, that 'Neither party [was] to enter into treaty with any prince without the consent of the other; and if any treaties exist or hereafter be made contrary to the effect of this, they shall be invalid without the

[205] Knecht, *The French Renaissance Court*, 72.
[206] Nichols, ed., *Chronicle of Calais*, 30.
[207] *CSPV* vol. 3, #50.
[208] *LP* vol. 3, #908 (10 July 1520).
[209] *LP* vol. 3, #908.

consent of both'.[210] This may sound like a dedicated pact, but, as Glenn Richardson observes, 'nothing in it [the treaty] contradicted the pre-existing Anglo-French alliance agreement and for Mary's marriage to the dauphin'.[211] He furthermore explains that, 'Both sides were evidently serious about a deal between them, but in the end the English were not serious enough because at this point Henry and Wolsey had more to gain by keeping Henry in the role of international arbiter'.[212]

Conclusion: 'Footprints in the snow'

In order to fully understand what took place during the banquets organized by Henry's servants for Charles and his followers during the 1520 and 1522 visits, we have had to draw together the snippets of information that we have to obtain a sense of the total experience of the multilevel, multimedia events that we know were organized with great effort and sparing no expenses. I here turn to Edward Muir's important observation regarding the study of rituals that were performed at specific moments in the past. Likening documentary evidence to 'footprints in the snow, signs that some animal we have chosen to call a "ritual" once passed by', Muir observes that 'traces of that animal', that is, the event, can be found in a variety of different source types.[213] He mentions pictorial evidence, 'prescriptive and descriptive texts', but also legal evidence in the form of 'criminal records from cases of rituals that turned violent'.[214] But most importantly for the purpose of this chapter, Muir underscores that, 'These images and texts followed their own rules of composition and evoked their own representational traditions, just as rituals did, but those rules and traditions were different from those that operated in ritual performances'.[215] We have seen this in the ways in which chronicle texts, festival books, and civic remembrance of hard work in preparation of events, each offer their own perspective

---

[210] *LP* vol. 3, #908.
[211] Glenn Richardson, 'The King, the Cardinal-Legate, and the Field of Cloth of Gold', *Royal Studies Journal* 4:2 (2017), 141–60 (153).
[212] Richardson, 'The King', 153–4.
[213] Muir, 'The Eye', 132.
[214] Muir, 'The Eye', 132.
[215] Muir, 'The Eye', 132.

following their own motifs, but when pasted together, a full reconstruction cannot be offered of an event, and this chapter has not provided a full record of each of the meetings between Henry and Charles. Muir warns that, 'one must never confuse the static visual representations or textual prescriptions or descriptions of rituals for that now long lost dynamic moment of a particular ritual performance'.[216] However, what this chapter *was* able to do was to use the important work previously conducted in food history and studies of drama, performance, and spectatorship, to employ a methodology that could tease out information on how Henry invested in his relationship with Charles V, how his hosting the emperor was used to build foreign relations, but also to signal to others that he could, indeed, host the emperor in a way that honoured his guest, while showing himself to be the relative equal to the at that moment most powerful man in Europe. The spectator galleries built in the temporary banqueting hall in Calais symbolize within this case study the need to show or indeed, *show off* Henry's foreign relations, with Henry as host very much in charge. Methodologically speaking, the study of food and consumption in this chapter has contributed to understanding some of Henry's tactics in foreign diplomacy. Within Tudor studies, research in food could, I believe, take a more prominent place if evidence of food and consumption were integrated more structurally into wider discussions, just as, for example, legal and ecclesiastical records are currently employed.

---

[216] Muir, 'The Eye', 132.

| 4 |

Fashion Victims

Picture perfect

Portraiture has long played a part in royal marriage negotiations. Johan Huizinga tells the story of Philip the Good, the Duke of Burgundy, sending painter Jan van Eyck all the way to Portugal to paint a representation of the *infanta* Isabella (1397–1467), the daughter of John I of Portugal and Philippa of Lancaster.[1] Maximizing the chances of this representation reaching the Burgundian Low Countries, two portraits were dispatched, taking different travel routes.[2] Similarly, it is likely that the painting of Bianca Maria Sforza, dated circa 1493 and painted by the Milanese artist Ambrogio de Predis,[3] was based on sketches produced so that King Maximilian I (later Habsburg Emperor) could catch a glimpse of his potential future wife.[4] And when the widower Henry

---

[1] Huizinga, *Herfsttij der Middeleeuwen*, 326.
[2] Kirsten O. Frieling, 'Dressing the Bride: Weddings and Fashion Practices at German Princely Courts in the Fifteenth and Sixteenth Centuries', in Erin Griffey, ed., *Sartorial Politics in Early Modern Europe: Fashioning Women* (Amsterdam: Amsterdam University Press, 2019), 75–92 (78, footnote 8).
[3] Ambrogio de Predis, 'Bianca Maria Sforza, probably 1493', Widener Collection, nr. 1942.9.53, National Gallery of Art, Washington, DC: https://www.nga.gov/collection/art-object-page.1192.html#inscription.
[4] Keith Christiansen and Stefan Weppelmann, eds., *The Renaissance Portrait from Donatello to Bellini*, Metropolitan Museum of Art (New Haven, CT: Yale University Press, 2011), 264: 'He [De Predis] was first asked to make a charcoal drawing of Bianca Maria,

VII in 1505 considered remarriage, portraits were exchanged between the English king and Margaret of Austria, although this did not, in the end, lead to a match.[5] Another unsuccessful attempt at courtship involving portraiture was made after the death of Jane Seymour, when Henry VIII was hoping to find a new wife and sent the painter Hans Holbein the Younger on a mission to the court of Margaret of Austria to capture the likeness of her kinswoman, Christina of Denmark, the Duchess of Milan.[6] Instructions from Thomas Cromwell to the diplomat *cum* English ambassador to the Habsburg Empire Philip Hoby provide an insight into such procedures. Hoby, arriving in Brussels with Holbein, after presenting himself to the duchess, was to pass on commendations made by Cromwell, and suggest she may have heard from the 'Lady Regent' [Margaret of Austria] about the reasons for his coming, after which he was to get to business:

> He shall then beg her to take the pain to sit that a servant of the King, who is come thither for that purpose, may take her physiognomy; and shall ask when Mr. Hanns [Holbein] shall come to her to do so. The said Philip shall as of himself express a wish that both for my Lord's reports of her virtues and for his own view of them, it might please the King, being now without a wife, to advance her to the honour of a queen of England. And he shall well note her answers, her gesture and countenance with her inclination, that he may at his return declare the same to the King's Majesty. Her picture taken, he and Hanns shall return immediately.[7]

which was then passed to a German agent working for the Duke of Saxony who had come to Milan to observe the young woman on Maximilian's behalf ... on a second trip to Milan the German agent asked for a "retracto colorito" (coloured portrait). The likely result of that request is the portrait of Bianca Maria, now in the National Gallery of Art, Washington, D.C.' For observation that the portrait itself was presumably made 'after her betrothal', see Sara van Dijk, *'Beauty Adorns Virtue': Dress in Portraits of Women by Leonardo da Vinci* (Unpublished doctoral thesis, University of Leiden, 2015), 88, footnote 102.

[5] Tracey A. Sowerby, '"A Memorial and a Pledge of Faith": Portraiture and Early Modern Diplomatic Culture', *The English Historical Review* 129:537 (2014), 296–331 (303).

[6] Hans Holbein the Younger, 'Christina of Denmark, Duchess of Milan', National Gallery, London: https://www.nationalgallery.org.uk/paintings/hans-holbein-the-younger-christina-of-denmark-duchess-of-milan.; Christiane Hertel, 'Engaging Negation in Hans Holbein the Younger's Portrait of Christina of Denmark, Duchess of Milan', in Andrea Pearson, ed., *Women and Portraits in Early Modern Europe* (London: Routledge, 2016), 107–36.

[7] *LP* vol. 13.1, #380. A letter sent from Mary of Austria to Eustace Chapuys reveals suspicion of the English, and notes that 'Cromwell has sent hither a man express and a message

Holbein was also sent to paint a portrait of Anne of Cleves, which reached Henry VIII in August 1539.[8] And it is to Anne of Cleves that we turn in this chapter.

Scholarship's hyper-focus on Anne of Cleves's appearance

There is always a discrepancy between that which account takers in the fifteenth and sixteenth centuries were interested in, and the concerns of scholars today. Then, importantly, there is also the question of scholarship's understanding of and interaction with the extant evidence. I here briefly refer to *The Face of Queenship* (2010) in which Anna Riehl has convincingly addressed the complex value placed on the facial and physical beauty of women in the context of the early modern court. Riehl has also reflected on the difficulties created by, 'a continual need to negotiate deception and honesty of display, both in real-life situations . . . and in representation when both the author and the audience have to contend with the difficulty of verbal description of faces and the unreliability of portraiture'.[9] Indeed, we have seen in Cromwell's instruction to Philip Hoby that Holbein's portrait was to

by Hauton (Hutton) for leave to the former to take the duchess of Milan's portrait, which she had granted, and the man has returned to England with it' (*LP* vol. 13.1, #419). Chapuys reports back to Mary of Austria that on 18 March 1538, 'the painter returned with the Duchess' likeness, which has pleased the King much, and put him in much better humour'. (*LP* vol. 13.1, #583). Rumours were also shared with Montmorency that Henry VIII was going to meet the Duchess of Milan at Calais after Easter. (*LP* vol. 13.1, #630).

[8] Hans Holbein the Younger, 'Portrait d'Anne de Clèves (1515–1557), reine d'Angleterre, quatrième épouse de Henri VIII', INV 1348; MR 756, Louvre, Paris: https://collections.louvre.fr/ark:/53355/cl010062615. In 1989 Candy Kuhl restored a painting by Bartolomaeus Bruyn the Elder (St John's College at the University of Oxford): https://www.sjc.ox.ac.uk/college-life/art/colleges-art-collection/. Peter Hacker and Candy Kuhl, 'A Portrait of Anne of Cleves', *The Burlington Magazine* 134:1068 (1992), 172–5 (173): 'It is plausible to suppose that this painting is a contemporary portrait of Anne of Cleves. In favour of this hypothesis its similarities to the Holbein may be adduced—in the head-dress, jewellery, bodice, and facial features. The conjecture that it might be of her sister Amelia can surely be rejected on the grounds of the improbability of both princesses possessing let alone sharing, the identical bejewelled collar, crucifix and gold chains, or even head-dress and pearl-embroidered bodice'.

[9] Anna Riehl, *The Face of Queenship: Early Modern Representations of Elizabeth I* (New York: Palgrave Macmillan, 2010), 2–3.

be accompanied by 'his own view of them [Christina's virtues]'.[10] And reverberating through ambassadorial dispatches and letters written by messengers we find writers commenting on the verisimilitude of representations in written, spoken, or painted form.[11] Yet whilst such issues generally played a role in international diplomacy in the sixteenth century, it is surprising that in the study of Anne of Cleves, they should so dominate the scholarly discussion, making the supposed *lack* of beauty of Anne of Cleves over-prominent in Tudor scholarship. Why is it, that when reading account books, for example, scholarship seems alert to an accountant's biases and omissions in their records, but that when reading descriptions of the appearances of early modern princesses and aristocratic women, these are still taken at face value? In the case of Anne of Cleves, it may be that the general narrative about her short marriage to Henry VIII seems to pivot around her 'looks'. Most readers will recall the uncomplimentary comments about Anne's physical appearance made by Thomas Cromwell when fearing for his life in the Tower, such as, 'he [Henry VIII] had felt her [Anne's] belly and breasts, and thought she was no maid'.[12] And perhaps the most persistent verbal image of Anne of Cleves is that of the 'Flanders mare', a phrase often attributed to Henry VIII himself, but which actually postdates her life and that of her contemporaries. It is important here to first get the 'Flanders mare' canard out of the way. The description cannot be found in recorded evidence earlier than bishop Gilbert Burnet's *The History of the Reformation of the Church of England* (1679)[13]:

[10] *LP* vol. 13.1, #380.

[11] A number of examples will be given in this chapter. See also, Gérard de Plaines, Seigneur de la Roche, working as an ambassador for Margaret of Austria, writing to his employer about Mary Tudor that he had 'never seen so beautiful a lady', and that 'Her [Princess Mary's] deportment is exquisite both in conversation and in dancing, and she is very lively'. In order to emphasise the truthfulness of his account, he added that he 'had refrained from writing about the Princess [Mary] till he had seen her several times' (*LP* vol. 1, #3041).

[12] *LP* vol. 15, #823.

[13] Retha M. Warnicke, *The Marrying of Anne of Cleves: Royal Protocol in Early Modern England* (Cambridge: Cambridge University Press, 2000), 256; Lisa Mansfield, 'Face-to-Face with the "Flanders Mare": *Fama* and Hans Holbein the Younger's *Portrait of Anne of Cleves*', in Claire Walker and Heather Kerr, eds., *'Fama' and her Sisters: Gossip and Rumour in Early Modern Europe* (Turnhout: Brepols, 2015), 115–35 (115). The verbal image is so pervasive and perhaps so engrained in the ways in which Anne of Cleves has been discussed, that even in a very positive review of Warnicke's book (in which she rightly

But when he had a sight of her, finding none of these charms which he was made believe were in her, he was so extreamly surprized, that he not only did not like her, but took an Aversion to her, which he could never after overcome. He swore they had brought over a *Flanders Mare* to him, and was very sorry he had gone so far, but glad it had proceeded no further. And presently he resolved, if it were possible, to break off the matter, and never to yoke himself with her.[14]

The term 'Flanders Mare' was subsequently picked up by Tobias Smollett, who in *A Complete History of England* (1748) writes,

the king no sooner heard she had landed at Rochester, than he went incognito, to see his future consort, and found her so different from her picture, which had been drawn by Hans Holbein, that in the impatience of his disappointment, he swore they had brought him a Flanders mare.[15]

Having exposed these records of Anne of Cleves's appearance as unfounded in contemporary evidence, we must now first briefly turn to contemporary reports of her appearance, which are problematic in a different way. Necessarily, those who favoured the Tudor-Cleves match and wished to encourage Henry VIII to pursue the relationship, such as Thomas Cromwell, would have acclaimed Anne's various—physical and behavioural—qualities. Thus when in March 1539 Cromwell wrote to Henry reporting that 'Everyone praises the lady's beauty, both of face and body. One said she excelled the Duchess [of Milan] as the golden sun did the silver moon', he was conveying a message constructed to suit his political goals.[16] Apart from Cromwell's clear agenda, the difficulty of

notes that the term 'Flanders Mare' was an invention by 'later observers' (256)), Charles Carlton states right at the start: 'Scorned as the "Flanders Mare", her ugliness was so well concealed in Hans Holbein's portrait that Henry VIII agreed to marry her by proxy in 1540.' Charles Carlton, 'Retha M. Warnicke. *The Marrying of Anne of Cleves: Royal Protocol in Early Modern England*. New York: Cambridge University Press. 2000. xiv, 343. $27.95', *The American Historical Review* 106:4 (2001), 1451.
[14] Gilbert Burnet, *The History of the Reformation of the Church of England*, vol. 1, part 1, 2nd edn. (London, 1681), 271. Note that the italics in the quote represent Burnet's emphasis.
[15] Tobias George Smollett, *A Complete History of England from the Descent of Julius Caesar to the Treaty of Aix la Chapelle*, vol. 4, 3rd edn. (London, 1758; 1st edn. 1748), 217–8.
[16] *LP* vol. 14.1, #552 (18 March 1539).

describing a woman's features in a way that conveyed an image, the subjective nature of any statement made about 'beauty', and of course the hyperbolic nature of this particular one, an important limitation can be found in the fact that Cromwell had not actually met Anne; his message was based on the opinions of unspecified persons rather than on his own perceptions. And as such it does not provide us with Cromwell's opinion of Anne, but with evidence of his need to present Henry with a particular notion, serving a clear political aim.

Given that Cromwell had not travelled to Germany it is only logical—and to be expected—that he had not seen Anne in person, but even those who did journey to foreign lands at times had to base their reports on observations made by others. This can be seen, for example, in the letter written by the diplomat Nicholas Wotton to Henry VIII sent from Duren on 11 August 1539 to report on Anne of Cleves. This letter, heavily scorched with burn marks but extant in British Library Cotton MS Vitellius B XXI, includes the well-known line about the lady being raised close to her mother's elbow, a phrase much-repeated in Tudor studies. The full description reads as follows:

> ... she hathe from her childhode (lyk as the Lady Sybille was, till she was marryd, *and* the Ladye Amelye has been and is) ben brought up with the Ladye Duchess her mother *and* yn manner never from her elbow, the Ladye Duchess being a wyse Ladye *and* one that verye strytlye looket to her children. All the gentlemen of the court, and other that I have askyd of, rapport her to be of verye lowlye *and* gentyll conditions.[17]

It may be emphasized here that Wotton did not claim to know of her 'conditions' from a first-hand encounter, but simply reported what the gentlemen of the court and others he has spoken with had told him. Wotton continues to describe the lady's accomplishments, unfortunately incomplete to us because of the fire-damage, which has caused parts of the letter to have been burned away. But we can see him mentioning that 'she occupieth her tyme most with the nedyll',[18] and 'she canne reede and wryte her ... [paper scorched away in the left-hand

---

[17] BL, Cotton MS Vitellius B XXI, fol. 204r. http://www.bl.uk/manuscripts/Viewer.aspx?ref=cotton_ms_vitellius_b_xxi_f204r.

[18] BL, Cotton MS Vitellius B XXI, fol. 204r.

corner] Frenche latyn or other langaige she [. . .] nor yet she canne not synge nor pleye . . . onye instrument for they take it heere yn Germanye for a rebuke *and* an occasion of lightnesse that gre[t] ladyes shuld be lernyd or have enye knowledge of musike.'[19] He calls her wit 'good', and subtly notes that he has asked around about her drinking habits, which he formulates as: 'I could never here that she is ynclyned to the good chere of this countrey'.[20] Again, the desirable quality of being moderate in drinking is reported as based on the information provided by others. It is also in this letter that Wotton writes that 'yo*ur* graces servant hanze albein hathe taken th'effigies of my ladye Anne *and* the ladye Amelye *and* hath expressyd theyr immaiges verye lyvelye'.[21] Had Wotton seen Anne and Amelia from close enough to make this observation of like-ness himself or did he again base himself on the assurance of others who had?[22]

As we have already seen in Chapter 3, the problem with ambassadors, diplomats, dignitaries, messengers, and other visitors sending reports to their colleagues or patrons, is that they—not always but certainly often—described situations or events that they either did not attend, or where they could not get close enough to the heart of the event to truly *see* what occurred. This would also mean that they may not always have had a chance to properly view the main persons involved in the event. Thus when the French ambassador to England Charles de Marillac on 5 January 1540 reported on the appearance of '*la reine d'Angleterre*' [Anne of Cleves] in a letter to Anne de Montmorency, he based his account '*au jugement de plusiers qui l'ont veue de près*' [on the judgement of those who have seen her from nearby].[23] In other words, he overtly presented a second-hand account. It is to these unnamed spectators that he ascribes the opinion that, '*Ne s'est trouvée si jeune qu'on pençoyt*' [she is not found as young as one/they thought], and, '*ny*

[19] BL, Cotton MS Vitellius B XXI, fol. 204v. http://www.bl.uk/manuscripts/Viewer. aspx?ref=cotton_ms_vitellius_b_xxi_f204v.

[20] BL, Cotton MS Vitellius B XXI, fol. 204v.

[21] BL, Cotton MS Vitellius B XXI, fol. 204v.

[22] The latter is implied in Elizabeth Norton, *Anne of Cleves: Henry VIII's Discarded Bride* (Stroud: Amberley, 2010), 36. See my Note 8 for the link to the painting by Bar-tolomaeus Bruyn the Elder, which is likely to have been the portrait referred to by Wotton.

[23] Jean Kaulek, ed., *Correspondance Politique de Mm. de Castillon et de Marillac, Ambassadeurs de France en Angleterre (1537–1542)* (Paris: Félix Alcan, 1885), 151.

de si grande beaulté que tout le monde affermoit'[24] [nor the great beauty that everyone affirmed]. In his dispatch to King Francis I sent on the same day, Marillac furthermore writes that, '*A ce qu'on peult juger, est de aaige d'environ trente ans, estant de stature de corps haute et gresle, de beaulté moyenne et de contenance fort asseuré et résolue'.*[25] [(As one/they can judge), she is about 30 years of age, tall and thin, of medium beauty, and of very assured and resolute countenance].[26] Again, this would have been based on other people's opinions of what they had seen looking at the new queen.

News travelled fast, and gossip was happily shared. Intelligence about Anne of Cleves's arrival in England made its way to the queen of France, Eleanor of Austria (1498–1558), who in turn shared the latest news with Alessandro Farnese. Farnese was the grandson of Pope Paul III, and was in early 1540 conducting diplomatic business as a Papal Legate, seeking to improve relations between Francis I and Charles V.[27] This involved travelling between the Low Countries and France, but also, it seems, allowed for savouring a bit of scandal. On the 7th of February Farnese wrote to Paul III: 'The queen of France tells me that ... the new Queen is worthy and Catholic, old and ugly, so that when the King saw her he was not pleased with her in that German dress, and made her dress in the French fashion'.[28] The cardinal was communicating an account that was *at least* third-hand, but it seems that he had hit the nail on the head regarding the importance of dress in the perceptions of Anne of Cleves.

---

[24] Kaulek, ed., *Correspondance Politique*, 151.

[25] Kaulek, ed., *Correspondance Politique*, 151. Curiously, Strickland in her *Lives of the Queens of England*, vol. 4 (Philadelphia, PA, 1847), 248, translated this as: 'From what one may judge ... she is about thirty years old [she was but twenty-four]. She is tall of stature, pitted with the small-pox, and with little beauty. Her countenance is firm and determined'. Strickland continued: 'The circumstance of her being marked with the small-pox explains the mystery of why Holbein's portrait pleased the king so much better than the original' (248). Given that research as well as pervasive opinions about historical figures continue to be based on or influenced by accessible nineteenth-century publications, such as Strickland, it is important to interrogate where certain notions come from. The French text by Marillac in any case does not suggest that Anne of Cleves had had small-pox.

[26] Modified from: *LP* vol. 15, #22 (5 January 1540).

[27] Richard Cooper, 'Legate's Luxury: The Entries of Cardinal Alessandro Farnese to Avignon and Carpentras, 1553', in Nicolas Russell and Hélène Visentin, eds., *French Ceremonial Entries in the Sixteenth Century: Event, Image, Text* (Toronto: Centre for Reformation and Renaissance Studies, 2007), 133–61 (134).

[28] *LP* vol. 15, #179 (7 February 1540).

Writing fashion, performing a genre

In what follows, a sartorial lens is used to investigate perceptions of Anne of Cleves's appearance, and to illustrate that the records detailing these perceptions are best understood in the context of a genre of writing about the outward appearances of princesses and noblewomen, in particular those originating from different countries. As will be obvious from this chapter, this research is especially indebted to the excellent collection of essays edited by Erin Griffey, titled *Sartorial Politics in Early Modern Europe* (2019), in particular the important work done by Kirsten O. Frieling, whose study of dress habits at the German princely courts has opened up avenues for further study.[29] Frieling addresses 'how the court and its surroundings reacted to foreign ways of dressing', and prioritizes the 'identity-forming and political implications of aristocratic female dress'.[30] Her work relies on two emerging streams in historical research: that which acknowledges and investigates 'the role of aristocratic and royal women as (politically) active agents in cultural transfer processes in the Middle Ages and, above all, the early modern period',[31] and another that 'analys[es] the significance of fashion and dress for social positioning'.[32] The latter is still an emerging field, even though intensive studies of wardrobe accounts, financial records,

---

[29] Frieling, 'Dressing the Bride, 75–92.
[30] Frieling, 'Dressing the Bride', 76.
[31] Readers new to this field are referred to the 'Queenship and Power' book series, edited by Carole Levin and Charles Beem (Palgrave Macmillan), e.g. Theresa Earenfight, *Queenship in Medieval Europe* (2013); Gillian B. Fleming, *Juana I: Legitimacy and Conflict in Sixteenth-Century Castile* (2018); Penelope Nash, *Empress Adelheid and Countess Matilda: Medieval Female Rulership and the Foundations of European Society* (2017); Zita Eva Rohr, *Yolande of Aragon (1381–1442) Family and Power* (2016); Estelle Paranque, *Elizabeth I of England Through Valois Eyes: Power, Representation and Diplomacy in the Reign of the Queen, 1558–1588* (2019); Erin Sadlack, *The French Queen's Letters: Mary Tudor Brandon and the Politics of Marriage in Sixteenth-Century Europe* (2011); Elena Woodacre, ed., *Queenship in the Mediterranean: Negotiating the Role of the Queen in the Medieval and Early Modern Eras* (2013); A number of excellent collections of essays include, among others, Anne J. Cruz and Maria Galli Stampino, eds., *Early Modern Habsburg Women: Transnational Contexts, Cultural Conflicts, Dynastic Continuities* (Farnham: Ashgate, 2013); Ana Maria S. A. Rodrigues, Manuela Santos Silva, and Jonathan Spangler, eds., *Dynastic Change: Legitimacy and Gender in Medieval and Early Modern Monarchy* (London: Routledge, 2019); Nadine Akkerman and Birgit Houben, eds., *The Politics of Female Households: Ladies-in-Waiting across Early Modern Europe* (Leiden: Brill, 2013).
[32] Frieling, 'Dressing the Bride', 76.

and material culture objects have been conducted—in Tudor Studies notably by Maria Hayward—demonstrating the clear and distinct value of a sartorial focus for wider explorations of court cultures.[33]

The sartorial focus is a particularly fruitful tool for the study of perceptions of Anne of Cleves, and is here used to show what fashions were in vogue at the Tudor court, but also crucially, how 'Dutch' style clothes were employed in the court context. In the second part of this chapter, we move beyond the notion of 'self-fashioning'. This term, coined by Stephen Greenblatt, has been usefully employed in many studies concerned with dress and clothing to show how the wearer of a garment or what we might now call 'outfit' used costly dress to present themselves as a person of substance, riches, and, perhaps, honour or virtue.[34] However, scholarship has in recent years importantly noted the limitations of studying garments or descriptions of fashions purely on what they *meant* to express. Benjamin Wild, for example, observed that, 'even the principle of strict sartorial hierarchy could not guarantee the successful reception of messages conveyed through dress. Clothes could reflect the wearer's status, but they did not necessarily convincingly

---

[33] For example, Maria Hayward, *Dress at the Court of King Henry VIII* (Leeds: Maney, 2007); Maria Hayward, *The Great Wardrobe Accounts of Henry VII and Henry VIII* (Woodbridge: London Record Society: The Boydell Press, 2012); Eleri Lynn, *Tudor Fashion* (New Haven, CT: Yale University Press, 2021). Other important studies include: Cornelia Aust, Denise Klein, and Thomas Weller, eds., *Dress and Cultural Difference in Early Modern Europe* (Berlin and Boston, MA: De Gruyter, 2019); Ann Rosalind Jones and Peter Stallybrass, *Renaissance Clothing and the Materials of Memory* (Cambridge: Cambridge University Press, 2000); Maria Hayward, *Rich Apparel: Clothing and the Law in Henry VIII's England* (Farnham: Ashgate, 2009); Ulinka Rublack, *Dressing Up: Cultural Identity in Renaissance Europe* (Oxford: Oxford University Press, 2011); Evelyn Welch, ed., *Fashioning the Early Modern: Dress, Textiles, and Innovation in Europe, 1500–1800* (Oxford: Oxford University Press, 2017). Regarding the still emerging status of the field, Elizabeth McMahon observes in a recent publication: 'While scholars from Roland Barthes to Valerie Steele have argued that clothing and dress are anything but shallow, the notion stubbornly persists . . . Consequently, the rich clothing which was such an important feature in the self-fashioning at Tudor courts has often been ignored in favour of records of governance and court structure'. Elizabeth McMahon, 'Accounting Legitimacy in Purple and Gold: Mary Tudor, Household Accounts, and the English Succession', in Valerie Schutte and Jessica S. Hower, eds., *Mary I in Writing* (Palgrave Macmillan, 2022), 189–217 (191).

[34] On the use of Greenblatt's 'self-fashioning' in studies of fashion, see, e.g., John Styles, 'Fashion and Innovation in Early Modern Europe', in Evelyn Welch, ed., *Fashioning the Early Modern: Dress, Textiles, and Innovation in Europe, 1500–1800* (Oxford: Oxford University Press, 2017), 33–55 (34–5).

reconstitute it'.[35] Also Susan Crane, following Bourdieu, reflected on the 'aesthetic value' of clothes as an 'aspect of social meaningfulness'. She importantly observed that aesthetic value 'is more susceptible to redefinition (in fashion trends, for example) than other meanings clothing can express (such as income and office)'.[36] In other words, one could wear an incredibly costly costume, reflective of wealth and position, and seek to 'self-fashion' oneself accordingly, but if those perceiving the outfit did not find it aesthetically pleasing, the message intended to be sent did not necessarily have to be received as such.

Our concern here is the act of *describing* the appearances of foreign princesses, which meant responding to a genre of writing that had particular typical attributes, and which, in a way constituted a performance. Following Erving Goffman's still influential self-presentation theory, and their perception of 'everyday life as a theatrical performance', Katherine Wilson has understood inventories to be 'subjective records, which need to be analysed through careful reconstruction of the immediate social context surrounding their creation'.[37] The same can be said for descriptions of worn attire as noted down by courtiers, ambassadors, and other account takers. These accounts cannot be read as 'innocent' representations of what was worn at an event or occasion, but were written to inform, persuade, curry favour, celebrate, or to entertain, or indeed, a combination of these. Interestingly, where any number of contexts can be reconstructed for inventory taking, the contexts of foreign royal brides being shown to their new populaces, often in the form of a procession, and the contexts of royal nuptial ceremony and celebration show great similarity across Europe, very much in line with the 'scriptedness' and performative aspect of ceremonial events referred to in the previous chapter. From this follows that records detailing the appearances of foreign princesses tell us more about fashions and expectations of *narrative* about royals than about the persons

---

[35] Benjamin Wild, 'Clothing Royal Bodies: Changing attitudes to royal dress and appearance from the Middle Ages to Modernity', in Elena Woodacre et al., eds., *The Routledge History of Monarchy* (London: Routledge, 2019), 390–407 (394).

[36] Susan Crane, *The Performance of Self: Ritual, Clothing, and Identity During the Hundred Years War* (Philadelphia, PA: University of Pennsylvania Press, 2002), 6.

[37] Katherine Anne Wilson, 'The Household Inventory as Urban "Theatre" in Late Medieval Burgundy', *Social History* 40:3 (2015), 335–59 (359). Wilson relies on Erving's sociological study *The Presentation of Self in Everyday Life* (first published 1956; London: Penguin, 1990).

depicted. Scrutinizing such accounts also takes us back to the observations made at the end of Chapter 3, that documentary evidence does not suffice to reconstruct an event or occasion, but that it can bring us closer to understanding more fully the transnational contexts of European court culture. Addressing this kind of performed spectatorship committed to the page reveals that comments on the appearance of Anne of Cleves that currently inform the backbone of most studies on Anne of Cleves should not be taken at face value, urging for a reconsideration of the narratives that have thus far steered scholarly attitudes to the 'Lady of Cleves', as she was addressed after her marriage to Henry VIII was dissolved.[38]

Skirting around the issue?

Several accounts that refer to Anne of Cleves's appearance make reference to her un-English sense of style. A letter from an unspecified sender to Lady Lisle refers to Anne having worn 'a rich attire upon her head of her own country fashion'.[39] Marillac to Francis I wrote that, '*ladite dame ... estant vestue à la mode du pays dont elle venoit*'.[40] [She was clothed in the fashion of the country from which she came].[41] And also Hall's account of Anne of Cleves's wedding attire makes mention of the outlandish fashion that was displayed, referring to a 'gowne of ryche cloth of gold set full of large flowers of great and Orient Pearle, made after the Duche fassion rownde'.[42] The 'Duche' style outfit had certainly been rich, and as such sufficiently splendid to show off her status and to present herself as a match worthy to be the king's wife. But if we read

[38] The marriage was dissolved by an act of parliament (32 Henry, c. 25): 'for the suertie and certaintye of his Highnes posteritie and succession as for the welth quietness rest and tranquillitie of this Realme'. T.E. Tomlins and W.E. Taunton, eds., *Statutes of the Realm* (London, 1817), vol. 3, 782. The new way of referring to Anne of Cleves is mentioned in a letter by Marillac to King Francis I. His phrase subtly notes the temporality of titles and ways of addressing: '*qui à ceste heure est dicte seullement madame de Clèves*' [who is at this moment called only Madame de Cleves]. Kaulek, ed., *Correspondance Politique*, 217.

[39] *LP* vol. 15, #18 (4 January 1540)

[40] Kaulek, ed., *Correspondance Politique*, 150.

[41] *LP* vol. 15, #22 (5 January 1540).

[42] Edward Hall, *The Triumphant Reigne of Kyng Henry the VIII*, ed. Charles Whibley (London: Jack, 1904), vol. 2, 302.

between the lines in Hall, it seems that the style of the clothes worn by
Anne, especially her headgear, was simply not *en vogue* at the English
court, and that somehow this style needed to be modified to something
more to the taste of the English. We read for example about the outfit worn after dinner, for Evensong, during supper with the king and a
number of festivities such as banquets, masks 'and dyuerse dysportes',
that Anne wore the following:

> And after dyner she chaunged into a gowne lyke a mannes gowne, of
> Tyssue with longe sleves gyrte to her, furred with ryche Sables, her
> narrowe sleves were very costly, but on her head she had a cap as she
> ware on the saturdaie before with a cornet of laune, which cap was so
> ryche of Perle and Stone, that it was judged to bee of great valew.[43]

Hall appears to imply that the gown 'lyke a mannes gowne', with
its expensive sables and fetching narrow sleeves, was fashionable
enough.[44] The rather explicit 'but' used before describing the 'cap' worn
on her head, however, suggests that this choice of head-cover—not customary at the English court—wasn't quite the thing. In his description
of the joust, another festive event under the auspices of the nuptial
celebrations, the change in headgear is overtly applauded:

> The Sonday after were kepte solempne Justes, which muche pleased
> the straungiers. On whiche daie she was *appareiled after the Englishe
> fashion, with a Frenche whode*, which so set furth her beautie and
> good vysage, that every creature rejoysed to behold her (emphasis
> added).[45]

This 'French' hood, Hall suggests, did wonders for showing off the lady's
beauty. The fact that a statement vis-à-vis the rejoicing of the crowds

[43] Hall, *The Triumphant Reigne*, 302–3.
[44] Sables were costly, and as Cinzia Maria Sicca observes, were subject to sumptuary
law (for men): 'only dukes could use cloth of gold for their attire or that of their horses,
and no one under the rank of an earl could wear sable'. Cinzia Maria Sicca, 'Fashioning
the Tudor Court', in Maria Hayward and Elizabeth Kramer, eds., *Textiles and Text: Re-
establishing the Links between Archival and Object-based Research* (London: Archetype
Publications, 2007), 93–104 (97). Hayward calls sable 'the most desirable fur of the period'.
Maria Hayward, 'Fashionable Fiction: The Significance of Costumes in The Tudors', in
William B. Robison, ed., *History, Fiction, and The Tudors* (New York: Palgrave Macmillan,
2016), 293–306 (297).
[45] Hall, *The Triumphant Reigne*, 303.

regarding her 'beautie and good visage' was not made when she had been dressed in her German clothes, may be another of Hall's subtle ways to record that it had not been deemed much of a success. Charles de Marillac expressed himself in not quite as diplomatic a tone, and overtly stated what was not admired about the German dress in his description of Anne's ladies who were wearing this style:

> De Ladite dame amène du pays son frère en sa compaignye jusques à douze ou quinze damoiselles, qui sont encores enférieures en beaulté à leur maistresse et sont d'ailleurs vestues d'une façon d'habit si lourd et mal sayant qu'à peine ne les trouverait-on que laydes quant ores bien elles seroient belles.[46]
>
> [The said lady has brought in her entourage from the country of her brother about twelve or fifteen young ladies/women, who are more inferior in terms of beauty than their mistress, and they are dressed in a type of dress so heavy and badly becoming that that they would almost be thought ugly even if they were beautiful].[47]

Henry VIII, we have seen in the intelligence shared between Cardinal Farnese and the pope, preferred the French *mode* over that of the Low Countries ('when the King saw her he was not pleased with her in that German dress, and made her dress in the French fashion'[48]). And Marillac clearly stated that the 'German' style dress was bulky and ill-fitting ('*lourd et mal sayant*').[49] But we have seen other rather 'bulky' fashions being received more enthusiastically at the Tudor court in previous years. Think for example of the gable hood that was reintroduced to the court by Jane Seymour, a style of headdress referred to by Maria Hayward as having been 'unfashionable compared to the smaller, neater, French hood that left the front of the wearer's hair uncovered'.[50] By adopting this style of hood that was at that moment in time rather *démodé*, Jane Seymour appears to have deliberately moved away from a style that had been favoured by Anne Boleyn,[51] and may have used it to

[46] Kaulek, ed., *Correspondance Politique*, 151.
[47] Translation adapted and modified from: *LP* vol. 15, #23 (5 January 1540).
[48] *LP* vol. 15, #179 (7 February 1540).
[49] Kaulek, ed., *Correspondance Politique*, 151.
[50] Hayward, 'Fashionable Fiction', 302.
[51] Anne Boleyn's supposed penchant for French fashion including the French hood is not shown on the commemorative lead medal, presumably celebrating her coronation, now in the British Museum (M.9010), that depicts Anne Boleyn instead in a gable

cultivate an appearance of modesty in comparison to her predecessor, as well as to liken herself through this choice of fashion to Katherine of Aragon, who had also worn the gable hood.[52] Note, however, that Jane Seymour seems to have been cunning enough to combine her bulky headdress with fetching gowns in the 'French' style, a combination of attire she is sporting in her portrait painted by Hans Holbein the Younger.[53] Another successful introduction of rather bulky fashion can be found in Katherine of Aragon's voluminously hooped skirts, described in an anonymous eye-witness account: 'beneth her [Katherine and her ladies'] wastes certayn rownde hopys beryng owte ther gownes from their bodies aftir their countray maner.'[54] Katherine's style of dress appears to have been received at court as a delightful fashion-statement in which foreignness was considered an asset.[55] Earenfight, for example, has observed that Katherine's 'wardrobe' by virtue of exuding a sense of 'foreignness', 'marked the move of the Tudor dynasty from an English stage to one far more broadly European in outlook and ambition.'[56] Hayward identifies Katherine as a trend-setter and the anonymous account of the hooped skirts as 'one of the earliest descriptions of the farthingale or *verdugado* being worn in England.'[57] And certainly, Katherine of Aragon showed her influence in making

hood with a veil hanging from it along her back. The medal bears the inscription: 'THE MOOST HAPPI . ANNO 1534'. https://www.britishmuseum.org/collection/object/C_M-9010.

[52] A portrait of Katherine of Aragon wearing a gable hood made by Johannes Corvus around 1510–20, is now lost. A later portrait following Corvus dates from the second half of the sixteenth century, 'Catherine of Aragon (1485–1536) (c. 1550–99)', oil on panel, 57.5×44.6 cm, RCIN 404746, Royal Collection: https://www.rct.uk/collection/404746/catherine-of-aragon-1485-1536.

[53] Hans Holbein the Younger (studio of), 'Portrait of Jane Seymour (1509?–1537)', oil on panel, 26.4×18.7 cm, Mauritshuis, The Hague: https://www.mauritshuis.nl/en/our-collection/artworks/278-portrait-of-jane-seymour-1509-1537/. The dress is identified as being in the French style in Lisa Monnas, 'All that Glitters: Cloth of Gold as a Vehicle for Display 1300–1550', in Christoph Brachmann, ed., *Arrayed in Splendour: Art, Fashion, and Textiles in Medieval and Early Modern Europe* (Turnhout: Brepols, 2019), 95–133 (129).

[54] *Receyt*, 43.

[55] Earenfight, 'A Precarious Household', 343.

[56] Earenfight, 'A Precarious Household', 343.

[57] Maria Hayward, 'Spanish Princess or Queen of England? The Image, Identity and Influence of Catherine of Aragon at the Courts of Henry VII and Henry VIII', in José Luis Colomer and Amalia Descalzo, eds., *Vestir a la española en las cortes europeas (siglos XVI y XVII) / Dressing the Spanish in the European courts (XVI and XVII centuries)* (2 vols.; Madrid: Centro de Estudios Europa Hispanica, 2014), 11–36 (19).

Spanish-type dress a prominent sight at the Tudor court, and by extension, at international interactions. For example, at the Field of Cloth of Gold conference she 'on one occasion', as Maria Perry notes, wore 'a Spanish headdress with her hair hanging down over one shoulder'.[58] Katherine also tried to get Henry to wear Spanish-type dress, for example, the Inventory of King Henry VIII's Wardrobe at London of 1520–21 (BL Harley MS 4217) shows that she presented her husband with a 'Spaynisshe cloke of Blak Frisado *with* a Border of Goldesmythis worke'.[59] Katarzyna Kosior has similarly observed that Bona Sforza (1494–1557) who married Sigismund I 'the Old' of Poland, attempted to persuade her husband to dress in the fashion of her country, as evidenced by the Italian-made shirts that travelled to Poland in Bona's trousseau to be presented as a gift to Sigismund.[60]

The Tudor court, over the years, proved itself rather flexible with regards to adopting fashions in different styles, and dress understood to be fashionable in particular regions or countries was used as a political tool in the formation of potential alliances. This can, for example, be seen in Princess Mary (later Queen Mary I; 1516–58) as a child being dressed in different styles, depending on the matches or alliances her father was planning in which she played a role.[61] For example, Alison Carter observed that in 1522 Henry and Charles V agreed to a marriage contract, 'which stipulated that Mary should now be educated in the customs of Spain, and dress in the Spanish fashion'.[62] In 1527, Hall records, Mary was shown to the French ambassadors with a view to a match with Henri Duke of Orleans (1519–59), the second son of Francis I. She and her ladies were 'appareled after the romayne fashion', that is

[58] Maria Perry, *Sisters to the King* (London: André Deutsch, 2002), 211.

[59] 'Item a Spaynisshe cloke of Blak Frisado *with* a Border of Goldesmythis worke geuen by the Quenes ["s" in "Quenes" appears blotched] grace to the king.' BL, Harley MS 4217, fol. 4v. http://www.bl.uk/manuscripts/Viewer.aspx?ref=harley_ms_4217_f004v.; Hayward, 'Fashionable Fiction', 301.

[60] Katarzyna Kosior, *Becoming a Queen in Early Modern Europe: East and West* (Unpublished doctoral thesis, University of Southampton, 2017), 48.

[61] Please note that this chapter refers to two royal women called Mary Tudor: the daughter of Henry VII and Queen of France, and the daughter of Henry VIII and later queen of England. To avoid confusion, I refer to the former as 'Mary Tudor' and to the latter as 'Princess Mary' or 'Mary I'.

[62] Alison J. Carter, 'Mary Tudor's Wardrobe', *Costume* 18:1 (1984), 9–28 (10).

to say, following the trends of the Burgundian court.[63] Here, it is possible that Henry VIII, infinitely competitive with Francis I, had ordered his daughter to be dressed in this particular mode of dress, perhaps in order not to appear to accept the French as leaders of style, and signalling an implicit threat that alliances could be made with Charles V should those with Francis prove unsatisfactory. In a similar vein, Mary was given 'a French gown with a long train' that she may have worn, as Carter notes, 'in December 1539 [when] she received Duke Philip of Bavaria as a prospective husband and on 6 January 1540 [when] Henry VIII married Anne of Cleves'.[64] Just as Mary had not adopted French dress when meeting the French ambassadors, she had not been apparelled in 'Dutch' or 'German' fashion when meeting Duke Philip, nor in honour of the arrival of her father's new bride. Was this to do with signposting Tudor superiority over, respectively, Duke Philip and Anne of Cleves, or was it simply that Dutch or German style attire was not worn as much at the Tudor court in the late 1530s and early 1540s?

'German' or 'Dutch' dress at the Tudor courts of Henry VIII and Mary I

Hayward observed that 'the English were not enamoured of the high-necked Netherlandish fashions for women favoured in Cleves'.[65] But we do see occasional references to this style of gown in the archival material referring to bespoke clothing. An example from 1543 shows a tailor's bill addressed to Katherine Parr, which refers to 'the making of Italian gowns... French, Dutch and Venetian gowns', as well as to 'Venetian sleeves' and 'French hoods' which had been ordered 'for your daughter'.[66] A relatively late example of Mary I as queen shows her to have owned a Dutch gown in 1557: 'Item For Makinge doewche gowne

[63] Cf; Carter, 'Mary Tudor's Wardrobe', 10.
[64] Carter, 'Mary Tudor's Wardrobe', 12.
[65] Hayward, *Dress at the Court of King Henry VIII*, 183.
[66] 'Henry VIII: April 1543, 21–25', in *Letters and Papers, Foreign and Domestic, Henry VIII, Volume 18 Part 1, January–July 1543*, ed. James Gairdner and R.H. Brodie (London, 1901), 254–72. *British History Online*, at: http://www.british-history.ac.uk/letters-papers-hen8/vol18/no1/pp254-272 [accessed 22.03.2023].

of purpulle Satten Embrodered with passhement of golde'.[67] Later references to her wardrobe reveal that she generally favoured 'frenche' gowns.[68] The latter type of gown also dominates Elizabeth's Inventory of the Royal Wardrobe from 1600 listing the 'Gownes late Queene Maries'.[69]

The examples of Mary's years as queen seem too late for the purpose of studying the attire worn by Anne of Cleves in late 1539. But the reason I address this, is twofold. First, the written records unfortunately do not always specify the cut or style of gowns, and at times only state the material of which a garment was made, such as we see in the Whitehall records detailing the attire previously worn by Queen Jane and returned to Henry VIII after her death.[70] Secondly, during her reign, Mary interestingly ordered the making of a relatively large number of Dutch style gowns. These were, however, not for her own use, but used to clothe her fool, Jane. During Mary's first year as queen, the following 'Douche gownes' were recorded to have been made:

> Item, for making of a Douche gowne for Jane our Foole of striped purple satten, the pleites lyned with frise and buckram, the bodyes lyned with fustian.
> Item for making of a Douche gowne for her of Crimson satten striped with golde, the bodyes lyned with fustian, the pleites lyned with freize and buckram.
> Item for making of a Douche gowne for her of crimson striped satten, the bodyes lyned with fustyan, the plate with frieze & buckram, and for sewing silk to the same.

---

[67] TNA, E 101/424 7, fol. 5, Item 7. Referred to in Hilary Doda, 'Of Crymsen Tissue': The Construction of A Queen: Identity, Legitimacy and the Wardrobe of Mary Tudor (Unpublished Master of Arts thesis, Dalhousie University, Halifax, Nova Scotia, 2011), 117–18. I am very grateful to Dr Hilary Doda for a photographic image of the relevant line in this record, and for a transcription, both generously shared via email in 2020. For reasons of consistency within this chapter, I changed the representation of abbreviations in this quotation. Any remaining errors are my own.

[68] For example, the transcriptions of E101/427/11 in Carter, 'Mary Tudor's Wardrobe', 23–8.

[69] British Library, Stowe MS 557: 'Inventory of the royal wardrobe, 1600'. Fol. 8r–8v. http://www.bl.uk/manuscripts/FullDisplay.aspx?ref=Stowe_MS_557&index=81.

[70] Maria Hayward, ed., The 1542 Inventory of Whitehall: The Palace and Its Keeper, vol. 2: The Transcripts (London: Illuminata Publishers for The Society of Antiquaries of London, 2004), 151–2.

Item for making of a Douche gowne for her of blew damaske chek-
ered, the bodyes lyned with fustyan, the pleight lyned with cotton and
buckram (...).[71]

Later still, during the first two years of Mary's marriage to Philip of
Spain the accounts show that Jane was again given clothing in this style:
'a douche gowne of fustian of Naples striped for Jane our foole', and
'a douche gowne for her of grene satten tyncelled with copper gold
frenges, the plaites lyned with cotton and Buckram the bodyes lyned
with white Fustyan & paste Buckram'.[72] In the same year a fool referred
to as 'Beden' was also presented with a gown of this type: 'Dowche
gowne of Cloth for Beden the foole, frenged, the plaits lined with friese
and buckram, and the bodyes lyned with fustyan'.[73] This suggests that
Mary used clothing cut in a Dutch style to sartorially distinguish her
fool—or fools, should 'Beden' not be an alias for 'Jane' but a separate individual—from other persons at court.[74] In other words, she
employed it as a livery. Hilary Doda remarks that this kind of attire
'present[ed] a visual punchline based on the English habit of using the
Dutch as the common butt of jokes'.[75]

Importantly, besides the obvious difference in fit and style that would
have made the wearer of a Dutch gown stand out in groups favouring
French or Italian style dress, the elaborate striped, checked or fringed
patterns on the dresses ordered for Jane the fool likely served to underscore her distinct position at court.[76] Raymond van Uytven, notably,
has observed that striped cloth 'was usually handed out to the lowest
ranks of the household'.[77] Striped cloth was cheaper than unicoloured
cloth, and Jane was not typically provided with fabrics as luxurious
as those worn by the more senior female members of the household.
However, we do see that on formal, ceremonial occasions, rich fabrics would have been worn by Mary's fools, as seen in the warrant for

[71] C.C. Stopes, *Shakespeare's Environment* (London: Bell and Sons, 1914), 261.
[72] Stopes, *Shakespeare's Environment*, 262–3.
[73] Stopes, *Shakespeare's Environment*, 263.
[74] A similar point is made in Doda, *'Of Crymsen Tissue'*, 153.
[75] Doda, *'Of Crymsen Tissue'*, 153.
[76] I thank Prof. Dr Pamela M. King for making this suggestion.
[77] Raymond van Uytven, 'Showing off One's Rank in the Middle Ages', in Wim Blockmans and Antheun Janse (eds.), *Showing Status: Representations of Social Positions in the
Late Middle Ages* (Turnhout: Brepols, 1999), 19–34 (33).

Mary I's coronation, sent to Sir Edward Walgrave, the knight of the Great Wardrobe. Signed 'Marye the quene' in the left-hand corner to bring into effect the warrant, it opens in the usual way ('We woll and commaunde you to deliver or cause to be delyuored . . .'), followed by a description of the items of clothing necessary for the persons mentioned ('our righte Dere and Entiorlye beloved the Ladye Elyzabethe' and 'our ryghte dere and Entyerlye beloved Coosin the Ladye Clifforde, etc.').[78] For our purpose, it is interesting to note that items of apparel were requested for 'William Sommer our foole' ('oon gowne and oon Coate'), and that an elaborate description is given detailing the apparel needed 'for Jane our Wooman Foole'[79]:

> twoo gownes and twoo kyrtelles oon gowne of purple golde tinsell toder gowne of Crimsin Satten Rayed withe thredde of golde oon kyrtell of blewe sylke Frendged with blewe sylke striped with golde and thoder kyrtell of blacke golde tinsell.[80]

The materials were costly and some of the colours used (purple, gold) were not typically associated with fools. But the fringes, stripes, and the specified, rather wild, combinations of colours would have signalled the fool's status, perhaps in combination with the style and pattern of the dress. Mary's coronation warrant does not specify whether Jane was to be dressed in Dutch, French, or another style dress, but based on the above, we can take it to have been unlikely to have matched the queen's or any of her ladies' style, and therefore cannot have been too

[78] TNA, SP 46/8, fol. 5: 'Sign manual warrant to Sir Edward Walgrave, master of the Great Wardrobe, for delivering robes (described) for the Coronation (. . .) William Sommer "our foole" and Jane "our woman foole"' (25 September 1553). I thank Zoe Screti for bringing this source to my attention and for photographic material. The transcription of the warrant is my own, and so are all remaining errors. Note that there is an interesting lack of a descriptor of the family relationship between Queen Mary and her half-sister, all the more striking as other relatives in this warrant are referred to as 'cousin'. The 'entyerlye beloved Coosin the Lady Clifford' refers to Lady Margaret Clifford, later Margaret Stanley, Countess of Derby (1540–96). She was the daughter of Lady Eleanor Brandon, and the granddaughter of Mary Tudor, Queen of France and Charles Brandon. The will of Henry VIII had included Margaret Clifford in the line of succession, should Henry's children Edward, Mary, and Elizabeth not provide heirs, and after the heirs of Lady Frances Grey, eldest daughter of Mary Tudor, Queen of France. See, Thomas Rymer, *Foedera*, vol. 15 (London, 1713), 113.
[79] TNA, SP 46/8, fol. 5.
[80] TNA, SP 46/8, fol. 5.

fashionable in cut. The warrant helpfully specifies that 'purple satten for oon Frenche gowne' was requested for Lady Clifford, cancelling that out for Jane's gown.[81] This is furthermore underscored by Antoine de Noailles's account of Mary I's coronation, about which he includes, '*madame Elizabeth, soeur de sa majesté, & madame de Cleves, vestues toutes deux d'argent d'une robbe à la Françoise*' [Madame Elizabeth, sister of her majesty, and Madame of Cleves, dressed both of them in silver in a gown in the French style].[82]

Scholarship has suggested that Jane the Fool also appeared in the painting titled 'The Family of Henry VIII', to be found at the 'Haunted Gallery' at Hampton Court.[83] In this painting a high-necked style of dress with puffed sleeves is worn by the female figure in the background who may be identified as Jane. This would thus represent a visual exemplification of a Dutch-style gown worn by a female fool towards the end of Henry VIII's reign. Susan James suggests that Jane can be seen in the documentation to have worn this type of cut *prior to* 1545:

> Jane's career in Mary's household can be documented by chamber accounts through to September 1544 . . .The listings suggest that her fool's uniform was a Dutch gown consisting of a kirtle with an upstanding collar worn over a pleated forepart, the pleats stiffened with buckram or linen.[84]

However, this suggestion appears to conflate the information presented in Mary's *Privy Purse Expenses* whilst she was still a princess with the warrants and accounts which recorded Mary's wardrobe expenses as queen.[85] Contrary to what James implies, *The Privy Purse Expenses*,

[81] TNA, SP 46/8, fol. 5.
[82] Antoine de Noailles, *Ambassades de Messieurs de Noailles en Angleterre*, vol. 2 (Paris, 1763), 197.
[83] 'The Family of Henry VIII' (c. 1545), RCIN 405796, Hampton Court Palace, Royal Collection Trust https://www.rct.uk/collection/405796/the-family-of-henry-viii. Susan James, 'Jane, The Queen's Fool (*fl.* 1535–1558), ODNB, Oxford University Press, published online 2019. https://doi.org/10.1093/odnb/9780198614128.013.112276: 'Such an outfit almost certainly identifies her as the left-hand figure in the portrait of the family of Henry VIII'. James identifies the male figure in the background as 'Will Somers, the king's fool'. In a (partly) alternative reading, the two figures in the background are identified as 'the king's jester and a maidservant' in Kevin Sharpe, *Selling the Tudor Monarchy: Authority and Image in Sixteenth-Century England* (New Haven, CT: Yale University Press, 2009), 139.
[84] James, in 'Jane, The Queen's Fool'.
[85] For a study of the latter: Doda, *'Of Crymsen Tissue'*, 159–211.

unfortunately, do not explicitly state the cut or style of the garments bought for Jane. For example, we learn that in 1537 20 d. was paid towards 'housen and shoes to Jane the fole'.[86] Fabrics were bought in April 1538, 'a yerde & a halfe of Damaske for Jane the Fole'.[87] In July 1538 10 s. was paid 'for a gowne for Jane the Fole',[88] in January 1542/3 'xj. d' was spent 'for making of Smocks for lucruce and Jane the fole',[89] in April 1543 Mary paid for 'a payr of Shoes for Jane the fole',[90] and in June of that year 'for a payr of housen for Jane the fole'.[91] The records do not specify that the damask bought was turned into a Dutch-style gown, or that the gown made in 1538 represented that particular cut.

It is thus a distinct possibility—but, importantly, not a certainty—that when Henry VIII watched the antics of his daughter's fool in the late 1530s, this fool was dressed in a livery in the 'Dutch' fashion. An unlucky coincidence for Anne of Cleves when she arrived at the English court, dressed in expensive regalia in the style of her homeland. The fool's potential wearing of this 'Dutch' style itself is here not presented as the reason this type of dress would have proved a *faux-pas* when worn by Anne of Cleves; indeed, I do not mean to suggest that Henry would have thought his new bride—in her splendid finery made of costly material in regal cloth of gold and dripping with pearls—was dressed as a fool. Rather, I suggest here that the fool's wearing this 'Dutch' style may serve as evidence that this type of cut was deemed unfashionable, or indeed simply *unusual* enough for it to be safely rendered into a fool's livery without likely causing offence to any of the ladies at court.

'Her own country fashion'

The political significance of 'foreign styles' worn at the European courts, and the implications of the sartorial choices made by foreign brides has been addressed in several studies. Frieling importantly observed,

---

[86] *PPE Mary*, 50.
[87] *PPE Mary*, 64.
[88] *PPE Mary*, 73.
[89] *PPE Mary*, 108.
[90] *PPE Mary*, 113.
[91] *PPE Mary*, 119.

Foreign fashions were always compared with the familiar dress style, because it was only through being contrasted with known local fashions that divergences and foreign elements of other fashions became apparent. Hence, foreign fashions were always viewed implicitly as a kind of alternative to familiar fashions.[92]

Indeed, the abovementioned comments on Anne of Cleves's attire can be placed in a larger collection of very similar accounts. Marillac's observation that *'ladite dame ... estant vestue à la mode du pays dont elle venoit'*,[93] [The same lady... was clothed in the fashion of the country from which she came] seems completely in line with other descriptions of royal and noble women wearing dresses in the fashions of their home countries. For example, Beatrice of Naples (1457–1508) married the King of Hungary Matthias Corvinus in 1476, and Frieling observes that Beatrice was reported by one chronicle writer to have 'attended the crowning shortly before her marriage *in iren waelischen klaydern* ("her Italian clothes") and attended her wedding with a veil *alsdann die Walhin tragen* ("how Italian women used to wear it")'.[94] A further example from around the same time can be found in Hans Oringen's description of the Landshut wedding of Hedwig Jagiellon (known in Polish as *Jadwiga Jagiellonka*) and George, Duke of Bavaria-Landshut in 1475.[95] Oringen, present at the event, recorded that after the ceremony in the church a dance took place at a house, and that during the dance, Hedwig was dressed in *'einen grünen damasche rock, weyt gemacht nach iren landes sitten'*[96] [a green damask skirt, made wide after the custom of their country] (emphasis added). And another chronicler also comments on Hedwig's wearing *'ain kostlich klaid auf polonischen fitten gemacht'* [an expensive dress made in the Polish style] during the

---

[92] Frieling, 'Dressing the Bride', 83.

[93] Kaulek ed., *Correspondance Politique*, 150.

[94] Frieling, 'Dressing the Bride', 78–9.

[95] For an excellent introduction to the Landshut wedding, see: Thomas Alexander Bauer, 'The Wedding of Duke Georg of Landshut in 1475—A Challenge for the Whole Town', *Terminus: Journal of Early Modern Literature and Culture* 11 (2009), 33–41.

[96] Thomas Alexander Bauer: Feiern unter den Augen der Chronisten. Die Quellentexte zur Landshuter Fürstenhochzeit von 1475. München 2008. Please refer to 247–267 (253); Frieling, 'Dressing the Bride', 83.

wedding.[97] Closer to home we may once more recall the anonymous eye-witness account of the entry of Katherine of Aragon into London in 1501, which informed the reader of the richness of the attire, and of its style typical for the princess's place of origin ('in riche apparell on her body aftir the manour of her contre').[98] And within the time-span of the reign of Henry VIII, we see the reports made on Mary Tudor's appearance on her marrying the French King Louis XII. For example, a letter dispatched on 14 October 1514 to Antonio Triulzi, who was the Bishop of Asti and French ambassador to the Signory of Venice, records that on 8 October, 'on entering the suburbs' of Abbeville, Mary Tudor appeared in a 'dress being cloth of gold on crimson with close English sleeves.'[99]

Similarly, the communication written to Lady Lisle that Anne of Cleves wore 'a rich attire upon her head of her own country fashion',[100] is not unusual a remark given that fashions in headdress differed significantly across the European royal and ducal courts, and invited close scrutiny in written accounts. By means of an example, we turn to Eleanor of Austria (1498–1558) who had first married King Manuel of Portugal and during this marriage retained her Flemish style. When she became queen of France after her marriage to François I, both her imperial family-connection—she was a Habsburg after all—and previous marriage can be seen to have influenced her attire during formal ceremonies.[101] For her entrée at Bayonne where she crossed the border into her new country, an eye-witness, Sebastién Moreau, reported that *'la dite dame'* [the said lady; Eleanor] was dressed in *'une fine robe de velour noir'* [a fine dress of black velvet] that was lined with satin in crimson, and was richly adorned.'[102] Interestingly, for

[97] Lorenz Westenrieder, ed., *Beyträge zur Vaterländischen Historie, Geographie, Statistie und Landwirtschaft*, vol. 2 (München, 1789), 142; Frieling, 'Dressing the Bride', 83.

[98] *Receyt*, 32.

[99] *CPSV* vol. 2, #511.

[100] *LP* vol. 15, #18 (4 January 1540)

[101] Janet Cox-Rearick, 'Power-Dressing at the Courts of Cosimo de' Medici and François I, The 'moda alla Spagnola' of Spanish Consorts Eléonore d'Autriche and Eleonora di Toledo', *Artibus et Historiae* 30:60 (2009), 39–69 (40).

[102] M.L. Cimber and F. Danjou, eds., *Archives curieuses de l'histoire de France*, ser. 1, vol. 2 (Paris: Beauvais, Membre de L'Institut Historique, 1835), 437. Also cited in Lisa Mansfield, 'Lustrous Virtue: Eleanor of Austria's Jewels and Gems as Composite Cultural

our purpose, Moreau further specified that her hair-style and adornments favoured the Iberian fashion: '*sa teste estoit accoustrée et habillée à la portugaloise*' [her head was adorned and dressed in the Portuguese style].[103] This likely means, as Cox-Rearick explains, that she was sporting '*papos*', 'side puffs decorated with narrow braids that were worn contemporaneously by Empress Isabella of Portugal'.[104] Correspondingly, when Eleanor and the king, her husband, visited Angoulême on 24 July 1530, her hair was dressed in the Spanish way ('*coyffée à la mode d'Espaigne*').[105] This likely means that she again wore the puffs of hair around her ears.

In the same way, when Mary Tudor married Louis XII of France, the new queen's clothes worn during appearances to the public were recorded in anonymous festival books. *S'ensuit l'ordre qui a este tenue a lentree de la royne a Abeville* (1514), for example, records that '*la dicte dame*' [the said lady; so, the English princess], '*estoit vestue dune robe de drap dargent*' [was dressed in a robe of cloth of silver]. But to the festival book writer, it was her headdress that merited special amplification in the narrative: '*la billement de la teste a la facon de son pays*'[106] [the billement on her head in the style of her country].[107] We see this mentioned again in a summary of two letters dated 8 and 9 October

Identity and Affective Maternal Agency', in Erin Griffey, ed., *Sartorial Politics in Early Modern Europe: Fashioning Women* (Amsterdam: Amsterdam University Press, 2019), 93–114 (106–7).

[103] Cimber and Danjou, eds., *Archives curieuses*, 437.

[104] Cox-Rearick, 'Power-Dressing', 40, and footnote 18. '*Papos*' are described as 'hair covering the ears' in Isabelle Paresys, 'Dressing the Queen at the French Renaissance Court: Sartorial Politics', in Erin Griffey, ed., *Sartorial Politics in Early Modern Europe: Fashioning Women* (Amsterdam: Amsterdam University Press, 2019), 57–74 (69). Paresys observes that 'her [Eleanor's] style was labelled Spanish rather than Portuguese or Castilian' (69).

[105] Jean François Eusèbe Castaigne, ed., *Entrées solennelles dans la ville d'Angoulême depuis François Ier jusqu'à Louis XIV* (Angoulême, 1856), 300; Cox-Rearick, 'Power-Dressing', 43.

[106] *S'ensuit l'ordre qui a este tenue a lentree de la royne a Abeville* (1514), Bibliothèque Mazarine, 8° 35478 [Res]. Permalink: https://bibnum.institutdefrance.fr/ark:/61562/mz17411, 2–3 when counting title page as 1.

[107] 'Billement' refers to goldsmith's work attached or worn together with a headdress, often with precious stones or pearls. See for example, the attire worn by Mary I during her royal entry, in a 'gowne of purple velvet French fashion ... with a rich bowdricke of gould, pearle, and stones about her necke, and a riche billement of stones and great pearle on her hoode ...' Cf; Sarah Duncan, *Mary I: Gender, Power, and Ceremony in the Reign of England's First Queen* (New York, NY: Palgrave Macmillan, 2012), 18.

1514, Abbeville, from the Sanuto Diaries recording that "The Queen [Mary Tudor] was very magnificently dressed, both her gown and head gear being of the English fashion, and very costly, both in jewels and goldsmiths" work."[108]

Princess make-over

Writing about the French court, Croizat observed that 'foreign queens had to choose whether or not to adopt French attire when making their debut'.[109] She explained, 'a queen's decision to wear her native fashions for her first public appearances may have been perceived as a sign of reluctance to embrace her new country'.[110] It is in this light that we may understand the section in the letter written to the Bishop of Asti recording the proceedings after the church ceremony and dinner on 9 October 1514:

> the most Christian King *had the Queen dressed in French costume*, and they gave a ball, the whole court banqueting, dancing, and making good cheer; and thus at the eighth hour, before midnight, the Queen was taken away from the entertainment by 'Madame', to go and sleep with the King (emphasis added).[111]

It can be inferred that Louis XII was happy to see Mary dressed in the fashion of her country on entering the town and showing herself off to her new subjects—presumably also to visually inform them of the new queen's English background—but that after the formal ceremony and during the evening leading up to the consummation of the match, she was expected to dress in the French fashion. Sentiments of expectation that a bride would at some point during the wedding ceremonies or festivities change into the apparel of her new country can be found in various reports of such events. This could, for example, occur in the form of a compliment made about the change of clothes when it happened, as found in the commemorative booklet *Lentree de la Royne a*

---

[108] *CPSV* vol. 2, #509.
[109] Yassana C. Croizat, 'Living Dolls: François Ier Dresses his Women', *RQ* 60 (2007), 94–130 (122, footnote 69).
[110] Croizat, 'Living Dolls', 122, footnote 69.
[111] *CSPV* vol. 2, #511.

Ableville (1514), which records Mary Tudor's adoption of French fashion, much to the appreciation of the anonymous writer: '*ung peu deuant
le soupper la royne a este acoustree a la mode de france. Laquelle il fasoit
meilleur veoir que a la mode dangleterre*'.[112] [A little before dinner the
queen was outfitted in the fashion of France, which was better to see
than the fashion of England]. This comment is very similar both in
expression and in attitude to Hall's observation that Anne of Cleves
looked better wearing a French-style headdress ('On whiche daie she
was appareiled after the Englishe fashion, with a Frenche whode, which
so set furth her beautie and good vysage, that every creature rejoysed
to behold her'[113]). We also, however, find implied criticism through
suggestions made that a bride would look even more stunning if she
were to change into the clothes of her new country. For example, Oringen's account detailing the appearance of Hedwig Jagiellon includes the
observation that the queen would be more beautiful and appropriate to
the task if dressed in German attire ('*so sie gecleydet wirt nach deuschen
sitten, so wirt sie ser ein wolgestalte vnd wolgeschikte furstin*' [if she is
dressed according to German customs, she will be a well-shaped and
well-suited duchess]).[114]

Genre performed

Perhaps the most complex aspect of descriptions detailing the appearances of foreign princesses, is that which conveys an image of their
entourage of ladies and women who accompanied her on her journey. Like descriptions of a princess's own dress and headgear such

---

[112] *Lentree de la royne a Ableville* (Paris: Guillaume Mart, 1514), Bibliothèque
Mazarine, 8° 35476 [Res]. Permalink: https://bibnum.institutdefrance.fr/ark:/61562/
mz17916, 7 counting title page as 1. Both remarks referred to in Note 105 and Note 112
in this chapter pertaining to Mary Tudor's attire are also referred to in Charles Giry-
Deloison, 'Une haquenée . . . pour le porter bientost et plus doucement en enfer ou en
paradis': The French and Mary Tudor's marriage to Louis XII in 1514', in David Grummitt, ed., *The English Experience in France c. 1450–1558: War, Diplomacy and Cultural
Exchange* (London: Routledge, 2002), 132–59 (159).
[113] Hall, *The Triumphant Reigne*, 303.
[114] Thomas Alexander Bauer: Feiern unter den Augen der Chronisten. Die Quellentexte zur Landshuter Fürstenhochzeit von 1475. München 2008, 257; Frieling, 'Dressing
the Bride', 84.

portrayals are typically formulaic and generally convey a number, or all, of the following few key points: the ladies have come along from princess's country; the ladies are dressed in the clothing fashionable in their native country; the ladies are less visually attractive than their mistress so that the princess by comparison, clearly outshines her ladies; ladies and women of different ranks are dressed accordingly to visually assert a hierarchy among them. Turning again to the letters from the Sanuto Diaries describing Mary Tudor's entry at Abbeville, we see the following:

> Next followed 12 ladies; the wives, sisters, and daughters of the lords, princes, and grandees who had accompanied her, all most richly arrayed *in the English fashion*, in cloth of gold; and after them came some 40 other damsels, well and sumptuously adorned in the English fashion. Three carriages, which the Queen brought from England, followed; they were very handsome and contained ladies (emphasis added).[115]

In this letter a clear hierarchy can be revealed through description of dress. As mentioned in the above, 'The Queen [Mary Tudor] was very magnificently dressed, both her gown and head gear being of the English fashion, and very costly, both in jewels and goldsmiths' work.'[116] The 'ladies' also in English clothes, are 'most richly arrayed', the damsels following, 'well and sumptuously adorned', and the 'handsome' carriages contained 'ladies' whose apparel is not specified, and it is implied that their clothing would have been inferior in riches. The ladies and women in Katherine of Aragon's entourage were described according to a similar pattern. The *infanta* on this occasion rode a mule, and so did her principal ladies. We learn that the first lady of Spain wore 'her heer hanging down abowte her neke, and a good large hatt upon her hed proporchyoned aftir the fachion of a cardenalles hatte as the Princes hade'. In other words, her headdress mirrored that of the princess, showing off her rank. Then followed four ladies, 'all in blake, called Lady Mastres, with kerchiers upon her hed, a blak thinge of clothe over her kerchiers like unto the fachion of a religious woman

---

[115] *CSPV* vol. 2, #509.
[116] *CPSV* vol. 2, #509.

aftir the maner of Spayne'.[117] Giles Tremlett notes that they wore these 'black dresses with long black mantilla-like head-dresses' out of diffidence to the princess, so that she might shine by comparison.[118] Further on in the procession followed 'ij other charys not so richely beseen', in other words, less handsomely decked-out carriages. These 'charys' contained 'Spanyssh women apparellyd aftir de Spanysshe fachion. Ther apparel was busteous [rustic, coarse] and marvelous, and they were not the fairest women of the company'.[119] Tremlett has interpreted the 'lesser Spanish Women' to have worn clothes 'rougher' than those of the princess and the more important ladies travelling more towards the front of the train.[120]

Processions followed a strict set of customs, sumptuary laws dictated what could be worn by persons of a certain rank, and brides should not be rivalled with in terms of beauty or splendour by their ladies and women. We have also seen that account takers at an event dispatched the information their absent patrons needed, and writers of celebrative festival books were meant to record that would bring most honour to their patrons. Given all of this, it is no surprise that describing the appearance of a foreign princess and her entourage followed the particular formulaic structure described above; after all, circumstance, custom of events, and the rationale for writing called for such an approach. That such a genre of writing was recognizable to contemporaries, and that perhaps young persons were taught which aspects to look for in a description of this type can be discerned from the problematic and extravagant description of Katherine's entourage by Thomas More in his letter to his former tutor John Holt, preserved in British Library Ms. Arundel 249, a letter already referred to in Chapter 1 of this book.[121] In this letter,

[117] *Receyt*, 32.
[118] Giles Tremlett, *Catherine of Aragon: Henry's Spanish Queen* (London: Faber and Faber, 2010), 79.
[119] *Receyt*, 33.
[120] Tremlett, *Catherine of Aragon*, 79.
[121] BL, Arundel MS 249. Transcribed in: Rogers, ed., *The Correspondence of Sir Thomas More*, 4–5. The letter is problematic because of its tone, choice of words, and what it appears to convey (see my Chapter 1). See also, Imtiaz Habib, who interpreted More's passage to express itself derisively of people of colour in Katherine of Aragon's train. He argued that, 'for More "Ethiopian" is a stand-in for African generally'. He continued, 'Even if the identifier seems neutral, however, it already appears negatively marked with the trailing qualifier "pigmy," with which it is conversely linked, the resulting compound

More referred to the pomp and splendour of the occasion, and commented that the 'apparatus' of England's nobles was so great it should be admired (*'Tantus erat nobelium nostrorum apparatus vt admiration esse posset'*). He then contrasted that with the Spanish party (*'At Hispanorum comitatus . . . qualis erat!'*), and made a reference to Holt's absence from the event by writing that if he [Holt] would have been there, he would have laughed at the Spanish party, *'ita ridiculi errant'* [so ridiculous they were]. He thus placed himself in the role of an intelligencer, and the communication in the context of letters in which an ambassador or messenger dispatches reports to a patron or colleague.

More continued to discuss the Spanish entourage, noting that, 'except for three or at most four faces, they were hardly tolerable' (*'facies praeter tres aut ad summum quattuor vix tollerabiles'*), and described the *infanta*'s followers as '*curvi . . . laceri, nudipedes, pigmei Aethiopes'* [crooked . . . torn/tattered, bare-footed, pygmy Ethiopians]. Continuing his ridicule of the party's appearance, he suggested that they looked as if they had escaped straight out of hell (*'ex inferis euasisse putauisses'*). More then reported positively on the princess's beauty using tones that led Thomas Penn in his bestseller *Winter King* to refer to More as 'positively dreamy'.[122] But actually, More was doing so much more than simply expressing his delight at the princess's appearance. When he wrote, '*At domina ipsa, mihi crede, omnibus habunde placuit'* [but the lady herself, believe me, was pleasing to all], and asserted that none of the qualities are missing that one finds in a beautiful maiden (*'pulcherrime virginis'*), he, within the genre of describing foreign princesses and their parties, contrasted the princess favourably against her attendants. His description of the princess's beauty is both copious and vague, as is typical in this kind of report. He also underlined the verisimilitude of his account of her beauty ('believe me'), and reported what others thought of her, perhaps also slightly tongue in cheek towards the genre, given that, as we have seen, such reports often had to rely on other peoples' statements. He emphasized, '*omnes denique eam laudabant maxime, nemo satis'* [all praised her highly, no-one enough], and

phrase itself being progressively arrived at from "ridiculous" to "barefooted"'. Habib, *Black Lives*, 24.

[122] Thomas Penn, *Winter King: The Dawn of Tudor England* (London: Penguin, 2012), 60.

ended on the hopes that the princely couple (here literally: 'the most famous couple in England' ('*celeberrimum coniugium Anglie*'), would be 'happy and prosperous' ('*felix faustumque*').

More's actual attitude to the Spanish entourage notwithstanding, he appears in this letter to have shown off his knowledge of a genre of writing that was sufficiently formulaic and answering to particular expectations so as to render writing a report like this a self-conscious performative act. In More's letter the hyperbole applied throughout can also be seen as self-conscious, and as possibly functioning as a witticism or comment on this kind of report. And perhaps this, although less bombastically written, is how we can also read Marillac's assertion of Anne of Cleves's ladies-in-waiting being '*enférieures en beaulté à leur maistresse*' [more inferior in terms of beauty than their mistress]. According to the formulae dominating this type of writing, Marillac could hardly have called the ladies *more* beautiful than their mistress, and given that the genre dictates that rich clothing equalled beauty, and the ladies were likely less dressed to impress than their patroness, Marillac's description when seen in context, makes perfect sense. The reversed compliment at Anne's address via the description of the ladies allowed Marillac to pronounce himself critical of the *mode* worn at the court of Cleves whilst minimizing negative expression about the new queen of England, as we have seen. The presence of a hyperbole in the account to Montmorency is visible if we compare it to Marillac's more nuanced reference to the attire of Anne's ladies in waiting and women in his letter to King Francis I:

> ayant admené jusques à douze ou quinze demoiselles d'honneur vestues de mesme sorte et d'habit qui a semblé à plusieurs chose estrange.[123]
>
> [She brought around twelve or fifteen ladies of honour who were clothed in the same sort of clothing, which to many looked like a strange thing].

In this letter it appears that the ladies all dressed in the same way— almost by means of a livery—that rendered their appearance strange to the eye. As they were all outfitted in the style fashionable at the house of Cleves, this would have given them a collective outlandishness to

---

[123] Kaulek, ed., *Correspondance Politique*, 151.

this French viewer. The bottom-line, however, is that however much Anne of Cleves and her ladies and women had attempted, according to their respective ranks, to 'self-fashion' in order to make an impression on the English and dignitaries and ambassadors from other countries, their clothes were assessed and redefined according to English and French fashions. After all, the records describing the princess's appearance clearly show that Anne's style was not appreciated in the way it was intended. At the same time, these records must be understood, keeping in mind that they appear to be following a clearly set-out pattern of expectation on how to respond to foreign dress worn by a princess and her retinue.

Some final thoughts

It appears that representing the physical appearance of Anne of Cleves both in portraiture and in the written word relied on both political agendas—such as in the case of Cromwell's praises—and on writing conventions so strong that they somewhat undermine the value of that which is represented. Hall can be seen to have simply repeated the descriptions of a display of wealth through costume, and a delight in a bride's changing her headgear to the fashion of her new country as was often seen in chronicles celebrating royal or ducal nuptials. The report written to Lady Lisle echoed descriptions of headgear worn by foreign brides across Europe. And Marillac's comments on Anne can be read as formulaic, following a clearly set-out genre of writing. How much does this really say about Anne of Cleves's beauty apart from it having been deemed relevant by those taking account of it? The sartorial approach in this chapter enables me to suspect, not that much. It is for that reason that scholarship, repeatedly returning to the idea of Anne of Cleves as Henry's 'ugly wife' would benefit from turning to more informative lenses and discussions. An excellent illustration of one such direction is given by Valerie Schutte, whose work in the field of book and manuscript studies in relation to Anne of Cleves is exemplary.[124]

---

[124] Valerie Schutte, 'Anne of Cleves in Book and Manuscript', *The Journal of the Early Book Society* 21 (2018), 123–47.

And with this we return to Chapter 1, in which we saw how we sometimes need to address additional source material to present new contexts in order to more fully understand the extant material regarding court customs, celebrations and ceremony, so that we can revisit the conclusions drawn from earlier interpretations. In the following chapter we continue to discuss Anne of Cleves, opening on a methodological issue that sits on the intersection between interlanguage, transnational, and inclusive scholarship: the question where information has come from (in terms of its source), and how this has been interrogated, shared, and eventually, adopted into the narratives that are shared about a historical person, event, or situation, and its contexts. A crucial follow-up question is how and where this primary and secondary source material can be accessed, and verified. These questions, as we have seen, are pertinent for all the themes covered in this book and have been silently applied throughout as existing perspectives have been interrogated and fresh perspectives offered. Methodologically speaking, however, they deserve more overt treatment, which they will get in Chapter 5.

| 5 |

Leaving an Impression

Introduction

In what follows we take as a starting point the annulment of the marriage of Anne of Cleves to Henry VIII. This concluded a piquant time
in Tudor marital history, during which Henry's advisors had worked
hard to render the match invalid on the basis of Anne's earlier precontract to Francis of Lorraine (1517–45). The precontract for all its
importance, however, was never produced at the English court. Scholarship has since referred to this document, but in doing so had to rely
on a nineteenth-century transcription by Karl W. Bouterwek.[1] This
edition—with the best intentions—was produced out of antiquarian
interest. The purpose of Bouterwek's work was to share interesting
archival finds with like-minded enthusiasts; not to guide scholars to
opportunities for further study or to direct them to source material.
Thus, Bouterwek did not consistently cite his sources, and for the
precontract, notably, he only provided a roughly contextual reference
by referring readers to T.J. Lacomblet's *Urkundenbuch* (1858); but the
'*urkunde*' in question is one of 13 June 1527, an agreement drawn up
between the Duke of Guelders (Charles II of Egmond; 1467–1538), and

---

[1] K.W. Bouterwek, 'Anna von Cleve, Gemahlin Heinrichs uiij, Königs von England',
Zeitschrift des Bergischen Geschichtsvereins, vol. 4 (Bonn: 1867), 337–413. For the transcription of an unspecified copy of the charter of 5 June 1527, see 385–91.

John III of Cleves (1490–1539), rather than the agreement of 5 June of the same year which Bouterwek transcribed.[2] In other words, this provides a 'dead end' for identifying Bouterwek's original source material. Given the context and purpose of Bouterwek's transcription, this is not necessarily a limitation in *his* work, but one that has had a notable effect on Tudor Studies. Indeed, the sporadic scholarly attention given to Anne of Cleves's precontract appears to refer to the existence of Bouterwek's transcription, but rarely shows any detailed engagement with the contents of the 1527 charter.[3] It is possible that in some cases the nineteenth-century transcription has not invited closer scrutiny because its origins lack transparency, so that its contents could not be verified. One can also easily see how a linguistic barrier may present itself when reading a text as formulaic and diplomatic as a marital charter in a language that is not necessarily accessible to all scholars of Tudor history.

The current chapter is the first to present an in-depth study of the 1527 agreement, through a material cultural analysis of what I will refer to as 'the Arnhem charter'. This original charter detailing the marital agreements in the match between Anne of Cleves and Francis of Lorraine has been hiding in plain sight at the Gelders Archief in Arnhem, the Netherlands.[4] The charter at Arnhem represents a unique third copy of

---

[2] T.J. Lacomblet, ed., *Urkundenbuch Für Die Geschichte Des Niederrheins Oder Des Erzstifts Cöln, Der Fürstenthümer Jülich Und Berg, Geldern, Meurs, Kleve Und Mark, Und Der Reichsstifte Elten, Essen Und Werden*, vol. 4 (Düsseldorf, 1858), 646–8, #526.

[3] A 'close study' of the 1527 document is mentioned in Warnicke, but she does not offer the reader an analysis of its text. Warnicke, *Anne of Cleves*, 243. David Starkey mentions the Cleves–Lorraine agreement in passing in his *Six Wives* (New York: Harper Collins, 2003), 639–40, citing Bouterwek as his source, although misspelling his initials.

[4] Gelders Archief, Arnhem (hereafter: GldA) 0001-1791, 'Akte van huwelijksvoorwaarden tussen Frans I, hertog van Lotharingen en Anna van Kleef'. 1 charter. Derde exemplaar, bestemd voor hertog Karel als bemiddelaar' (5 June 1527). Following my request to the archive, the document has been made available to the general public, and can be accessed online at: https://permalink.geldersarchief.nl/ EF04470A01224E599BC3D91D7E5578B2. I thank Dr Clare Egan for studying the charter and its seals with me at the Gelders Archief, and for her sharp and critical eye. Further thanks should go to Laura Marienus; we are currently preparing a full transcription of the charter to enable further research on this topic. A reference to the existence of this charter has long been available to readers of Dutch, since a one-line 'summative statement' ['*regest*'] of this charter is offered in Isaak Anne Nijhoff, ed., *Gedenkwaardigheden uit de geschiedenis van Gelderland: door onuitgegevene oorkonden opgehelderd en bevestigd* (Arnhem, 1862), vol 6.2, 877, #1425. The archival reference in Nijhoff (#1425) does

the agreement, a fair copy drawn up for the administration of Charles of Egmond, who served as the broker of the betrothal (see Figure 5.1 and 5.2).[5] 'Reading' the charter as a material object, this chapter reveals that Anne of Cleves had not been a stakeholder in the agreement made

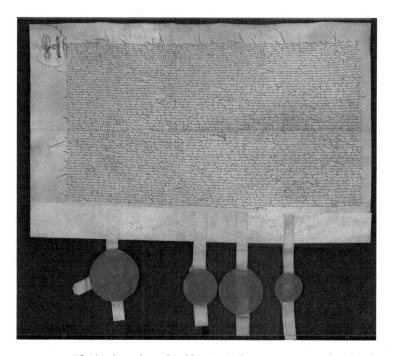

FIGURE 5.1   The 'Arnhem charter'. Gelders Archief: 0001-1791r. Reproduced with permission.

not, however, correspond to the charter's current reference number due to archival reorganization. Consulting the concordance drawn up by M. Flokstra and F.J.W. Kan enables readers to find the new archival numbers for the original source material referred to by Nijhoff: https://permalink.geldersarchief.nl/9711FAD88B0A4125830738458E352552.

[5] I refer to Charles Duke of Guelders as Charles of Egmond, following among others, Remi van Schaïk, 'Taxation, Public Finances and the State-Making Process in the Late Middle Ages: The Case of the Duchy of Guelders', *JMH* 19 (1993), 251–71; G. Kalsbeek, *De betrekkingen tusschen Frankrijk en Gelre tijdens Karel van Egmond* (Wageningen: Veenman, 1932). Scholarship at times uses 'Charles Duke of Guelders' and 'Charles of Egmond' interchangeably, such as, for example, in Aart Noordzij, 'Against Burgundy. The Appeal

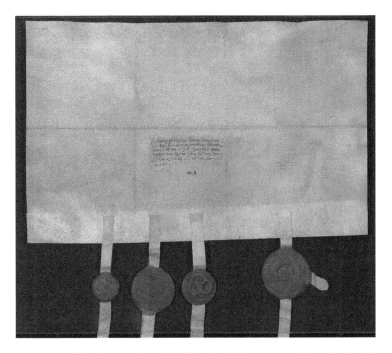

FIGURE 5.2 The 'Arnhem charter'. Gelders Archief: 0001-1791v. Reproduced with permission.

with the house of Lorraine, and that she had not consented to the match. The visual aspects of the charter made this very clear to anyone who had access to the document, regardless of the languages they could read. The evidence leads to the conclusion that Anne of Cleves had not pressed for the charter to be delivered to England once it had become clear that Henry VIII wanted his marriage annulled; after all, the 1527 charter would have shown the king and anyone else looking at it—without the need of a German translator or interpreter—that the Lorraine match did not form an impediment to his own marriage to Anne, and this was not what Henry needed to hear at that moment in time. The evidence

of Germany in the Duchy of Guelders', in Robert Stein and Judith Pollmann, eds., *Networks, Regions and Nations: Shaping Identities in the Low Countries, 1300–1650* (Leiden: Brill, 2010), 111–29.

thus suggests Anne of Cleves to have been more of a strategist than has previously been supposed.

The question of Anne of Cleves's precontract

In June 1540 Henry VIII was eager to be released from his marriage to his fourth wife but concerned that a divorce or dissolving the match would negatively affect international relations. What if her brother, William of Cleves, took offence and aligned himself with Henry's enemies *du moment*, the King of France, and the Habsburg Emperor Charles V?[6] Indeed, a formal, official, reason was required for the match to be undone, and this presented itself in the form of Anne's precontract with Francis of Lorraine, drawn up in June 1527.[7]

Roughly one year earlier, Thomas Cromwell had been at pains to establish whether Anne would make a suitable candidate for marrying Henry VIII, and this, at the time, balanced on the question of her having consented to her betrothal to the son of Lorraine in 1527. Two ambassadors, Nicholas Wotton (who we have already seen in the previous chapter) and Richard Berde had been tasked with reporting to Cromwell what they had learned about this matter. Thus in May 1539 they reported that the Vice-Chancellor of Cleves, Henry Olisleger, had emphatically stated that the marital deal had been an agreement between Anne's father and the Duke of Lorraine, who had been 'yn communicacion togither for the mariaige of the Marquyse, the duke of Loraynes sonne, *and* the said ladye Anne'.[8] Commenting on the contractual implications of the agreement, Olisleger had apparently said, 'that they hadde gone so ferre that wrytinges wer made *and* sealyd up on

---

[6] For this concern, see *LP* vol. 15, #823 (30 June 1540), as recorded by Thomas Cromwell.

[7] Warnicke, *Anne of Cleves*, 144–5.

[8] British Library, Cotton MS Vitellius B XXI, fol. 197v, http://www.bl.uk/manuscripts/ Viewer.aspx?ref=cotton_ms_vitellius_b_xxi_f197v. Note that this is also the same letter in which Wotton and Berde complain that they could not properly see Anne and her sister because of their substantial garments and headcoverings: 'We sayde, we hadde not seene theym, for to see but a parte of theyr faces, *and* that under suche a monstruouse habyte *and* apparell, was no syght, neither of they[r] [word crossed out] [inserted: faces] nor of theyr [word crossed out] [inserted: persones]. Why quod he, wolde yow see theym nakydde?' fols. 196v–197r. Calendared in *LP* vol. 14.1, #920 (3 May 1539).

hit, and that the Duke of Cleves hadde payed therupon to the Duke of Gheldres by the said agreement certeyn so*mm*es of money. *And* hadde fulfille[d] on his parte all thinges, saving that the lady Anne was not yet maryed to the said Marquyse'.[9] The Vice-Chancellor had also rebutted protestations made by the ambassadors that in this case Anne might not be considered as a future wife for Henry VIII, by asserting that 'these promyses wer made onelye betwixte the fathers. And the partyes as yet have not gyven theyr consen[tes]. But ar at theyr libertye to do what they Wille'.[10] Thomas Cromwell only had Olisleger's word to go by, presented through a second-hand narrative, but this appears to have persuaded him, given that he continued to pursue Anne for Henry. The intelligence gathered by Wotton and Berde would again resurface when Henry found that he did not want to be married to Anne of Cleves.

Then, in June 1540, a set of memoranda written by Stephen Gardiner, with additional notes made by Thomas Wriothesley, documented the strategy undertaken to rid Henry of his wife. An important avenue to explore was 'An ensearch to be made to attain knowledge [of] the contract made with the prince of Lor[raine], whether it was *de præsenti* or *de futuro*'.[11] The reasoning behind this was that if the 1527 marriage contract had been of the '*per verba de futuro*' variety, it would have been relatively easy to dissolve. But this would have presented an outcome unfavourable to Henry, who at this point in time needed the Lorraine match to have been binding. As David Loades explains, the '*per verba de futuro*' contract type represented 'the normal approach used in diplomatic matches, when both parties wished to preserve their freedom of action, and when the principals were probably infants'.[12] And, as we will see next, studying the 1527 document makes clear that this is indeed the type of agreement that had been made at the time.

Another item on Gardiner's agenda was, 'To see and search for the instrument [of renunciation] made since her [Anne of Cleves's] coming into England'.[13] And indeed, earlier that year, on 26 February 1540, a copy of a notarial document had been produced that confirmed that

[9] BL, Cotton MS Vitellius B XXI, fol. 197v. Calendared in *LP* vol. 14.1, #920.

[10] BL, Cotton MS Vitellius B XXI, fol. 197v. Calendared in *LP* vol. 14.1, #920.

[11] *LP* vol. 15, #821 (29 June 1540).

[12] David Loades, *The Six Wives of Henry VIII* (Stroud: Amberley, 2009), 13.

[13] *LP* vol. 15, #821 (29 June 1540).

in February 1535 the Lorraine–Cleves match had been renunciated.[14] This document had been stamped with a seal depicting a beer pot. Given Henry VIII's clear wishes, the only politic response to this document within the context of the Tudor court would have been to deem it unacceptable as evidence. It is therefore no surprise that Gardiner's memorandum reveals that the document was considered suspicious on the basis of its beer pot seal: 'The instrument signed with the bere pot containeth no m[anner] of discharge at all, but rather ministereth matter of m[uch] doubt'.[15]

A betrothal *per verba de praesenti* was legally binding if a ceremony had been held, also if the match had not been consummated. But in the latter case it could still be dissolved, for example, if one of the parties had not consented to the marital agreement. If no ceremony had been held but the betrothal had been consummated, it could not be undone.[16] And indeed, we see in June 1540 that the Lorraine–Cleves pact was being treated as if it had been *per verba de praesenti*, on the basis of 'evidence' provided for and in cooperation with Henry VIII himself. For example, consummation of the Lorraine match was helpfully suggested by Thomas Cromwell, held in the Tower under attainder, who conveniently remembered that Henry had told him that 'he [Henry] had felt her [Anne's] belly and breasts, and thought she was no maid'.[17] This likely served to suggest that she had consummated the Lorraine marital deal, thus implying it to have been *per verba de praesenti*. The other 'evidence' came to Henry in the form of his conscience. Cromwell again obligingly noted in a (now heavily scorched) letter to Henry that could be used in the case that 'ye hadde done all that ye cowlde to move nature . . . consent to have done with her as is pertenent to . . . yet ever there was an obstacle [heavy crossing out] and th[at your Grace] [t]hought before god she was not your wyffe [lawful]'.[18] Here it is helpful to note that in the same letter Cromwell also pleaded for his life,

[14] *LP* vol. 15, #267 (26 February 1540).

[15] *LP* vol. 15, #821.

[16] Loades, *The Six Wives*, 13.

[17] *LP* vol. 15, #823.

[18] BL Cotton MS Otho C X, fol. 250r. http://www.bl.uk/manuscripts/Viewer. aspx?ref=cotton_ms_otho_c_x_f250r. '[at your Grace]' and '[lawful]' are additions suggested in *LP* vol. 15, #824, in which the letter is calendared.

'upon my knees prostrate ... King pardon mercye and ... Christ', which
perhaps can be seen to have coloured his impartiality in the matter.[19]

We see that sometime between the end of June when Cromwell committed this 'evidence' to the page, and 7 July 1540 when depositions were
taken from a number of key witnesses, the narrative of what had happened between Henry and Anne took a bit of a turn. The depositions by
Sir Thomas Hennege and Anthony Denny presented a narrative similar to that of Cromwell's letter to Henry. Denny, for example, signed the
following statement:

> how indeed his highnes could not induce himself to have affection
> to the quene, for that she was not as she was reported, but had her
> brests so slake, & other parts of body in such sort, that his highnes
> somewhat suspected her virginity, & concluded that her body was
> of such indisposition to his, that he could never in her company be
> provoked and stered to know her carnally.[20]

Doctor John Chamber, however, presented the non-consummation in a
way that emphasized the king's lack of consent without overtly suggesting that Anne had previously consummated her marriage with another
man: 'how his grace found her body in such a sort disordered & indis-
posed to excite & provoke any lust in hym ... that his majesty could
not in any wise overcome that lothsomeness, ne in her company be
provoked or stered to that act'.[21] The 'King's declaration' about his marriage relied on Cromwell to testify to the king's 'lack of consent' and
'also the lack of the will and power to consummate the same', and refers
to the declarations of others to this effect, although leaving in the middle whether Anne of Cleves had come to him as a virgin ('nor yet, if
she brought maidenhead with her, took any from her by true carnal

[19] BL Cotton MS Otho C X, fol. 250v. http://www.bl.uk/manuscripts/Viewer.
aspx?ref=cotton_ms_otho_c_x_f250v. Calendared in *LP* vol. 15, #824.

[20] *LP* vol. 15, #850. The deposition is quoted from: John Strype, *Ecclesiastical Memorials*, vol. 6: Appendix (London, 1816), 218. For a list of the depositions see: 'Cecil Papers:
1306–1541', in *Calendar of the Cecil Papers in Hatfield House: Volume 1, 1306–1571* (London,
1883), 1–16, #66. *British History Online* http://www.british-history.ac.uk/cal-cecil-papers/
vol1/pp1-16 [accessed 30.03.2023].

[21] Strype, *Ecclesiastical Memorials*, 220–1.

copulation').[22] Anne of Cleves herself had been approached by Gardiner and Thomas Audeley but did not produce a statement.[23] But by a stroke of genius someone—perhaps Thomas Wriothesley, one of the king's secretaries[24]—formulated a statement signed jointly by Lady Rutland, Lady Rocheford, and Lady Edgecomb, in which they testified to Anne's complete ignorance of all matters sexual:

> First, al they being together, they wished her grace with child. And she answered & said she knew wel she was not with child. My Lady Edgecomb said, How is it possible for your grace to know that, & ly every night with the king? I know it wel I am not said she. Than said my Lady Edgecomb, I think your grace is a mayd stil. With that she laughed. And than said my Lady Rocheford, By our Lady, Madam, I think your grace is a mayd stil, indeed. How can I be a mayd, said she, & slepe every night with the king? There must be more than that, said my Lady Rocheford, or els I had as leve the king lay further. Why, said she, whan he comes to bed he kisses me, & taketh me by the hand, & byddeth me, Good night, swete hart: & in the morning kisses me, & byddeth me, Farewel, darling. Is not thys enough? Than said my Lady Rutland, Madam there must be more than this, or it will be long or [sic] we have a Duke of York, which al this realm most desireth. Nay, said the quene, is this not enough? I am contented with this, for I know no more.[25]

Although it is, 'highly doubtful', to use Warnicke's words,[26] that Anne would have said these things in conversation with the three ladies, this over-the-top narrative included a number of elements crucial to the settling of the divorce issue. It included the king's subjects' concern with the succession, and their overtly articulated desire (here expressed by Lady Rocheford) for the king to marry someone else should he not consummate the marriage with his current wife; it confirmed the non-consummation of the marriage, while presenting the relations between

---

[22] *LP* vol. 15, #825. He also refers to the royal physicians, 'the lord Privy Seal that now is, Hennage and Denny' being able to 'testify according to truth'.

[23] Norton, *Anne of Cleves*, 102.

[24] Warnicke, *Anne of Cleves*, 235: 'They [the three ladies] either conspired together . . . or one of the king's ministers, perhaps Wriothesley, devised this single deposition for each to sign'.

[25] Strype, *Ecclesiastical Memorials*, 221–2.

[26] Warnicke, *Anne of Cleves*, 234.

Henry and Anne in a flattering light; and it offered an alternative account in which Anne rather than Henry could be blamed, and, importantly, in the most politically-sensitive manner possible, as the account did not feature a suggestion of shared blame on part of Anne's family or the house of Lorraine in the form of the issue of the precontract.

Two days after the testimonies were given, the marriage between Henry VIII and Anne of Cleves was formally annulled in a charter—bearing the seals of Thomas Cranmer, the archbishop of Canterbury, and Edward Lee, the archbishop of York—extant in British Library Cotton Ch x 13.[27] The marriage was deemed void by an act of parliament (32 Henry, c. 25) 'for the suertie and certaintye of his Highnes posteritie and succession as for the welth quietnes rest and tranquillitie of this Realme'.[28] By mentioning the 'succession', the Act delicately implied that the Lady Anne would not secure the country with an heir, and indeed, the nonconsummation of the marriage is stated as the main reason for declaring the marriage invalid. Anne of Cleves assented, as the act of parliament specifies:

> The said lady Anne ... Did then of her owne free will assent and consent thereunto, and moreover sithens that tyme having knowledge and clere understanding of the resolution diffinition and determination with the particularities therof made by the said archebishops bishops and clergie, hathe in presence of certaine noblemen as the same noble men have openly in the Courte of parlament testified and declared, not only truly confessed and knowledged amonge other circumstances that she remayneth not carnally knowen of the Kinges Highnes body, but also hathe agreed and fully submitted herself to the same determination as to a thinge purely truely justly indifferently and honorably doon diffyned and determined by the said Archebishops bishoppis and clergy; And her said confession and agreement she hath also signified by a lettre subscribed with her awne hande whiche lettre and instrument hath ben openly redd declared and publishid to the said lordis and commons in this present parlament assembled in both houses of the said parlament.[29]

---

[27] BL Cotton Ch X 13. http://www.bl.uk/manuscripts/FullDisplay.aspx?ref=Cotton_Ch_X_13.

[28] Tomlins and Taunton, eds., *Statutes of the Realm*, vol. 3, 782.

[29] Tomlins and Taunton, eds., *Statutes of the Realm*, vol. 3, 782. An example of contemporary sniggers about the affair can be found in the correspondence of Richard Hilles, a

Henry sought a way out of the marriage, and Anne gave him his way out. She was at this point Henry's fourth consort, of whom the first, Katherine of Aragon, had been divorced and had died in relative isolation, separated from her daughter, as we have seen in Chapter 2. The second wife, Anne Boleyn, had been beheaded; and the third, Jane Seymour, had died after giving birth to the wished-for heir.[30] Anne of Cleves's cooperative attitude to Henry's wishes suggests it to be unlikely that she had not considered what would happen to her once Henry cast his eye over a new marital candidate whom he preferred, and she appears to have sought for a way to escape a future that looked gloomy at best. Indeed, providing Henry with his desired outcome resulted in Anne of Cleves becoming the consort who, in a way, profited most from her marriage. The 'provision' made for her by the king included her being 'considered as the King's sister, and have precedence over all ladies in England, after the Queen and the King's children', and she was given 'an annual income of 8,000 nobles', the manors of Richmond and Blechingley, 'hangings, plate, and furniture', clothes, jewels, and pearls, as well as means to take on sufficient staff to take care of her needs.[31] Furthermore, the relationship between the king and his new 'sister' was likely cordial after their marriage had been annulled, as is suggested by their keeping each other cheerful company, but also by hints of friendly or familial intimacy seen from little gestures, such as Henry's concocting

Protestant living in London, who was to write that the archbishop of Canterbury and the other bishops 'found Anne of Cleves was still a maid'; to which he commented: 'that is a likely thing indeed! Who, judging of the King by his fruits, would believe him to be so chaste?' *LP* vol. 16, #578.

[30] Katherine of Aragon is discussed in Chapters 1 and 2. Some influential studies on Henry's second and third queen are listed here: G.W. Bernard, *Anne Boleyn: Fatal Attractions* (New Haven, CT: Yale University Press, 2010); Eric Ives, *The Life and Death of Anne Boleyn* (Oxford: Blackwell, 2004); Gordon Kipling, '"He That Saw It Would Not Believe It": Anne Boleyn's Royal Entry into London', in Alexandra F. Johnston and Wim Hüsken, eds., *Civic Ritual and Drama* (Amsterdam: Rodopi, 1997), 39–79; Greg Walker, 'Rethinking the Fall of Anne Boleyn', *HJ* 45:1 (2002), 1–29; Retha M. Warnicke, *The Rise and Fall of Anne Boleyn* (Cambridge: Cambridge University Press, 1989). For the death of Jane Seymour, see: Samuel Lurie, 'Was Queen Jane Seymour (1509–1537) Delivered by a Cesarean Section?', *Endeavour* 41:1 (2017), 23–8; See also, Aidan Norrie, 'Jane Seymour: Saintly Queen', in Aidan Norrie, Carolyn Harris, J.L. Laynesmith, Danna R. Messer, and Elena Woodacre, eds., *Tudor and Stuart Consorts: Power, Influence, and Dynasty* (New York: Palgrave Macmillan, 2022), 79–100.

[31] *LP* vol. 15, #899.

'A plaster for my ladye Anne of Cleve to mollifie, and resolve, conforte and cease payne of colde and wyndie causses'.[32]

In all of this, it is not surprising that although Henry VIII after Anne's arrival in England repeatedly asked to see documents *renunciating* the Cleves–Lorraine betrothal—which could subsequently be undermined—such requests were not made for the 1527 documents, or copies thereof, *establishing* the betrothal. The 1527 documents had been requested prior to his choosing Anne as his future wife, but at this time, in August 1539, ambassador Wotton communicated back to England that he had not been able to procure them despite earlier promises from Anne's brother William that he would provide them as evidence.[33] Retha M. Warnicke reads William's later 'failure to send the documents' as 'puzzling'. She writes, 'for a close study of them indicates that Francis and she [Anne] were sworn in *per verba de futuro* vows only. When they were to come to an appropriate age, but without a definite date specified, they were to conclude the union in a nuptial ceremony'.[34] Warnicke does, unfortunately, not provide her readers with a 'close study' of the agreement, which she accessed in the nineteenth-century edition prepared by Bouterwek, but she does suggest reasons for the documents not to have been sent to England after the Tudor–Cleves marriage had taken place. 'Perhaps', Warnicke suggests, 'her brother's ministers had thought it was unnecessary to forward the documents to England because they held the misguided belief that Henry had consummated the union and that all was well with the royal couple'.[35] The other potential reason Warnicke puts forward is that 'diplomatic silence both about the receipt of the beer bot document and about the need for further information concerning the Lorraine union must have misled Anne's family about the real state of affairs'.[36]

What has perhaps been overlooked is that once married to Henry, Anne could have pressed for these documents to be provided, but she did not follow up on this, presumably because she was aware that they

[32] BL Sloane MS 1047, fol. 30v. http://www.bl.uk/manuscripts/Viewer.aspx?ref=sloane_ms_1047_f030v.
[33] Warnicke, *Anne of Cleves*, 87 and 93.
[34] Warnicke, *Anne of Cleves*, 243.
[35] Warnicke, *Anne of Cleves*, 243.
[36] Warnicke, *Anne of Cleves*, 243.

represented a match '*per verba de futuro*', and that she had never consented to be married to Francis of Lorraine. This shows her to have been
astute in her knowledge of the laws concerning matrimony, and to have
had a clear understanding of how to stay on the right side of those laws
that positively affected her well-being, once she had realized Henry's
determination to end their marriage. It is not for nothing that Anne
of Cleves has been referred to in previous scholarship as 'the survivor
queen'.[37]

Next follows the first material study of the 1527 document agreeing
to the *per verba de futuro* betrothal of Anne of Cleves and Francis of
Lorraine.[38] The exquisitely preserved seals attached to the document
reveal, even to readers who do not read Low German, the language of
the document, that Anne was not a stakeholder in this betrothal.[39] Consequently, the document, if it *had* been viewed by English eyes at the
Tudor court, would have made clear that Anne had never consented to
marrying Francis of Lorraine.

The 'Arnhem charter': An unstudied material culture object

The Arnhem charter and the four wax seals attached to the document have been incredibly well preserved. The seals provide a key to

[37] See for example, Valerie Schutte, 'Anne of Cleves: Survivor Queen', in Aidan Norrie,
Carolyn Harris, J.L. Laynesmith, Danna R. Messer, and Elena Woodacre, eds., *Tudor and
Stuart Consorts: Power, Influence, and Dynasty* (New York: Palgrave Macmillan, 2022),
101–17.

[38] Seals form an important type of evidence in current material culture studies. A
good starting point for understanding its value can be found in Jitske Jasperse, *Medieval
Women, Material Culture, and Power: Matilda Plantagenet and her Sisters* (Leeds: ARC
Humanities Press, 2020), Chapter 2, 37–62.

[39] The language used is also classified as 'Low German' in Warnicke, *Anne of Cleves*,
243. For an excellent study of the languages spoken in the region, see Luc de Grauwe,
'Emerging Mother-Tongue Awareness: The Special Case of Dutch and German in the
Middle Ages and the Early Modern Period', in Andrew R. Linn and Nicola McLelland,
eds., *Standardization: Studies from the Germanic Languages* (Current Issues in Linguistic Theory no. 235; Amsterdam: John Benjamins, 2002), 99–115. Cleves appears to
have been part of the 'Nederlantsche' area rather than of the 'Overlantsche' area (which
today is referred to as 'Oberdeutsch'). I thank Prof. Dr Raphael Berthele for sharing this
information.

understanding the document, as they reveal which parties were formally involved, but also, where applicable, how they related to one another, for example through shared heraldry. Utilizing personal seals enabled the participating parties to perform their cultural heritage, their territorial and political power or agency, as well as their recent or historical relationships with other political entities, and one could say that by stamping the wax, participant parties literally *and* figuratively made an impression.[40]

The two red seals attached to the bottom of the document (respectively left and mid-left when looking at the recto side of the document) belong to Anthoine, Duke of Lorraine and Bar, father of the groom-to-be, and to Charles of Egmond, whose seal is symbolically placed in the middle between those of the two parties he was to unite through this document. The two yellow wax seals (respectively mid-right and right) represent Anne of Cleves's parents: John III of Cleves and Maria of Jülich-Berg. Interestingly, the omission of seals representing individuals in this particular instance may be just as telling as the preservation of the seals that *were* attached to the document. Thus we see that Francis's mother, Renée de Bourbon-Montpensier, did not—and did not have to—consent to her son's marriage. Her exclusion from any official role in the marital agreement may at first sight seem incongruous with both of Anne's parents consenting to the match, leaving one to wonder why Anne was represented by two co-sealing parties, while her future husband was only represented by his father. But the reason for Francis's mother not being formally involved was that the marriage contract sealed a deal revolving around the inheritance of lands that specifically concerned both of Anne's parents and Antoine, Duke of Lorraine. Renée had no claim to this inheritance, and was therefore not a relevant party within the context of the agreement.

This may require some further explanation; Charles of Egmond did not have—legitimate—offspring to whom he could leave his lands, and as a result several parties were keen to secure this coveted piece of

---

[40] This point is made about an earlier time of seal-use in: Brigitte Bedos-Rezak, 'In Search of a Semiotic Paradigm: The Matter of Sealing in Medieval Thought and Praxis (1050–1400)', in Noël Adams, John Cherry, and James Robinson, eds., *Good Impressions: Image and Authority in Medieval Seals* (London: British Museum, 2008), 1–7 (1): '... seals were experienced as, and acted as, impressions'. An excellent introduction to seals can be found in: Brigitte Bedos-Rezak, *When Ego was Imago: Signs of Identity in the Middle Ages* (Leiden: Brill, 2011).

northern Europe, and to add Guelders to their own.[41] Jülich neigh-
boured Guelders, and had once been part of the same territory, so
that John III of Cleves, by virtue of being Maria of Jülich-Berg's husband, could be considered a potential heir to Charles's lands lands *de
jure auxoris* [by right of [the] wife]. And there were other sharks in the
pond: Anthoine, the Duke of Lorraine and Bar, was a kinsman of the
Duke of Guelders; his mother Philippa was Charles of Egmond's sister.[42] Anthoine's claim was therefore based on blood-ties rather than on
territory and tradition, and he too made for a logical heir. Meanwhile,
Charles V also saw clear benefits in holding this area.[43] A solution to
avoid potential conflicts that could be caused by numerous parties chas-
ing after the Guelders lands was that John III would give up his claim
in favour of his daughter Anne, and that the Duke of Lorraine would do
the same for his son; their children could then marry, and the inheritance would stay 'in the family'. And so it was decided. The opening of
the charter introduces the main parties binding themselves through the
document:

> Wir Anthoni herβog zu Valabrien Lothringen und Bar marggrave
> Marggrave Zu Pontamessen Grave zu Provenβe und Widdemont *etc.*
> Unnd van derselber gnaden Wir Johann herβogh zu Cleve Guylich
> und Bergh Grave zu der Marke unnd zu Ravennsbergh *etc.* Auch wir
> Maria gebornn van Guylich herβoginne zu Cleve . . .[44]

---

[41] An accessible introduction to the background of this 'deal' can be found in Norton,
Anne of Cleves, 13.

[42] They are mentioned as siblings in: J.A.E. Kuijs, 'Catharina van Gelre (geb.
Omstreeks 1440—gest. Geldern 25-1-1497', *Digitaal Vrouwenlexicon van Nederland* (Den
Haag: Instituut voor Nederlandse Geschiedenis, 2007), http://hdl.handle.net/2066/
43877.

[43] He would eventually do so following the Treaty of Venlo in 1543. See, Van Schaïk,
'Taxation, Public Finances and the State-Making Process', 256. Note that Charles of
Egmond had been an agent for Francis I at the time of the imperial election. For the
charter formalizing this appointment, see: GldA 0001–2042: 'Akte waarbij Frans I, koning van Frankrijk hertog Karel benoemt tot zijn gevolmachtigd vertegenwoordiger bij de
keurvorsten van het Duitse Rijk, 1519.01.16. 1 charter'. https://permalink.geldersarchief.nl/
518364546BA34A3A891EBB7ED014989F. This appointment is referred to in J.E.A.L. Struick, *Gelre en Habsburg, 1492–1528* (Utrecht: Smits, 1960), 267. See also Struick's Chapter 5
for the relations between Guelders and the Habsburgs during the years 1524–28.

[44] GldA 0001–1791. Readers wishing to consult the original charter using the link
above who are unused to reading this type of document in (Low) German are pointed
towards a helpful introduction to German palaeography offered by the Staatlichen
Archive Bayerns, München, titled 'Digitale Schriftkunde'. https://www.gda.bayern.de/
DigitaleSchriftkunde/index.html. Note that 'marggrave' is repeated in the charter, but not
in Bouterwek.

[We, Anthoine, Duke of Calabria, Duke of Lorraine, and Marquess of Bar, Marquess of Pont-à-Mousson, Count of Provence and
Vaudémont *etc*. And by the same grace, We John Duke of Cleves,
Jülich and Berg, Count of Mark and of Ravensberg *etc*. Also we Maria
born of Jülich, Duchess of Cleves . . .].

Here again, we see that Renée de Bourbon-Montpensier was not
included. It is also interesting to note that Anne's mother, Maria, was
both represented by her current title of '*herβoginne zu Cleve*' [Duchess
of Cleves], as well as being referred to by the house of her birth:
'*Guylich*' [Jülich]. Her family background was important to emphasize
given that the potential inheritance of Guelders relied on the Jülich
connection.

The charter next introduces Charles of Egmond's role in the agreement ('*Durch . . . mittel deβ hochgebornen fürsten. Unnsers beson-
dern lieben Dhu[?]es Nevens unnd Swagers hernn Carls herβogenn
zu Gheldernen etc*').[45] [Through the high-born prince, our especially
beloved Duke(?) Nephew/Cousin and Brother-in-law Lord Charles
Duke of Guelders]. Here the word '*Nevens*' [nephew, or cousin] is
indicative of the family relationship between Charles and Anthoine.
The word '*Swager*' [literally: 'brother-in-law'] should be read more
loosely in this context; technically, Charles was not a brother-in-
law to any of the other parties involved. He was not married to a
sister of any of the parties, nor was he a brother to any of their
wives. Here the more distant understanding of a remote relative
applies.[46] The relative vagueness of the term is useful within the
context of the charter, as it enables Anthoine of Lorraine and the
parents of Anne of Cleves to present themselves as equals in their
relationships to Charles of Egmond, and does not prioritize the Lorraine party over the Cleves party, nor by implication, the Lorraine
claim over Charles's territories above the claim to these lands by
Cleves.

---

[45] GldA 0001–1791. Note that 'hernn' here is fashioned with a flourish rather than a
diacritical mark or abbreviation.

[46] DWDS clarifies for 'Schwager, der': 'Noch bis zum 18. Jh. kann Schwager jeden
angeheirateten männlichen Verwandten bezeichnen'. See: *DWDS—Digitales Wörterbuch
der deutschen Sprache. Das Wortauskunftssystem zur deutschen Sprache in Geschichte und
Gegenwart,* hrsg. v. d. Berlin-Brandenburgischen Akademie der Wissenschaften, https://
www.dwds.de/.

As for the bride and groom, Anne and Francis were not direct heirs to the Guelders lands, but the point of the whole exercise was that through this agreement they *would be*. Thus the charter makes overt the relationship between Athoine, John, and Maria with the future bride and groom. Anne and Francis are referred to as '*unnser beider kinderen*' [children of us both], and the charter documents their respective places in their parents' households, relevant for the transaction that was to follow: Anthoine's son is documented to have carried the '*Marggrave*' [Marquess] title and his being the Duke of Lorraine eldest son is given prominence in the charter ('*aldsten Sone Franciscus Marggraven*'). The *herβog* and *herβogynne* of Cleves specifically note that they offer in marriage 'another and second daughter, Anna' ('*anderer unnd zweiter dochter Anna*'),[47] rather than their first-born daughter Sibylle, who had married John Frederick I of Saxony in February 1527.[48] Nowhere in the charter do either Anne or Francis affirm or agree to what was decided; they are only spoken about. This is completely in line with their not being represented by individual seals attached to the charter. Here it is good to remember that, although Anne's later prominence as a Tudor consort may lead present-day readers to approach the charter with the assumption that she would have been one of the key players in the Lorraine–Cleves agreement, in 1527 Anne was only 11 years old and her groom-to-be Francis was even younger.

Seals: Leaving an impression

Turning to the seals as material objects reveals that the heraldic depictions found pressed into the wax tell an eloquent story about the territorial powers and connections between the stakeholders in the agreement.[49] They thus represent a visual type of 'documentation' in their own right, complementing and consolidating the written words in the charter that state the names, statuses, and lands of the

[47] GldA 0001–1791.
[48] Frieling, 'Dressing the Bride', 86.
[49] For an introduction to heraldry I refer readers to the old but still useful: Joseph Edmondson, *A Complete Body of Heraldry*, vol. 1 (London, 1780), from 161 onwards; Kathryn James, *English Paleography and Manuscript Culture: 1500–1800* (New Haven, CT: Yale University Press, 2020), 200–3 on heraldry, and 204–6 on charters and deeds.

parties involved, as well as the relationships between these parties when applicable.

Anthoine's seal is by far the largest of the four—its diameter an impressive 100 mm—and pictorially the most spectacular (see Figure 5.3).[50] The seal, circular in form, depicts on its obverse side an armoured man on horseback wearing a helmet, raising a sword in one of his hands, and a shield in the other displaying the Lorraine arms, which are also represented on the horse's caparison. The stance of the body in the design is reminiscent of depictions of knights at a tourney, such as, for example, the *seigneur appellant* [lord appellant][51] in the *Traité de la forme et devis comme on peut faire les tournois* preserved in BnF MS Français 2695 (see Figure 5.4).[52] Minute details in the seal's design have been preserved, allowing us to observe the horse's fine plumed headdress, and the saddle sticking out underneath the man's leg. Susan M. Johns, although discussing an earlier century, importantly remarks that 'on the seals of male nobility the equestrian figure was the most enduring and dominant form of iconography which symbolized 'feudal lordship'.[53] And it is good to keep in mind here that although Anthoine's seal is notably different from the three others associated with this particular charter, it was completely conventional, even to the extent of using red wax on which to make its impression.[54] Around the seal's edges the inscription (or legend) can be seen. The inscription is difficult to read as it is rather worn in places, but it can be reconstructed as: '+ ANTHONIID 6 CALABR L[OTHO]R ET BAR DVC[I] PONTIS MON MARQ PVIE VAVDEMON COM[ITIS]'.[55] The other, reverse side of the seal reveals

[50] GldA 0001–1791/1. https://permalink.geldersarchief.nl/86D4C2368CF24A0B94CD 5B1EBFC7AA7C.

[51] In the joust a seigneur appellant would combat a seigneur defendant. See for example, *Traictié de la forme et devis d'ung tournoy* (*A Treatise on the Form and Organization of a Tournament*), *King René's Tournament Book*, ed. Elizabeth Bennett (1998), Princeton. https://www.princeton.edu/~ezb/rene/compare.html.

[52] BnF MS Français 2695, e.g., fol. 45v and fol. 101r. https://gallica.bnf.fr/ark:/12148/ btv1b84522067.

[53] Susan M. Johns, *Noblewomen, Aristocracy and Power in the Twelfth-century Anglo-Norman Realm* (Manchester: Manchester University Press, 2003), 122.

[54] See also, Johns, *Noblewomen, Aristocracy and Power*, 125 and 137.

[55] 'Of Anthony Duke of Calabria, Lorraine, and Bar, Marquess of Pont-à-Mousson Count of Provence and Vaudémont'. The word '*sigillum*' [seal] is implied in front of the name. Please note that my reading of the inscription differs from the interpretation suggested by Gelders Archief: https://permalink.geldersarchief.nl/

a counterseal,[56] a phenomenon defined by Johns as 'the application of a further distinct impression from a smaller seal to the reverse of the impression of the (great) seal', which she notes, 'added extra authentication to documents'.[57] Anthoine's counterseal does not bear a textual inscription. It does, however, show an angel holding up a shield that represents the same arms as those found on the other side of the seal.[58]

Although perhaps in some ways less visually dramatic than Anthoine's, the other three seals are certainly not less revealing in what they sought to communicate. As seen in Figure 5.5, Egmond's seal with an intersection of 64 mm is notably smaller than both Lorraine's and that of the Duke of Cleves. The text encircling the seal, where preserved, reads: 'SIGILLVM KAROLI DVCIS GELRIE COMITIS ZVTPHANIE'.[59] The seal displays *escutcheons* [shields] with the two *lions rampant* of the arms of Guelders, facing one another. The two jousting helmets shown above the shields are elaborately decorated; one with a crown and one with a feathered elevation.

It is worth comparing Egmond's seal to a representation of the arms of Guelders in BnF, Bibliotheque de l'Arsenal MS 4790 réserve (see Figure 5.6). In the latter image, the forms of the lions' tails are more visibly defined, and we can recognize one of the *lions rampant* in the Guelders' arms to underscore their historical alliance with the house of Jülich (Gold, with a black lion, a red tongue, and red claws).

John of Cleves's seal (see Figure 5.7) has a diameter of 85 mm, and reads around its edge: 'SIGILLV. D.NI. IOHA] NNIS/ DVCIS

86D4C2368CF24A0B94CD5B1EBFC7AA7C. My reconstruction of the legend as comparative material uses the pictorial representation of the complete seal and counterseal of Anthoine of Lorraine from: Augustin Calmet, *Histoire de Lorraine qui comprend ce qui s'est passé de plus memorable dans l'Archevêché de Tréves, & dans les Evêchés de Metz, Toul & Verdun, depuis l'entrée de Jules César dans les Gaules, jusqu'à la Cession de la Lorraine, arrivée en 1737, Inclusivement* (Nancy, 1748), vol. 2, vii.

[56] GldA 0001-1791/1C. https://permalink.geldersarchief.nl/FB71C2227DAB4E44B1A04BD1C078E940.

[57] Johns, *Noblewomen, Aristocracy and Power*, 132. Note that although Johns refers to an earlier time in her work, the practices cited here are still applicable in the context studied in this chapter.

[58] Note that this is the only of the four seals attached to the document to display a formal counterseal. The reverse sides of the other seals show simple notches made into the wax.

[59] 'Seal of Charles Duke of Gelders Count of Zutphen'. For an image of the seal which enables close study, and a transcription of the inscription: GldA 0001-1791/2. https://permalink.geldersarchief.nl/5813C22607D2433CB4CC858A4D646821.

FIGURE 5.3 Gelders Archief: 0001-1791, Seal of Anthoine of Lorraine, attached to the 'Arnhem charter' (photograph by the author).

Source gallica.bnf.fr / Bibliothèque nationale de France. Département des Manuscrits. Français 2695

FIGURE 5.4 Reproduced with permission from: Bibliothèque nationale de France, Département des Manuscrits. MS Français 2695, fol. 45v.

FIGURE 5.5 Gelders Archief: 0001-1791, Seal of Charles of Egmond, and a fragment of the seal of John III of Cleves, attached to the 'Arnhem charter' (photograph by the author).

Source gallica.bnf.fr / Bibliothèque nationale de France. Bibliothèque de l'Arsenal. Ms-4790 réserve

FIGURE 5.6 Reproduced with permission from: Bibliothèque nationale de France, Bibliothèque de l'Arsenal, MS 4790 réserve, fol. 42v.

FIGURE 5.7 Gelders Archief: 0001-1791, Seal of John of Cleves, attached to the 'Arnhem charter' (photograph by the author).

CLIVENSIS. IVLIE ET MONTENSIS: COMITIS MARCKENS. ET. RAVENSBVRGENSIS. ETC'.[60] The representations on the seal display the heraldic history of the merging of the lands of the houses of Mark-Cleves and Jülich-Berg after the duke's marrying Maria of Jülich-Berg; it represents five *escutcheons* [shields] each crowned with an elevation. The *escutcheons* display an *escarbuncle* [carbuncle; wheel-like construction] for Cleves,[61] the lion of Jülich—which as we have already seen, was a heraldic symbol he shared with Charles of Egmond—and a crowned lion with a forked tail for Berg.[62] And two of the *escutcheons* contain *ordinaries* [geometric figures], one displaying a *fess* [horizontal stripe] with *charges* [emblems] in the form of three check-like rows for Mark, and one depicting three *chevrons* [roof-like stripe pointing upwards] for Ravensberg. Again, decorated helmets are displayed above the shields, and the one at the top right (for Berg) can be seen to sport magnificently preserved peacock feathers.[63]

The fourth seal, belonging to Maria of Jülich-Berg (see Figure 5.8), has an intersection of 50 mm. It depicts an *escutcheon* held up, as if hugged, by two small hands on either side. The shield is divided in four compartments. Sections 1 and 4 represent a lion for Jülich, and sections 2 and 3 show a crowned lion with a double tail for Berg. At the centre of the *escutcheon* we find another representation of a small shield

---

[60] 'Seal of the lord [note: "D.NI" is a title abbreviation, in which "D" stands for "Dominus"] John Duke of Cleves, Jülich and Berg: Count of Mark. And Ravensberg, etc.' For an image of the seal which enables close study, and a transcription of the inscription: https://permalink.geldersarchief.nl/807C8C73F68D4FEC8B975B7493E23EE6.

[61] Henry Gough, *A Glossary of Terms used in Heraldry* (Oxford and London, 1894), 238.

[62] From the quality of the seal it is difficult to establish whether a *lion rampant* (holding up two front legs, and lifting a third leg a bit lower) or a *lion passant* (as if walking, holding up one leg) is represented. To compare, a manuscript image of John of Cleves's crest from the Münchener Digitale Bibliothek can be consulted. Bayerische Staatsbibliothek, München Cod.icon. 326: *Wappen der zu Regensburg zur Reichsversammlung 1594 anwesenden Fürsten* (Regensburg?, 1594), image 71. https://daten.digitale-sammlungen.de/~db/0001/bsb00011882/images/index.html?seite=71&fip=193.174.98.30. The helmet with the peacock feathers is well-turned out in the manuscript image, and confirms what we see in the seal. Note that where the heraldic images are combined in one shield in the manuscript image, the *escarbuncle* of Cleves sits in the top middle, whereas when each symbol is presented in a separate shield in the wax seal, the *escarbuncle* is shown in the top left shield.

[63] GldA 0001–1791/3. https://permalink.geldersarchief.nl/807C8C73F68D4FEC8B975B7493E23EE6.

FIGURE 5.8 Gelders Archief: 0001-1791, Seal of Maria of Jülich-Berg, attached to the 'Arnhem charter' (photograph by the author).

with three chevrons in reference to Ravensberg. Interestingly, where the seals of Anthoine, Charles and John bear inscriptions in the Latin genitive form following, or at times, implying the word '*sigillum*' [seal], as is often seen in legends on seals, Maria's inscription is written in Low German. It reads: 'MARIE GEBORE HERTOCHIN ZU GVILG VN BERG ETC. CLEIF VN GRAIVINE ETC.'[64] Just as in the charter text the patronymic reference to the prestige of her family is prominently presented, taking precedence before the title associated with her marriage. The placing of the word '*graivine*' [countess] in the seal's inscription may, however, pose a question of interpretation, as on her husband's seal, John III is presented as '*comitis*' [count] of Mark and Ravensburg, but as '*ducis*' [duke] of Cleves, Jülich, and Berg. We may therefore expect

---

[64] 'Maria born duchess of Jülich and Berg, etc. of Cleves, a countess, etc.' For an image of the seal which enables close study, and a transcription of the inscription: GldA 0001-1791/4. https://permalink.geldersarchief.nl/7B3CD7DB2D7A4F058B6C341CA8A8CD7E.

Maria to be presented as *duchess* of Cleves, also in line with the language used to describe Maria in the charter: '*Auch wir Maria gebornn van Guylich herβoginne zu Cleve*'.[65] But it is possible that the word '*Cleif*' in the inscription should be read as connected to '*Hertochin*' [duchess], and that '*graivine: + ETC*' may represent the lands thus far omitted in the inscription but present in the heraldic design in the seal: that is, Ravensberg.

In *The Marrying of Anne of Cleves*, Retha Warnicke—presumably—follows Vice-Chancellor's Olisleger in his statement that the 1527 documents of 5 and 13 June were 'signed off' by 'the dukes of Lorraine, Jülich-Cleves and Guelders', omitting the participation of Anne's mother in the agreement.[66] However, I have here shown that returning to the original charter gives a fuller appreciation of the parties involved, their agency, and their self-representation. It was significant that Anne's parents co-sealed the document, and that the duke of Lorraine did not, and did not need to, involve his wife in this transaction. Furthermore, as we have seen from Maria of Jülich-Berg's seal, her self-representation proudly advertised the identity and territorial claims of the family in which she was born, and served as a manifestation of the agency she could exercise, and from which her husband, and children, could enjoy the benefits.

Beyond Bouterwek

We have in this chapter focused on the historical value and implications of the Arnhem charter of 1527, but within the context of this book it is worth briefly returning to its methodological value. The text of the Arnhem charter can be seen to bear close resemblance to a transcription produced by Bouterwek in 1867.[67] He may have studied the same charter copy as the one that I consulted at the Gelders Archief in Arnhem, or he may have based his transcription on the copy of the charter written out for Anne's parents, or on the one belonging to the Duke of Lorraine.[68] When comparing the original charter text to the transcription prepared

[65] GldA 0001–1791.
[66] Warnicke, *Anne of Cleves*, 81.
[67] Bouterwek, 'Anna von Cleve', 385–91.
[68] I have not been able to find a location for these two charters.

by Bouterwek, the differences that can be detected are largely cosmetic, where he probably wanted to render the text easier to read for his contemporary, German-language audience. It is, however, also possible that these in part represent scribal differences between two different versions of the charter.

By addressing the materiality of the Arnhem charter, the 1527 agreement becomes more accessible as a source to scholars of Tudor studies. As we have seen, the significance of the original charter at Arnhem as a material object in part lies in the wealth of information that can be inferred from it—about the parties involved, their status, and territorial relevance, and the nature of the 'transaction' that the charter represented—before we even read a word of the language in which it was written. And indeed, the meaning of the charter as an object performing identity in conjunction with the written text it holds (but also separately from this text), its information transcending linguistic boundaries, would have been exactly why Anne of Cleves, when she realized that Henry was adamant in his wish for a divorce, did not actively pursue access to this document. Its physical attributions would have made it more than evident that the Lorraine agreement had not been an impediment to Henry's own marriage to Anne, and would thus have stood in the way of a divorce.

Anne of Cleves' 'place' in historical narratives appears to have been shaped by a number of decisions made by those writing about her, all of which are symptomatic of larger questions of both the accessibility and the treatment of source information. Bluntly said, one may argue that the Anne of Cleves-shaped hole in Tudor history was caused by both a lack of accessible sources,[69] and scholarly dismissal of Anne herself

---

[69] For Anne's accounts as queen, see TNA E101/422/15 and TNA E101/422/16. English-language source material on Anne is scant, due to the brevity of her marriage to Henry VIII, so that scholarship does not have the benefit of years' worth of traces of a queen's presence and activity—in financial accounts such as the Tudor Chamber Books, choices of style in Great Wardrobe accounts, or accounts of her participation in courtly activity in, for example, ambassadorial reports, or international correspondence, among other sources helpful to studying queenship. Recent popular historian work on Anne of Cleves has not always recognized the limitations posed by the extant material, and has sometimes sought to extensively flesh out their narrative by providing generalist backgrounds on the political manoeuvres of Anne's family, religion, and general customs at court, such as for example, in the recent commercial biography by Heather R. Darsie, *Anna, Duchess of Cleves* (Stroud: Amberley, 2019).

as largely politically irrelevant.[70] But we have seen in this chapter that new source material is still resurfacing, and also that making political decisions, or indeed, having any kind of socio-political impact, can take different forms. The Arnhem charter proves that contrary to what has previously been thought, Maria of Jülich-Berg, Anne of Cleves's mother, had a clear voice in the 1527 agreement. And by not urging that a copy of this agreement was shared with Henry, Anne made an informed decision affecting her status, personal wealth, and also her well-being. Indeed, history would have presented a different narrative if she had *not* granted Henry his annulment.

---

[70] Anne's having been 'overlooked in studies of Henry VIII and his wives' is addressed in Schutte, 'Anne of Cleves in Book and Manuscript', 123. Anne is called a 'diplomatic footnote' in David Loades, *The Tudor Queens of England* (London: Continuum, 2009), 112. References to Anne of Cleves in scholarship have for a long time carried an implicit, undermining, light mocking tone, betraying a line of thinking that has become engrained in ways in which 'history' has treated Anne of Cleves. For example, see the hyperbole in Rory McEntegart, *Henry VIII, the League of Schmalkalden and the English Reformation* (Woodbridge: Royal Historical Society: The Boydell Press, 2002), 191: 'That is to say, ten days after Henry's disastrous meeting with Anne at Rochester, four days after their wedding, and just three days after Henry's revelations as to *how Anne had terrorised him so in the nuptial bed*' (emphasis added). It should be noted here that even Henry VIII's less than complimentary references to the marital bed did not invite this emotive choice of words in scholarship.

Afterword

This book has set out to trace how Henry VIII's court—in all its 'Englishness'—responded to, and was shaped by, transcultural exchanges. The project was sparked by my coming across a document preserved at the Archivo General de Simancas (AGS), Valladolid, from 1503, which had been categorized by the archive as *'ayuda de costa a Alonso de Valdenebro y otro por su ida a Inglaterra'*,[1] [gratification on top of a salary given to Alonso de Valdenebro and another for his going to England]. The 'other' (*'otro'*) in question refers to Francisco de Dueñas, *atabalero* [kettle drummer]. That the trumpeter and drummer had been to England with Katherine of Aragon piqued my interest and struck me as an intriguing starting point to revisit what we already knew about Katherine's entourage, and about the formalities and festivities surrounding her marriage to Arthur Tudor. De Baeza's financial accounts and similar sources of information, such as Morales's *Data*, were read alongside the English-language Tudor Chamber Books and Records of Early English Drama as a way to cross-reference the evidence, and to fill hiatuses typically found in financial records such as these, which were, first and foremost, practical documents managing money, in which account takers were seen to be economical with their words, as well as displaying what they either experienced as 'normative' or 'regular', or what they assumed was necessary for conveying the information in the record in a usable way, in which case their choices may have catered for the understanding or biases of other users of the accounts. We have seen this, for example, in the English Chamber Book accounts not distinguishing between those on the payroll of Queen Isabella of Castile and those in the service of King Ferdinand of Aragon; all were referred to as 'Spanish'. Furthermore, hiatuses can be found

---

[1] MINISTERIO DE CULTURA Y DEPORTE Archivo General de Simancas, Cámara de Castilla, CCA, CED, 6, 101, 4 (15 May 1503), available at: http://pares. mcu.es/ParesBusquedas20/catalogo/description/2313716?nm [Accessed 20.05.2020]. In Chapter 1, *Cuentas* vol. 2, 583 was cited to refer to this transaction.

Intercultural Explorations and the Court of Henry VIII. Nadia T. van Pelt, Oxford University Press.
© Nadia T. van Pelt (2024). DOI: 10.1093/oso/9780192863447.003.0006

which suggest a lack of information. The payment to the musical staff working for the 'Erle of Spayne' in Records of Early English Drama suggests that maybe the account taker either did not know the name of the earl [the Conde de Cabra, as we saw in Chapters 1 and 3], or possibly, that only his rank mattered to keep a sufficiently workable record of the payment. We have also seen the obscuring of information within collective payments, in which a drummer, or, in the Castilian accounts, *atabalero*, may be found in a list of trumpet players.

Cross-referencing the English and Castilian financial records has furthermore prompted the discovery that, behind the Anglophone payment record, material evidence of persons of African descent might be obscured by records of group payments. And, at a methodological level, I found that there is a strong likelihood that the presence of more persons of African descent will be encountered in the Tudor court if the English material is systematically cross-referenced with Francophone Burgundian and Spanish material. Thus we saw that, prior to the arrival in the English court records of the now-famous Black trumpeter John Blanke, another trumpet player of African descent, Alonso (or Alfonso) de Valdenebro, can be identified to have performed at the court of Henry VII.[2]

These initial findings have informed the general approach of this book in which the research is based on a wide range of primary and secondary sources extending beyond the Anglophone material to which much of the scholarship on the court of Henry VIII has relied. The performativity of court life has formed the thematic backbone to the book. Across its five chapters, court musicians, court fools, food, dress, and the use of seals have been studied. These aspects of court life may seem peripheral to some readers, but I have shown their potential to help unwrap major political issues and dynamics. For example, we saw in Chapter 1 that court musicians moved across Europe, representing their royal patrons at moments of ceremony and celebration.

---

[2] An observation, as acknowledged in Chapter 1, shared also in Tess Knighton's work on early music, in which she noted Alonso to be 'one of four trumpeters who travelled to England with Katherine of Aragon in 1501'. Tess Knighton, 'Instruments, Instrumental Music and Instrumentalists: Traditions and Transitions', in Tess Knighton, ed., *Companion to Music in the Age of the Catholic Monarchs* (Leiden: Brill, 2017), 97–144 (116).

The relationships between patron and performer were based on trust and, at times, strong family ties. Sometimes musicians joined a court on a more permanent basis after having spent time there as visitors. In such cases, an earlier-established connection could be banked upon by a current patron, such as when Henry VIII sent John de Cecil to accompany Lord Darcy's visit to Ferdinand of Aragon under the auspices of the 'African war'. De Cecil's having previously worked for Ferdinand would have been a valuable diplomatic asset. Also in line with unpacking political issues through the study of aspects of court life, fools, studied in Chapter 2, have been recognized for their abilities and functions beyond bringing fun and entertainment, either as potential intelligencers, or as household officials able to make or contribute to political matters. For example, we have seen that a fool might stand in for an ambassador, as demonstrated by Chapuys's fool when the Imperial Ambassador was denied access to Katherine of Aragon at Kimbolton. Fools might also complement an act of political or diplomatic solidarity, as evidenced by Chapuys's fool's presence at Katherine of Aragon's deathbed.

Food, in Chapter 3, has been recognized as a major element in diplomacy. Banquets in the context of the European courts were 'multimedia' events comprising all manner of entertainment, and culinary, visual and auditory delights, alongside an intricate web of semi-scripted human interactions. Examples such as that of Henry VIII, Charles V and Katherine of Aragon sharing a hand-washing basin reveal the intricacy of the levels of ritual and expectation attached to seemingly basic aspects of court behaviour. Also, turning to the banqueting house in Calais, Chapter 3 demonstrated the scriptedness of the banquet as an event, as well as its being fashioned to cater for spectatorship. Participants at the banquet would have been visually delighted by all there was to absorb in terms of splendour and entertainment, but the builders of the banqueting house also erected lofts from which non-participants could watch the festivities below. The political and diplomatic value of narratives of such shared events cannot be underestimated, and it is clear that this was facilitated by the court in numerous ways, including as we have seen here, through the architectural design of a temporary construction made for an international encounter.

Chapter 4 has turned to dress as it was worn to 'self-fashion', but also as it was reported in letters and chronicle texts. It appears that Anne of

Cleves may have arrived at a court where her style of clothing was associated with fools' livery. Importantly, readings of her attire should be considered within a wider context of ambassadors and other account takers commenting on foreign brides, to show that these accounts are incredibly revealing of this genre, more so than about Anne of Cleves's personal 'looks'. Chapter 5, continuing to address the much-overlooked Anne of Cleves, returned 'ad fontes' to a charter kept at the Gelders Archief in Arnhem.[3] The charter details the marital agreement between Anne and Francis de Lorraine and provides insights into her premarital life and her mother's important voice in the Lorraine match. Anne of Cleves's not bringing up the charter as evidence when she found that Henry VIII sought a divorce furthermore suggests her astute understanding of marital politics at the English court.

Apart from a focus on the performativity of court culture and a cross-language and transnational approach, this book has presented an interdisciplinary contribution to interpreting and at times reconstructing the habits and customs which underpinned and determined court culture, including ceremony and ritual. I have sought to renew perspectives or to arrive at source material from non-traditional angles in the hope of sparking fresh discussions and yielding alternative understandings. The methodological lenses or foci employed can be used to supplement current dominant approaches to Tudor history, and the great value of more systematically using, for example, Food History or Sartorial Studies, is underlined. The major conclusion of the book therefore concerns its methodology: aiming to give a nuanced account of English matters from a variety of European perspectives, the readings in this book function as demonstrations of what Tudor scholarship has, at times, missed out on, and suggest further avenues that can be explored. The outcomes of these chapters suggest that the Henrician court was a space of transcultural encounters; a place significantly in touch with the wider world.

[3] I am grateful to the anonymous reviewers at Oxford University Press for their recognition of my work returning 'ad fontes', and borrow their phrasing here.

BIBLIOGRAPHY

Primary sources

Anderson, J.J., ed., *Records of Early English Drama: Newcastle upon Tyne* (Toronto: University of Toronto Press, 1982).

Archivo General de Simancas, Cámara de Castilla.

Archivo General de Simancas, Patronato Real, Capitulaciones con Inglaterra.

Archivo General de Simancas, Real Cancillería de los Reyes de Castilla.

Armin, Robert, *Foole vpon Foole, or Six Sortes of Sottes* (London, 1600; STC (2nd edn.): 772.3), Early English Books Online, https://eebo.chadwyck.com/home

Ashbee, Andrew, ed., *Records of English Court Music: 1485–1558*, volume 7 (London: Routledge, 1993).

Bayerische Staatsbibliothek (München), Cod.icon. 326: *Wappen der zu Regensburg zur Reichsversammlung 1594 anwesenden Fürsten* ([Regensburg?], 1594), https://daten.digitale-sammlungen.de/~db/0001/bsb00011882/images/index.html?seite=71&fip=193.174.98.30

Bergenroth, G. A., et al., eds., *Calendar of State Papers, Spain* (19 vols; London, 1862– 1954).

Beschreibung der einreittung Auch Krönung des Großmechtigsten Fürsten vnd Römischen Könings Caroli des fünften mit sampt aller andern Fürsten vnd herrn einreitten jetz Neülich beschehen zu Ach in Niderlandt im Jar Christi. M.vc.xx. (Mainz, 1520; BL General Reference Collection 1315.c.18), British Library 'Treasures in Full: Renaissance Festival Books', https://www.bl.uk/treasures/festivalbooks/BookDetails.aspx?strFest=0079

Bibliothèque Nationale de France, Bibliotheque de l'Arsenal MS 4790 réserve. ark:/12148/btv1b55009806h

Bibliothèque Nationale de France, MS Français 2695, https://gallica.bnf.fr/ark:/12148/btv1b84522067

Blatcher, Marjorie, ed., *Report on the Manuscripts of the Most Honourable The Marquess of Bath Preserved at Longleat, Volume IV: Seymour Papers, 1532–1686* (London: Her Majesty's Stationary Office, 1968).

Bouterwek, K.W., 'Anna von Cleve, Gemahlin Heinrichs uiij, Königs von England', *Zeitschrift des Bergischen Geschichtsvereins*, volume 4 (Bonn, 1867), 337–413.

Brewer, J.S., J. Gairdner, R.H. Brodie, eds., *Letters and Papers, Foreign and Domestic, of the Reign of Henry VIII* (21 vols. in 32 parts; London, 1862–1932).

British Library, Add MS 5016, http://www.bl.uk/manuscripts/FullDisplay.aspx?ref=Add_MS_5016

British Library, Arundel MS 249.

British Library, Cotton Ch X 13, http://www.bl.uk/manuscripts/FullDisplay.aspx?ref=Cotton_Ch_X_13

British Library, Cotton MS Otho C X, http://www.bl.uk/manuscripts/Viewer.aspx?ref=cotton_ms_otho_c_x_fs001r

British Library, Cotton MS Vitellius B XXI, http://www.bl.uk/manuscripts/Viewer.aspx?ref=cotton_ms_vitellius_b_xxi_fs001r

British Library, Harley MS 279.

British Library, Harley MS 4217, http://www.bl.uk/manuscripts/Viewer.aspx?ref=harley_ms_4217_fs001r

British Library, Sloane MS 1047, http://www.bl.uk/manuscripts/Viewer.aspx?ref=sloane_ms_1047_fs001r

British Library, Stowe MS 557: 'Inventory of the royal wardrobe, 1600', http://www.bl.uk/manuscripts/FullDisplay.aspx?ref=Stowe_MS_557

Brown, Rawdon, et al., eds., *Calendar of State Papers Relating To English Affairs in the Archives of Venice* (38 vols; London, 1864–1947).

Bruyn the Elder, Bartolomaeus, 'Anne of Cleves', St John's College, University of Oxford: https://www.sjc.ox.ac.uk/college-life/art/colleges-art-collection/

Burnet, Gilbert, *The History of the Reformation of the Church of England*, volume 1, part 1, 2nd edn. (London, 1681).

Calmet, Augustin, *Histoire de Lorraine qui comprend ce qui s'est passé de plus memorable dans l'Archevêché de Tréves, & dans les Evêchés de Metz, Toul & Verdun, depuis l'entrée de Jules César dans les Gaules, jusqu'à la Cession de la Lorraine, arrivée en 1737, Inclusivement*, volume 2 (Nancy, 1748).

Castaigne, Jean François Eusèbe, ed., *Entrées solennelles dans la ville d'Angoulême depuis François Ier jusqu'à Louis XIV* (Angoulême, 1856).

Calendar of the Cecil Papers in Hatfield House: Volume 1, 1306–1571 (London, 1883), *British History Online*, https://www.british-history.ac.uk/cal-cecil-papers/vol1

The Chamber Books of Henry VII and Henry VIII, 1485–1521, eds. M.M. Condon, S.P. Harper and L. Liddy, and S. Cunningham and J. Ross (Winchester: University of Winchester, 2017), https://www.tudorchamberbooks.org/

Castil-Blaze, *Chapelle-Musique des Rois de France* (Paris, 1832).

Cavendish, George, *The Life of Cardinal Wolsey*, ed. Samuel Weller Singer (London, 1827).

Cavendish, George, *The Life and Death of Thomas Woolsey, Cardinal, Once Arch Bishop of York and Lord Chancellour of England* (London, 1667; Wing: 1618), Early English Books Online, https://eebo.chadwyck.com/home

Cavendish, George, *The Negotiations of Thomas Woolsey, the Great Cardinall of England, Containing His Life and Death* (London, 1641; Wing: C1619aA), Early English Books Online, https://eebo.chadwyck.com/home

Cavendish, George, *The Negotiations of Thomas Woolsey, the Great Cardinall of England Containing his Life and Death* (London, 1650; Wing: C1619A), Early English Books Online, https://eebo.chadwyck.com/home

Chmel, Joseph, ed., *Die Handschriften der K.K. Hofbibliothek in Wien*, volume 2: *Handschriften* (Vienna, 1841).

Cimber, M.L., and F. Danjou, eds., *Archives curieuses de l'histoire de France*, ser. 1, volume 2 (Paris: Beauvais, Membre de L'Institut Historique, 1835).

La description et ordre du camp et festiement et ioustes des trescrestiens et tres puissans roys de France et Dangleterre (Paris, 1520), British Library 'Treasures in Full: Renaissance Festival Books', https://www.bl.uk/treasures/festivalbooks/BookDetails.aspx?strFest=0006

Douglas, Audrey, and Peter Greenfield, eds., *Records of Early English Drama: Cumberland/ Westmorland/ Gloucestershire* (Toronto: University of Toronto Press, 1986).

Edmondson, Joseph, *A Complete Body of Heraldry*, volume 1 (London, 1780).

Erasmus, Desiderius, *Colloquiorum Desiderii Erasmi Roterodami familiarium opus aureum. Cum scholiis quibusdam antehac non editis . . . etc.* (London, 1683).

Erasmus, Desiderius, *Moriae Encomium* (Paris: Jocodus Badius, 1519).

Finot, Jules, ed., *Collection des Inventaires des Archives Communales Antérieures a 1790*, volume 1, part 1 (Lille, 1899).

Finot, Jules, ed., *Collection des Inventaires des Archives Communales Antérieures a 1790*, volume 8 (Lille, 1895).

Gelders Archief (Arnhem), 0001–1791, 'Akte van huwelijksvoorwaarden tussen Frans I, hertog van Lotharingen en Anna van Kleef. 1 charter. Derde exemplar, bestemd voor hertog Karel als bemiddelaar', https://permalink.geldersarchief.nl/EF04470A01224E599BC3D91D7E5578B2

Gelders Archief (Arnhem), 0001–2042: 'Akte waarbij Frans I, koning van Frankrijk hertog Karel benoemt tot zijn gevolmachtigd vertegenwoordiger bij de keurvorsten van het Duitse Rijk, 1519.01.16. 1 charter', https://permalink.geldersarchief.nl/518364546BA34A3A891EBB7ED014989F

Gibson, James M., ed., *Records of Early English Drama: Kent* (3 vols; Toronto: University of Toronto Press, 2002).

Giuseppi, M.S., ed., *Calendar of the Cecil Papers in Hatfield House*, volume 17 (London, 1938).

Giustinian, Sebastian, *Four Years at the Court of Henry VIII*, ed. Rawdon Brown (2 vols; (London, 1854).

Gough, Henry, *A Glossary of Terms used in Heraldry* (Oxford and London, 1894).

Greenfield, Peter, and Jane Cowling, eds., *Records of Early English Drama: Hampshire* (2020), https://ereed.library.utoronto.ca/collections/hamps/.

Hall, Edward, *The Triumphant Reigne of Kyng Henry the* VIII, ed. Charles Whibley, volumes 1 and 2 (London: Jack, 1904).

Haus-, Hof-, und Staatsarchiv (Vienna), Staatenabteilungen, England, Berichte, Karton 7, 1535.

Hayward, Maria, ed., *The 1542 Inventory of Whitehall: The Palace and Its Keeper*, volume 2: *The Transcripts* (London: Illuminata Publishers for The Society of Antiquaries of London, 2004).

Here begynneth the boke of keruynge (London, 1508; Cambridge University Library, Sel.5.19.), University of Cambridge Digital Library, https://cudl.lib.cam.ac.uk/view/PR-SEL-00005-00019/1.

Holbein the Younger, Hans, 'Christina of Denmark, Duchess of Milan', National Gallery, London, 1538. https://www.nationalgallery.org.uk/paintings/hans-holbein-the-younger-christina-of-denmark-duchess-of-milan.

Holbein the Younger, Hans, 'Portrait d'Anne de Clèves (1515–1557), reine d'Angleterre, quatrième épouse de Henri VIII', Louvre, Paris, C. 1539. https://collections.louvre.fr/ark:/53355/cl010062615.

Holbein the Younger, Hans (studio of), 'Portrait of Jane Seymour (1509?–1537)', Mauritshuis, The Hague: https://www.mauritshuis.nl/en/our-collection/artworks/278-portrait-of-jane-seymour-1509-1537/.

Hume, Martin A. Sharp, ed. and trans., *Chronicle of King Henry VIII: Being a Contemporary Record of Some of the Principal Events in the Reigns Henry VIII and Edward VI. Written in Spanish by an unknown hand* (London: George Bell and Sons, 1889).

Ingram, R.W., ed., *Records of Early English Drama: Coventry* (Toronto: University of Toronto Press, 1981).

Jerdan, William, ed., *Rutland Papers: Original Documents Illustrative of the Courts and Times of Henry VII and Henry VIII, selected from the private archives of His Grace the Duke of Rutland* (London: Camden Society, 1842).

Kaulek, Jean, ed., *Correspondance Politique de Mm. de Castillon et de Marillac, Ambassadeurs de France en Angleterre (1537–1542)* (Paris, 1885).

Kipling, Gordon, ed., *The Receyt of the Ladie Kateryne*, Early English Text Society, Original Series 296 (Oxford: Oxford University Press, 1990).

Lacomblet, T.J., ed., *Urkundenbuch Für Die Geschichte Des Niederrheins Oder Des Erzstifts Cöln, Der Fürstenthümer Jülich Und Berg, Geldern, Meurs, Kleve Und Mark, Und Der Reichsstifte Elten, Essen Und Werden*, volume 4 (Düsseldorf, 1858).

Lalaing, Antoine de, *Collection des voyages des souverains des Pays-Bas*, ed. Louis Prosper Gachard, volume 1 (Brussels, 1876).

Leland, John, *Collectanea*, editio altera (6 vols; London, 1774).

Lentree de la royne a Ableville (Paris, 1514; Bibliothèque Mazarine, 8° 35476 [Res]), https://bibnum.institutdefrance.fr/ark:/61562/mz17916

Louis, Cameron, ed., *Records of Early English Drama: Sussex* (Toronto: University of Toronto Press, 2000).

Madden, Frederick, ed., *Privy Purse Expenses of the Princess Mary* (London, 1831).

Marche, Olivier de la, *Collection Complète des Mémoires Relatifs a l'Histoire de France: Olivier de la Marche*, volume 2 (Paris, 1825), *Gallica*, BnF, ark:/12148/bpt6k363643

Meredith, Peter, and John E. Tailby, eds., *The Staging of Religious Drama in Europe in the Later Middle Ages: Texts and Documents in English Translation* (Kalamazoo, MI, Medieval Institute Publications, 1983).

Mostaert, Jan Jansz, *Portret van een Onbekende Man* [Portrait of an Unknown Man], Rijksmuseum Amsterdam, C. 1525–1530. https://www.rijksmuseum. nl/nl/collectie/SK-A-4986

The National Archives, LC 2/1.

The National Archives, LC 9/50.

The National Archives, E101/417/2, #105; *Anglo-American Legal Tradition*, http://aalt.law.uh.edu/AALT7/E101/E101no0417/E101no0417no2/IMG_0158. htm

The National Archives, E101/417/6, #50; *Anglo-American Legal Tradition*, http://aalt.law.uh.edu/AALT7/E101/E101no0417/E101no0417no6/IMG_0161. htm

The National Archives, E101/417/6, #57 [filed a few documents further on]; *Anglo-American Legal Tradition*, http://aalt.law.uh.edu/AALT7/E101/ E101no0417/E101no0417no6/IMG_0169.htm

The National Archives, E101/424/7.

The National Archives, SP 46/8.

Nelson, Alan H., and John R., Elliott Jr, eds., *Records of Early English Drama: Inns of Court* (3 vols; Cambridge: D.S. Brewer, 2010).

Nichols, J.G. ed., *The Chronicle of Calais in the Reigns of Henry VII and Henry VIII, to the Year 1540* (London, 1846).

Nichols, J.G. ed., *Chronicle of the Grey Friars of London* (London, 1852).

Nicolas, Nicholas Harris, ed., *Privy Purse Expenses of Elizabeth of York: Wardrobe Accounts of Edward IV, with a Memoir of Elizabeth of York* (London, 1830).

Nicolas, Nicholas Harris, ed., *Privy Purse Expenses of King Henry VIII* (London, 1827).

Nijhoff, Isaak Anne, *Gedenkwaardigheden uit de geschiedenis van Gelderland: door onuitgegevene oorkonden opgehelderd en bevestigd*, volume 6.2: *Karel van Egmond, Hertog van Gelre, Graaf van Zutphen (1514–1528)* (Arnhem, 1862).

Noailles, Antoine de, *Ambassades de Messieurs de Noailles en Angleterre*, volume 2 (Paris, 1763).

Oviedo, Gonzalo Fernández de, *El libro de la cámara Real del Principe Don Juan e officios de su casa e servicio ordinario*, ed. J.M. Escudero de la Peña (Madrid: Sociedad de Bibliófilos Españoles, 1870).

Pilkinton, Mark C., ed., *Records of Early English Drama: Bristol* (Toronto: University of Toronto Press, 1997).

Pollard, A.F., ed., *The Reign of Henry VII from Contemporary Sources* (3 vols; London: Longmans, Green and Co., 1913–14).

Predis, Ambrogio de, 'Bianca Maria Sforza, probably 1493', National Gallery of Art, Washington, C. 1493. https://www.nga.gov/collection/art-object-page.1192.html#inscription.

Rincius, Bernardinus, *Le liure et forest de messire Bernardin Rince … conentant et explicant briefuement lappareil, les ieux, et le festin de la Bastille* (Paris, 1518; BL General Reference Collection DRT Digital Store 811.d.31.(1.), British Library 'Treasures in Full: Renaissance Festival Books', https://www.bl.uk/treasures/festivalbooks/BookDetails.aspx?strFest=0004

Rogers, Elizabeth Frances, ed., *The Correspondence of Sir Thomas More* (Princeton, NJ: Princeton University Press, 1947).

RUMEU DE ARMAS, Antonio, ed., *Itinerario de los Reyes Católicos, 1474–1516* (Madrid: Consejo Superior de Investigaciones Científicas, 1974).

Russell, John, *The Boke of Nurture Folowyng Englondis Gise … Edited from the Harleian MS. 4011 in the British Museum*, in Frederick J. Furnivall, ed., *Early English Meals and Manners*, EETS, o.s. 32, 1–112 (London: Oxford University Press, 1931; reprint of 1868 edn.)

Rymer, Thomas, *Foedera*, volume 15 (London, 1713).

S'ensuit l'ordre qui a este tenue a lentree de la royne a Abeville (1514?; Bibliothèque Mazarine, 8° 35478 [Res]), https://bibnum.institutdefrance.fr/ark:/61562/mz17411

Smollett, Tobias George, *A Complete History of England from the Descent of Julius Caesar to the Treaty of Aix la Chapelle*, volume 4, 3rd edn. (London, 1758; 1st edn. 1748).

Somerset, J. Alan B., ed., *Records of Early English Drama: Shropshire* (2 vols; Toronto: University of Toronto Press, 1994).

Sponsler, Claire, ed., *John Lydgate: Mummings and Entertainments* (Kalamazoo, MI: Medieval Institute Publications, 2010).

Stow, John, *Annales, or a General Chronicle of England*, ed. Edmund Howes (London, 1631).

Strickland, Agnes, *Lives of the Queens of England*, volume 4 (Philadelphia, 1847).

Strype, John, *Ecclesiastical Memorials*, volume 6: Appendix (London, 1816).

Testamento y Codicilo de Isabel la Católica (Madrid: Ministerio de Asuntos Exteriores, 1956).

Thomas, A.H., and I.D. Thornley, eds., *The Chronicle of London* (Gloucester: Alan Sutton, 1983).

Tomlins, T.E., and W.E. Taunton, eds., *Statutes of the Realm*, volume 3 (London, 1817).

TORRE, Antonio de la, ed., *La Casa de Isabel la Católica* (Madrid: Consejo Superior de Investigaciones Científicas, 1954).

TORRE, Antonio de la, and E.A. de la TORRE, eds., *Cuentas de Gonzalo de Baeza, Tesorero de Isabel la Católica* (2 vols; Madrid: Consejo Superior de Investigaciones Científicas, 1955–1956).

Traictié de la forme et devis d'ung tournoy (*A Treatise on the Form and Organization of a Tournament*), *King René's Tournament Book*, ed. Elizabeth Bennett (1998), Princeton, NJ.

The Traduction & Mariage of the Princesse (London: Richard Pynson, 1500; STC (2nd edn.)/ 4814), Early English Books Online, https://eebo.chadwyck.com/home

Tydeman, William, ed., *The Medieval European Stage, 500–1550* (Cambridge: Cambridge University Press, 2001).

Wasson, John M., ed., *Records of Early English Drama: Devon* (Toronto: University of Toronto Press, 1986).

Weiditz, Christoph, *Trachtenbuch*, Germanisches Nationalmuseum Digitale Bibliothek, Nürnberg, http://dlib.gnm.de/Hs22474/168

Westenrieder, Lorenz, ed., *Beyträge zur Vaterländischen Historie, Geographie, Statistie und Landwirthschaft*, volume 2 (München, 1789).

Wie vnd in wellicher gestalt Kay. May. von Bruck auss gen Lunden in Engeland gezogen/ ankommen und Empfangen worden ist (Augsburg, 1522; General Reference Collection DRT Digital Store C.33.e.3.), British Library 'Treasures in Full: Renaissance Festival Books', https://www.bl.uk/treasures/festivalbooks/BookDetails.aspx?strFest=0082

Wilson, Thomas, *The Arte of Rhetorike for the Vse of All Suche as are Studious of Eloquence, Sette Foorthe in Englishe, by Thomas Wilson. 1553* (London, 1584; STC (2nd edn.): 25805), Early English Books Online, https://eebo.chadwyck.com/home

Secondary sources

Ailes, Adrian, 'Machado, Roger [Ruy]', *Oxford Dictionary of National Biography*, Oxford University Press, 2004, https://doi.org/10.1093/ref:odnb/17527

Akkerman, Nadine, and Birgit Houben, eds., *The Politics of Female Households: Ladies-in-Waiting across Early Modern Europe* (Leiden: Brill, 2013).

Albala, Ken, *The Banquet: Dining in the Great Courts of Late Renaissance Europe* (Urbana and Chicago, IL: University of Illinois Press, 2007).

Albala, Ken, ed., *A Cultural History of Food in the Renaissance* (London and New York: Berg, 2012).

Andrés Díaz, Rosana de, *El ultimo decenio del reinado de Isabel I a través de la tresorería de Alonso de Morales (1495–1504)* (Valladolid: Secretariado de Publicaciones e Intercambio Editorial, Universidad de Valladolid, 2004).

Anglo, Sydney, 'Archives of the English Tournament: Score Cheques and Lists', *Journal of the Society of Archivists* 2:4 (1961), 153–62. https://doi.org/10.1080/00379816009513719

Anglo, Sydney, 'The Court Festivals of Henry VII: A Study Based Upon the Account Books of John Heron, Treasurer of the Chamber' *Bulletin of John Rylands Library* 43 (1960/1961), 12–45.

Anglo, Sydney, 'Financial and Heraldic Records of the English Tournament', *Journal of the Society of Archivists* 2:5 (1962), 183–95. https://doi.org/10.1080/00379816009513730

Anglo, Sydney, *The Great Tournament Roll of Westminster: A Collotype Reproduction of the Manuscript* (2 vols.; Oxford: Clarendon Press, 1968).

Anglo, Sydney, 'Ill of the Dead. The Posthumous Reputation of Henry VII', *Renaissance Studies* 1:1 (1987), 27–47. https://doi.org/10.1111/j.1477-4658.1987.tb00121.x

Anglo, Sydney, 'The London Pageants for the Reception of Katherine of Aragon: November 1501', *Journal of the Warburg and Courtauld Institutes* 26:1/2 (1963), 53–89. https://doi.org/10.2307/750570

Anglo, Sydney, 'William Cornish in a Play, Pageants, Prison, and Politics', *The Review of English Studies* 10:40 (1959), 347–60.

Aram, Bethany, 'Juana "the Mad's" Signature: The Problem of Invoking Royal Authority, 1505–1507', *Sixteenth Century Journal* 29:2 (1998), 331–58. https://doi.org/10.2307/2544520

Arnade, Peter, *Realms of Ritual: Burgundian Ceremony and Civic Life in Late Medieval Ghent* (Ithaca, NY, and London: Cornell University Press, 1996).

Aurell, Jaume, *Medieval Self-Coronations* (Cambridge: Cambridge University Press, 2020).

Aust, Cornelia, Denise Klein, and Thomas Weller, eds., *Dress and Cultural Difference in Early Modern Europe* (Berlin and Boston, MA: De Gruyter, 2019).

Backerra, Charlotte, and Peter Edwards, 'Introduction: Rank and Ritual in the Early Modern Court', *The Court Historian* 26:1 (2021), 1–10. https://doi.org/10.1080/14629712.2021.1887598

Bak, János M., ed., *Coronations: Medieval and Early Modern Monarchic Ritual* (Berkeley, CA: University of California Press, 1990).

Barker, Hannah, *That Most Precious Merchandise: The Mediterranean Trade in Black Sea Slaves, 1260–1500* (Philadelphia, PA: University of Pennsylvania Press, 2019).

Barnett, Eleanor, 'Reforming Food and Eating in Protestant England, c. 1560–c. 1640', *The Historical Journal* 63:3 (2020), 507–27. https://doi.org/10.1017/S0018246X19000426

Bauer, Thomas Alexander: Feiern unter den Augen der Chronisten. Die Quellentexte zur Landshuter Fürstenhochzeit von 1475. München 2008.

Bauer, Thomas Alexander, 'The Wedding of Duke Georg of Landshut in 1475—A Challenge for the Whole Town', *Terminus: Journal of Early Modern Literature and Culture* 11 (2009), 33–41.

Bedos-Rezak, Brigitte, 'In Search of a Semiotic Paradigm: The Matter of Sealing in Medieval Thought and Praxis (1050–1400)', in Noël Adams, John Cherry, and James Robinson, eds., *Good Impressions: Image and Authority in Medieval Seals* (London: British Museum, 2008), 1–7.

Bedos-Rezak, Brigitte, *When Ego was Imago: Signs of Identity in the Middle Ages* (Leiden: Brill, 2011).

Beer, Michelle L., *Queenship at the Renaissance Courts of Britain: Catherine of Aragon and Margaret Tudor, 1503–1533* (Woodbridge: Boydell and Brewer, 2018).

Bellis, Joanna, 'The dregs of trembling, the draught of salvation: the dual symbolism of the cup in medieval literature', *Journal of Medieval History* 37:1 (2011), 47–61. https://doi.org/10.1016/j.jmedhist.2010.12.003

Bennett, Philip E., Sarah Carpenter, and Louise Gardiner, 'Chivalric Games at the Court of Edward III', *Medium Ævum* 87:2 (2018), 304–42.

Bernard, G.W., *Anne Boleyn: Fatal Attractions* (New Haven, CT: Yale University Press, 2010).

Bernard, G.W., *The King's Reformation: Henry VIII and the Remaking of the English Church* (New Haven, CT: Yale University Press, 2005).

Bernard, G.W., *Who Ruled Tudor England: Paradoxes of Power* (London: Bloomsbury, 2022).

Billington, Sandra, *A Social History of the Fool* (Brighton: Harvester Press, 1984).

Blockmans, Wim, *Keizer Karel V: De Utopie van het Keizerschap* (Leuven: Van Halewyck, 2001).

Blockmans, Wim, and Esther Donckers, 'Self-Representation of Court and City in Flanders and Brabant in the Fifteenth and Early Sixteenth Centuries', in Wim Blockmans and Antheun Janse, eds., *Showing Status: Representation of Social Positions in the Late Middle Ages* (Turnhout: Brepols, 1999), 81–111.

Blumenthal, Debra, *Enemies and Familiars: Slavery and Mastery in Fifteenth-Century Valencia* (Ithaca, NY: Cornell University Press, 2009).

Bober, Phyllis Pray, *Art, Culture, and Cuisine: Ancient and Medieval Gastronomy* (Chicago, IL: University of Chicago Press, 1999).

Boffey, Julia, *Henry VII's London in the Great Chronicle* (Kalamazoo: TEAMS, 2019).

Boogaard, Ernst van den, 'Christophle le More, Lijfwacht van Karel V?', *Bulletin van het Rijksmuseum* 53:4 (2005), 412–33.

Boom, Ghislaine de, *De Reizen van Karel V*, trans. G. de Negris (Haarlem: Tjeenk Willink, 1960).

Bowles, Edmund A., 'Musical Instruments at the Medieval Banquet', *Revue belge de Musicologie* 12:1/4 (1958), 41–51. https://doi.org/10.2307/3686453

Brannen, Anne, 'Intricate Subtleties: Entertainment at Bishop Morton's Installation Feast', *Records of Early English Drama Newsletter* 22:2 (1997), 2–11.

Brigden, Susan, 'Henry Howard, Earl of Surrey, and the "Conjured League"', *The Historical Journal* 37:3 (1994), 507–37. https://doi.org/10.1017/S0018246X00014862

Bourne, W.R.P., 'The Birds and Animals Consumed when Henry VIII Entertained the King of France and the Count of Flanders at Calais in 1532', *Archives of Natural History* 10:2 (1981), 331–33. https://doi.org/10.3366/anh.1981.10.2.331

Byrne, Aisling, 'Arthur's Refusal to Eat: Ritual and Control in the Romance Feast', *Journal of Medieval History* 37:1 (2011), 62–74. https://doi.org/10.1016/j.jmedhist.2010.12.009

Carlton, Charles, 'Retha M. Warnicke. *The Marrying of Anne of Cleves: Royal Protocol in Early Modern England* (New York: Cambridge University Press, 2000), xiv, 343. $27.95', *The American Historical Review* 106:4 (2001), 1451.

Canova-Green, Marie-Claude, Jean Andrews, Marie-France Wagner, eds., *Writing Royal Entries in Early Modern Europe* (Turnhout: Brepols, 2013).

Carpenter, Sarah, 'Gely Wyth Tharmys of Scotland England': Word, Image and Performance at the Marriage of James IV and Margaret Tudor', in Janet Hadley Williams and J. Derrick McClure, eds., *'Freshe Fontanis': Studies in* the Culture of Medieval and Early Modern Scotland (Newcastle: Cambridge Scholars Press, 2013), 165–77.

Carpenter, Sarah, 'Laughing at Natural Fools', Theta 11, Théâtre Tudor (2013), 3–22, at: THETA11-01-Carpenter.pdf (univ-tours.fr)

Carpenter, Sarah, 'The Places of Foolery: Robert Armin and fooling in Edinburgh', Medieval English Theatre 37 (2015), 11–26.

Cartellieri, Otto, The Court of Burgundy, trans. Malcolm Letts (1st edn. 1929; London: Routledge, 1996).

Carter, Alison J., 'Mary Tudor's Wardrobe', Costume 18:1 (1984), 9–28. https://doi.org/10.1179/cos.1984.18.1.9

Chapman, Matthieu A., 'The Appearance of Blacks on the Early Modern Stage: Love's Labour's Lost's African Connections to Court', Early Theatre 17:2 (2014), 77–94. https://doi.org/10.12745/et.17.2.1206

Checa Cremades, Fernando, and Laura Fernández-González, eds., Festival Culture in the World of the Spanish Habsburgs (London: Routledge, 2016).

Chrimes, S.B., Henry VII (New Haven, CT: Yale University Press, 1999).

Christiansen, Keith, and Stefan Weppelmann, eds., The Renaissance Portrait from Donatello to Bellini, Metropolitan Museum of Art (New Haven, CT: Yale University Press, 2011).

Classen, Albrecht, 'Spain and Germany in the Late Middle Ages: Christoph Weiditz paints Spain (1529): A German artist traveller discovers the Spanish Peninsula', Neuphilologische Mitteilungen 105:4 (2004), 395–406.

Cohn, Henry Jacob, 'Did Bribes Induce the German Electors to Choose Charles V as Emperor in 1519?' German History 19:1 (2001), 1–27.

Cole, Denise E., 'Edible performance: feasting and festivity in early Tudor entertainment', in Sally Banes and Andre Lepecki, eds., The Senses in Performance (London: Routledge, 2012), 101–13.

Constable, Olivia Remie, To Live Like a Moor: Christian Perceptions of Muslim Identity in Medieval and Early Modern Spain (Philadelphia, PA: University of Pennsylvania Press, 2018).

Cooper, Richard, 'Legate's Luxury: The Entries of Cardinal Alessandro Farnese to Avignon and Carpentras, 1553', in Nicolas Russell and Hélène Visentin, eds., French Ceremonial Entries in the Sixteenth Century: Event, Image, Text (Toronto: Centre for Reformation and Renaissance Studies, 2007), 133–61.

Costa Gomes, Rita, The Making of a Court Society: Kings and Nobles in Late Medieval Portugal (Cambridge: Cambridge University Press, 2003).

Cox-Rearick, Janet, 'Power-Dressing at the Courts of Cosimo de' Medici and François I: The "moda alla Spagnola" of Spanish Consorts Eléonore d'Autriche and Eleonora di Toledo', Artibus et Historiae 30:60 (2009), 39–69.

Crane, Susan, *The Performance of Self: Ritual, Clothing, and Identity During the Hundred Years War* (Philadelphia, PA: University of Pennsylvania Press, 2002).

Croizat, Yassana C., 'Living Dolls: François Ier Dresses his Women', *Renaissance Quarterly* 60 (2007), 94–130. https://doi.org/10.1353/ren.2007.0027

Cruz, Anne J., and Maria Galli Stampino, eds., *Early Modern Habsburg Women: Transnational Contexts, Cultural Conflicts, Dynastic Continuities* (Farnham: Ashgate, 2013).

Cuenca Rodríguez, María Elena, 'Patrocinio Musical en el Viaje de Felipe y Juana a la Península Ibérica a Través la Crónica de Viena', *Revista de Musicología* 42:1 (2019), 17–42. https://doi.org/10.2307/26661392

Darsie, Heather R., *Anna, Duchess of Cleves: The King's 'Beloved Sister'* (Stroud: Amberley, 2019).

Davies, C.S.L., and John Edwards, 'Katherine [Catalina, Catherine, Katherine of Aragon] (1485–1536)', *Oxford Dictionary of National Biography* (Oxford: Oxford University Press, 2004). https://doi.org/10.1093/ref:odnb/4891

Dillon, Janette, *The Language of Space in Court Performance, 1400–1625* (Cambridge: Cambridge University Press, 2010).

Doorslaer, G. van, 'Lachapelle musicale de Philippe le Beau', *Revue belge d'archeologie et d'histoire de l'art* 4 (1934), 21–57.

Duggan, Mary Kay, 'Queen Joanna and Her Musicians', *Musica Disciplina* 30 (1976), 73–95.

Dumitrescu, Theodor, *The Early Tudor Court and International Musical Relations* (Aldershot: Ashgate, 2007).

Duncan, Sarah, *Mary I: Gender, Power, and Ceremony in the Reign of England's First Queen* (New York, NY: Palgrave Macmillan, 2012).

Dursteler, Eric R., 'Food and Politics', in Ken Albala, ed., *A Cultural History of Food in the Renaissance* (London and New York: Berg, 2012), 83–100.

Earenfight, Theresa, 'A Precarious Household: Catherine of Aragon in England, 1501–1504', in Theresa Earenfight, ed., *Royal and Elite Households in Medieval and Early Modern Europe: More than Just a Castle* (Leiden: Brill, 2018), 338–56. http://dx.doi.org/10.1163/9789004360761_016.

Earenfight, Theresa, *Queenship in Medieval Europe* (New York, NY: Palgrave Macmillan, 2013).

Earenfight, Theresa, 'Raising Infanta Catalina de Aragón to be Catherine, Queen of England', *Anuario de Estudios Medievales* 46:1 (2016), 417–43, https://doi.org/10.3989/aem.2016.46.1.13.

Earenfight, Theresa, 'The Shoes of an *Infanta*: Bringing the Sensuous, Not Sensible, "Spanish Style" of Catherine of Aragon to Tudor England', in Tracy Chapman Hamilton and Mariah Proctor-Tiffany, eds., *Moving Women*

Moving Objects (400–1500) (Leiden: Brill, 2019), 293–317. https://doi.org/10. 1163/9789004399679_015

Elston, Timothy G., 'Widow Princess or Neglected Queen? Catherine of Aragon, Henry VIII, and English Public Opinion, 1533–1536', in Carole Levin and Robert Bucholz, eds., *Queens and Power in Medieval and Early Modern England* (Lincoln, NE: University of Nebraska Press, 2009), 16–30.

Earle T. F., and K. J. P. Lowe, eds., *Black Africans in Renaissance Europe* (Cambridge: Cambridge University Press, 2005).

Edwards, John, *Mary I* (New Haven, CT: Yale University Press, 2011).

Epstein, Robert, 'Eating their Words: Food and Text in the Coronation Banquet of Henry VI', *Journal of Medieval and Early Modern Studies* 36:2 (2006), 355–77. https://doi.org/10.1215/10829636-2005-005

Epstein, Steven A., *Speaking of Slavery: Color, Ethnicity, and Human Bondage in Italy* (Ithaca, NY: Cornell University Press, 2001).

Ferer, Mary Tiffany, *Music and Ceremony at the Court of Charles V* (Woodbridge: The Boydell Press, 2012).

Ferer, Mary Tiffany, 'Queen Juana, Empress Isabel, and Musicians at the Royal Courts of Spain (1505–1556)', *Tijdschrift van de Koninklijke Vereniging voor Nederlandse Muziekgeschiedenis* 65:1/ 2 (2015), 13–36.

Fernández Alvarez, Manuel, *Charles V: Elected emperor and hereditary ruler*, trans. J.A. Lalaguna (London: Thames and Hudson, 1975).

Finlay, Robert, 'Politics and History in the Diary of Marino Sanuto', *Renaissance Quarterly* 33:4 (1980), 585–90.

Fleming, Gillian B., *Juana I: Legitimacy and Conflict in Sixteenth-Century Castile* (New York, NY: Palgrave Macmillan, 2018).

Forse, James H., 'Advertising Status and Legitimacy: or, Why Did Henry VIII's Queens and Children Patronize Travelling Performers?', *Early Theatre* 16:2 (2013), 59–90. https://doi.org/10.12745/et.16.2.4.

Fraser, Antonia, *The Six Wives of Henry VIII* (London: Weidenfeld & Nicolson, 1992).

Frieling, Kirsten O., 'Dressing the Bride: Wedding and Fashion Practices at German Princely Courts in the Fifteenth and Sixteenth Centuries', in Erin Griffey, ed., *Sartorial Politics in Early Modern Europe: Fashioning Women* (Amsterdam: Amsterdam University Press, 2019), 75–92.

Fryer, Peter, *Staying Power: The History of Black People in Britain* (London: Pluto Press, 2018).

Gadd, Derek, and Tony Dyson, 'Bridewell Palace Excavations at 9–11 Bridewell Place and 1–3 Tudor Street, City of London, 1978', *Post-Medieval Archaeology* 15:1 (1981), 1–79. https://doi.org/10.1179/pma.1981.001

Gandoulphe, Pascal, 'Quelques réflexions sur Germaine de Foix (1488–1536), dernière reine d'Aragon, et sa fortune historiographique', *Cahiers d'études romanes* 42 (2021), 189–209. https://doi.org/10.4000/etudesromanes.12295

Gentilcore, David, *Food and Health in Early Modern Europe: Diet, Medicine, and Society, 1450–1800* (London: Bloomsbury Academic, 2016).

Giry-Deloison, Charles, 'Une haquenée... pour le porter bientost et plus doucement en enfer ou en paradis': The French and Mary Tudor's marriage to Louis XII in 1514', in David Grummitt, ed., *The English Experience in France c. 1450–1558: War, Diplomacy and Cultural Exchange* (London: Routledge, 2002), 132–59.

Grauwe, Luc de, 'Emerging Mother-Tongue Awareness: The Special Case of Dutch and German in the Middle Ages and the Early Modern Period', in Andrew R. Linn and Nicola McLelland, eds., *Standardization: Studies from the Germanic Languages* (Current Issues in Linguistic Theory no. 235; Amsterdam: John Benjamins, 2002), 99–115.

Gunn, Steven, 'Henry VII in Context: Problems and Possibilities', *History* 92:3 (2007), 301–17. https://doi.org/10.1111/j.1468-229X.2007.00397.x

Habib, Imtiaz, *Black Lives in the English Archives, 1500–1677: Imprints of the Invisible* (London: Routledge, 2008).

Hacker, Peter, and Candy Kuhl, 'A Portrait of Anne of Cleves', *The Burlington Magazine* 134:1068 (1992), 172–75.

Hammer, Carl I., 'A Hearty Meal? The Prison Diets of Cranmer and Latimer', *Sixteenth Century Journal* 30:3 (1999), 653–80.

Hanawalt, Barbara, and Kathryn Reyerson, eds., *City and Spectacle in Medieval Europe* (Minneapolis, MN: University of Minnesota Press, 1994).

Hayward, Maria, *Dress at the Court of King Henry VIII* (Leeds: Maney, 2007).

Hayward, Maria, 'Fashionable Fiction: The Significance of Costumes in The Tudors', in William B. Robison, ed., *History, Fiction, and The Tudors* (New York: Palgrave Macmillan, 2016), 293–306.

Hayward, Maria, *The Great Wardrobe Accounts of Henry VII and Henry VIII* (Woodbridge: The Boydell Press for London Record Society, 2012).

Hayward, Maria, *Rich Apparel: Clothing and the Law in Henry VIII's England* (Farnham: Ashgate, 2009).

Hayward, Maria, 'Spanish Princess or Queen of England? The Image, Identity and Influence of Catherine of Aragon at the Courts of Henry VII and Henry VIII', in José Luis Colomer and Amalia Descalzo, eds., *Vestir a la española en las cortes europeas (siglos XVI y XVII)/Dressing the Spanish in the European courts (XVI and XVII centuries)* (2 vols.; Madrid: Centro de Estudios Europa Hispanica, 2014), 11–36.

Henisch, Bridget Ann, *The Medieval Cook* (Woodbridge: The Boydell Press, 2009).

Hertel, Christiane, 'Engaging Negation in Hans Holbein the Younger's Portrait of Christina of Denmark, Duchess of Milan', in Andrea Pearson, ed., *Women and Portraits in Early Modern Europe* (London: Routledge, 2016), 107–36.

Hondius, Dienke, 'Black Africans in Seventeenth-Century Amsterdam', *Renaissance and Reformation* 31:2 (2008), 87–105.

Huizinga, Johan, *Herfsttij der Middeleeuwen*, ed. Anton van der Lem (Leiden: Olympus, 2004; first edition 1919).

Hunt, Alice, *The Drama of Coronation: Medieval Ceremony in Early Modern England* (Cambridge: Cambridge University Press, 2008).

Ives, Eric, *The Life and Death of Anne Boleyn* (Oxford: Blackwell, 2004).

Jacquot, Jean, ed., *Les Fétes de la Renaissance* (Paris: Éditions du Centre National de la Recherche, Scientifique, 1956).

James, Kathryn, *English Paleography and Manuscript Culture: 1500–1800* (New Haven, CT: Yale University Press, 2020).

James, Susan, 'Jane, the Queen's Fool (fl. 1535–1558)', *Oxford Dictionary of National Biography* (Oxford: Oxford University Press, 2019). https://doi.org/10.1093/odnb/9780198614128.013.112276

Janssen, K.P.S. and Van Pelt, Nadia T., 'Royal epistolary courtship in Latin? Arthur Tudor's "love letter" to Katherine of Aragon at the Archivo General de Simancas and Francesco Negri's *Ars Epistolandi*', *Renaissance Studies* (2023) https://doi.org/10.1111/rest.12864

Jasperse, Jitske, *Medieval Women, Material Culture, and Power: Matilda Plantagenet and her Sisters* (Leeds: ARC Humanities Press, 2020).

Jeanneret, Michel, *A Feast of Words: Banquets and Table Talk in the Renaissance*, trans. Jeremy Whiteley and Emma Hughes (Cambridge: Polity Press, 1991).

Jensen, De Lamar, 'The Ottoman Turks in Sixteenth Century French Diplomacy', *Sixteenth Century Journal* 16:4 (1985), 451–70. https://doi.org/10.2307/2541220

Johns, Susan M., *Noblewomen, Aristocracy and Power in the Twelfth-century Anglo-Norman Realm* (Manchester: Manchester University Press, 2003).

Johnson, Lauren, 'Catalina of Motril (fl. 1501–1531)', *Oxford Dictionary of National Biography* (Oxford: Oxford University Press, 2019). https://doi.org/10.1093/odnb/9780198614128.013.369157

Johnston, Mark Albert, *Beard Fetish in Early Modern England: Sex, Gender, and Registers of Value* (London: Routledge, 2016).

Jones, Ann Rosalind, and Peter Stallybrass, *Renaissance Clothing and the Materials of Memory* (Cambridge: Cambridge University Press, 2000).

Jordan, Annemarie, 'Images of Empire: Slaves in the Lisbon Household and Court of Catherine of Austria', in T.F. Earle and K.J.P. Lowe, eds., *Black Africans in Renaissance Europe* (Cambridge: Cambridge University Press, 2005), 155–80.

Kalinowska, Anna, and Jonathan Spangler, with Pawl Tyszka, eds., *Power and Ceremony in European History: Rituals, Practices and Representative Bodies since the Late Middle Ages* (London: Bloomsbury, 2021).

Kalsbeek, G., *De betrekkingen tusschen Frankrijk en Gelre tijdens Karel van Egmond* (Wageningen: Veenman, 1932).

Kaufmann, Miranda, *Black Tudors* (London: Oneworld, 2017).

Kaufmann, Miranda, 'John Blanke (*fl.* 1507–1512)', *Oxford Dictionary of National Biography* (Oxford: Oxford University Press, 2014). https://doi.org/10.1093/ref:odnb/107145

Kennedy, Kirstin, 'Sharing and Status: The Design and Function of a Sixteenth-Century Spanish Spice Stand in the Victoria and Albert Museum', *Renaissance Studies* 24:1 (2010), 142–55. https://doi.org/10.1111/j.1477-4658.2009.00636.x

Kipling, Gordon, 'Brussels, Joanna of Castile, and the Art of Theatrical Illustration (1496)', *Leeds Studies in English* 32 (2001), 229–53.

Kipling, Gordon, *Enter the King: Theatre, Liturgy, and Ritual in the Medieval Civic Triumph* (Oxford: Clarendon Press, 1998).

Kipling, Gordon, '"He That Saw It Would Not Believe It": Anne Boleyn's Royal Entry into London', in Alexandra F. Johnston and Wim Hüsken, eds., *Civic Ritual and Drama* (Amsterdam: Rodopi, 1997), 39–79.

Kipling, Gordon, *The Triumph of Honour: Burgundian Origins of the Elizabethan Renaissance*, Publications of the Sir Thomas Browne Institute, General Series 6 (The Hague: Leiden University Press, 1977).

Kissane, Christopher, *Food, Religion and Communities in Early Modern Europe* (London: Bloomsbury Academic, 2017).

Knecht, Robert J., *Francis I* (Cambridge: Cambridge University Press, 1982).

Knecht, Robert J., *The French Renaissance Court, 1483–1589* (New Haven, CT: Yale University Press, 2008).

Knighton, Tess, 'Instruments, Instrumental Music and Instrumentalists: Traditions and Transitions', in Tess Knighton, ed., *Companion to Music in the Age of the Catholic Monarchs* (Leiden: Brill, 2017), 97–144. https://doi.org/10.1163/9789004329324_005

Knighton, Tess, 'Introduction', in Tess Knighton, ed., *Companion to Music in the Age of the Catholic Monarchs* (Leiden: Brill, 2017), 1–20. https://doi.org/10.1163/9789004329324_002

Knighton, Tess, 'Northern Influence on Cultural Developments in the Iberian Peninsula during the Fifteenth Century', *Renaissance Studies* 1:2 (1987), 221–37. https://doi.org/10.1111/j.1477-4658.1987.tb00129.x

Knighton, Tess, and Carmen Morte García, 'Ferdinand of Aragon's Entry into Valladolid in 1513: The Triumph of a Christian King', *Early Music History* 18 (1999), 119–63. https://doi.org/10.1017/S0261127900001856

Knighton, Tess, and Kenneth Kreitner, *The Music of Juan de Anchieta* (London: Routledge, 2019).

Kovács, Lenke, 'Frightened or Fearless: Different Ways of Facing Death in the Sixteenth Century Majorcan Play Representacio de la Mort', in Sophie Oosterwijk and Stefanie A. Knöll, eds., *Mixed Metaphors: The Danse Macabre in Medieval and Early Modern Europe* (Cambridge: Cambridge Scholars, 2011), 207–36.

Koziol, Geoffrey, *Begging Pardon and Favor: Ritual and Political Order in Early Medieval France* (Ithaca, NY: Cornell University Press, 1992).

Kuijs, J.A.E., 'Catharina van Gelre (geb. Omstreeks 1440 – gest. Geldern 25-1-1497', *Digitaal Vrouwenlexicon van Nederland* (Den Haag: Instituut voor Nederlandse Geschiedenis, 2007), at: http://hdl.handle.net/2066/43877

Labrador Arroyo, Félix, 'From Castile to Burgundy: The Evolution of the Queens' Households during the Sixteenth Century', in Anne J. Cruz and Maria Galli Stampino, eds., *Early Modern Habsburg Women: Transnational Contexts, Cultural Conflicts, Dynastic Continuities* (Farnham: Ashgate, 2013), 119–48.

Ladero Quesada, M.F., 'Recibir princesas y enterrar reinas (Zamora 1501 y 1504)', *Espacio Tiempo Y Forma. Serie III, Historia Medieval* 13 (2000), 119–37.

Lancashire, Anne, *London Civic Theatre: City Drama and Pageantry from Roman Times to 1558* (Cambridge: Cambridge University Press, 2002).

Lloyd, Paul S., 'Dietary Advice and Fruit-Eating in Late Tudor and Early Stuart England', *Journal of the History of Medicine and Allied Sciences* 67:4 (2012), 553–86. https://doi.org/10.1093/jhmas/jrr042

Loach, Jennifer, 'The Function of Ceremonial in the Reign of Henry VIII', *Past & Present* 142 (1994), 43–68. https://doi.org/10.1093/past/142.1.43

Loades, David, *The Six Wives of Henry VIII* (Stroud: Amberley, 2009).

Loades, David, *The Tudor Queens of England* (London: Continuum, 2009).

Lowe, Kate, 'The Stereotyping of Black Africans in Renaissance Europe', in T.F. Earle and K.J.P. Lowe, eds., *Black Africans in Renaissance Europe* (Cambridge: Cambridge University Press, 2005), 17–47.

Lowe, Kate, 'Visible Lives: Black Gondoliers and Other Black Africans in Renaissance Venice', *Renaissance Quarterly* 66:2 (2013), 412–52. https://doi.org/10.1086/671583

Lurie, Samuel, 'Was Queen Jane Seymour (1509–37) Delivered by a Cesarean Section?', *Endeavour* 41:1 (2017), 23–28. https://doi.org/10.1016/j.endeavour.2016.10.002

McEntegart, Rory, *Henry VIII, the League of Schmalkalden and the English Reformation* (Woodbridge: The Boydell Press for Royal Historical Society, 2002).

McGavin, John J., 'Close Kin to a Clean Fool: Robert Armin's Account of Jack Miller', *Theta* 12, Théâtre Tudor (2016), 39–56, at: THETA12-03-McGavin.pdf (univ-tours.fr)

McGavin, John J., and Greg Walker, *Imagining Spectatorship: From the Mysteries to the Shakespearean Stage* (Oxford: Oxford University Press, 2016).

McMahon, Elizabeth, 'Accounting Legitimacy in Purple and Gold: Mary Tudor, Household Accounts, and the English Succession', in Valerie Schutte and Jessica S. Hower, eds., *Mary I in Writing* (New York, NY: Palgrave Macmillan, 2022), 189–217.

Mansfield, Lisa, 'Face-to-Face with the 'Flanders Mare': *Fama* and Hans Holbein the Younger's *Portrait of Anne of Cleves*', in Claire Walker and Heather Kerr, eds., *'Fama' and her Sisters: Gossip and Rumour in Early Modern Europe* (Turnhout: Brepols, 2015), 115–35.

Mansfield, Lisa, 'Lustrous Virtue: Eleanor of Austria's Jewels and Gems as Composite Cultural Identity and Affective Maternal Agency', in Erin Griffey, ed., *Sartorial Politics in Early Modern Europe: Fashioning Women* (Amsterdam: Amsterdam University Press, 2019), 93–114.

Martín Casares, Aurelia, 'Free and Freed Black Africans in Granada in the Time of the Spanish Renaissance', in T.F. Earle and K.J.P. Lowe, eds., *Black Africans in Renaissance Europe* (Cambridge: Cambridge University Press, 2005), 247–60.

Massip, Francesc, 'The Cloud: A Medieval Aerial Device, Its Origins, and Its Use in Spain Today', in Clifford Davidson, ed., *The Dramatic Tradition of the Middle Ages* (New York, NY: AMS Press, 2005), 262–74.

Mattingly, Garrett, *Catherine of Aragon* (London: Jonathan Cape, 1963).

Mauss, M., 'Essai sur le don. Forme et raison de l'échange dans les sociétés archaïques', *L'Année Sociologique*, 2nd ser. 1 (1923–4), 30–186.

Metzler, Irina, *Fools and Idiots? Intellectual Disability in the Middle Ages* (Manchester: Manchester University Press, 2016).

Monnas, Lisa, 'All that Glitters: Cloth of Gold as a Vehicle for Display 1300-1550', in Christoph Brachmann, ed., *Arrayed in Splendour: Art, Fashion, and Textiles in Medieval and Early Modern Europe* (Turnhout: Brepols, 2019), 95–133.

Montanari, Massimo, *Medieval Tastes: Food, Cooking, and the Table*, trans. Beth Archer Brombert (New York, NY: Columbia University Press, 2015).

Morris, Paul N., 'Patronage and Piety: Montserrat and the Royal House of Medieval Catalonia-Aragon', *Mirator* 10 (2000), 1–15.

Muir, Edward, 'The Eye of the Procession: Ritual Ways of Seeing in the Renaissance', in Nicholas Howe, ed., *Ceremonial Culture in Pre-Modern Europe* (Notre Dame, IN: University of Notre Dame Press, 2007), 129–53.

Muir, Edward, *Ritual in Early Modern Europe*, 2nd edn. (Cambridge: Cambridge University Press, 2005).

Mullini, Roberta, '*Fulgens and Lucres*: A Mirror held up to Stage and Society', *European Medieval Drama* 1 (1997), 203–18. https://doi.org/10.1484/J.EMD.2.301064

Mulryne, J.R., Maria Ines Aliverti, and Anna Maria Testaverde, eds., *Ceremonial Entries in Early Modern Europe: The Iconography of Power* (London: Routledge, 2015).

Nash, Penelope, *Empress Adelheid and Countess Matilda: Medieval Female Rulership and the Foundations of European Society* (New York, NY: Palgrave Macmillan, 2017).

Noordzij, Aart, 'Against Burgundy. The Appeal Of Germany In The Duchy Of Guelders', in Robert Stein and Judith Pollmann, eds., *Networks, Regions and Nations: Shaping Identities in the Low Countries, 1300–1650* (Leiden: Brill, 2010), 111–29.

Normore, Christina, *A Feast for the Eyes: Art, Performance & the Late Medieval Banquet* (Chicago, IL: University of Chicago Press, 2015).

Norrie, Aidan, 'Jane Seymour: Saintly Queen', in Aidan Norrie, Carolyn Harris, J.L. Laynesmith, Danna R. Messer, and Elena Woodacre, eds., *Tudor and Stuart Consorts: Power, Influence, and Dynasty* (New York, NY: Palgrave Macmillan, 2022), 79–100. https://doi.org/10.1007/978-3-030-95197-9_6

Norton, Elizabeth, *Anne of Cleves: Henry VIII's Discarded Wife* (Stroud: Amberley, 2010).

Nubia, Onyeka, *Blackamoores: Africans in Tudor England, their Presence, Status and Origins* ([London?]: Narrative Eye, 2013).

Nubia, Onyeka, *England's Other Countrymen: Black Tudor Society* (London: Zed, 2019).

Nubia, Onyeka, 'Why Diversity in Tudor England Matters', in Suzannah Lipscomb and Helen Carr, eds., *What is History, Now?* (London: Weidenfeld & Nicolson, 2021), 169–77.

Ohajuru, Michael, 'The John Blanke Project', in Gretchen H. Gerzina, ed., *Britain's Black Past* (Liverpool: Liverpool University Press, 2020), 7–25.

Oliveira Alves, Rui Pedro de, 'The Trombone as Portrayed in Portuguese Iconography During the Sixteenth and Early Seventeenth Centuries', *Scottish Journal of Performance* 2:1 (2014), 55–85. https://doi.org/10.14439/sjop.2014.0201.04

Otele, Olivette, *African Europeans: An Untold Story* (London: Hurst & Company, 2020).

Otto, Beatrice K., *Fools Are Everywhere: The Court Jester around the World* (Chicago, IL: University of Chicago Press, 2001).

Paranque, Estelle, *Elizabeth I of England through Valois Eyes: Power, Representation and Diplomacy in the Reign of the Queen, 1558–1588* (New York, NY: Palgrave Macmillan, 2019).

Paresys, Isabelle, 'Dressing the Queen at the French Renaissance Court: Sartorial Politics', in Erin Griffey, ed., *Sartorial Politics in Early Modern Europe: Fashioning Women* (Amsterdam: Amsterdam University Press, 2019), 57–74.

Penn, Thomas, *Winter King: The Dawn of Tudor England* (London: Penguin, 2012).

Perry, Maria, *Sisters to the King* (London: André Deutsch, 2002).

Rastall, Richard, 'The Minstrels of the English Royal Households, 25 Edward I – 1 Henry VIII: An Inventory', *R.M.A. Research Chronicle* 4 (1964), 1–41.

Rastall, Richard, and Andrew Taylor, *Minstrels and Minstrelsy in Late Medieval England* (Woodbridge: Boydell Press, 2023).

Richardson, Glenn, *The Field of Cloth of Gold* (New Haven, CT: Yale University Press, 2013).

Richardson, Glenn, 'The King, the Cardinal-Legate, and the Field of Cloth of Gold', *Royal Studies Journal* 4:2 (2017), 141–60. http://doi.org/10.21039/rsj.v4i2.164

Richardson, Glenn, *Renaissance Monarchy: The Reigns of Henry VIII, Francis I and Charles V* (London: Arnold, 2002).

Riehl, Anna, *The Face of Queenship: Early Modern Representations of Elizabeth I* (New York, NY: Palgrave Macmillan, 2010).

Rodrigues, Ana Maria S.A., Manuela Santos Silva, and Jonathan Spangler, eds., *Dynastic Change: Legitimacy and Gender in Medieval and Early Modern Monarchy* (London: Routledge, 2019).

Rohr, Zita Eva, *Yolande of Aragon (1381–1442) Family and Power* (New York, NY: Palgrave Macmillan, 2016).

Ross, L.B., 'Beyond Eating: Political and Personal Significance of the *Entremets* at the Banquets of the Burgundian Court', in Timothy J. Tomasik and Juliann M. Vitullo, eds., *At the Table: Metaphorical and Material Cultures of Food in Medieval and Early Modern Europe* (Turnhout: Brepols, 2007), 145–66. https://doi.org/10.1484/M.ASMAR-EB.3.3048

Rublack, Ulinka, *Dressing Up: Cultural Identity in Renaissance Europe* (Oxford: Oxford University Press, 2011).

Ruiz, Theofilo F., *A King Travels: Festive Traditions in Late Medieval and Early Modern Spain* (Princeton, NJ, and Oxford: Princeton University Press, 2012).

Sadlack, Erin, *The French Queen's Letters: Mary Tudor Brandon and the Politics of Marriage in Sixteenth-Century Europe* (New York, NY: Palgrave Macmillan, 2011).

Şahin, Kaya, 'Staging an Empire: An Ottoman Circumcision Ceremony as Cultural Performance', *American Historical Review* 123:2 (2018), 463–92. https://doi.org/10.1093/ahr/123.2.463

Scarisbrick, J. J., *Henry VIII* (New Haven, CT: Yale University Press, 1997).

Schaïk, Remi van, 'Taxation, Public Finances and the State-Making Process in the Late Middle Ages: The Case of the Duchy of Guelders', *Journal of Medieval History* 19 (1993), 251–71. https://doi.org/10.1016/0304-4181(93)90016-6

Schiedlausky, Günther, *Essen und Trinken: Tafelsitten bis zum Ausgang des Mittelalters* (München: Prestel Verlag, 1956).

Screti, Zoe, '"A Motley to the View": The Clothing of Court Fools in Tudor England', *Midlands Historical Review* 2 (2018), 1–16.

Schutte, Valerie, 'Anne of Cleves in Book and Manuscript', *The Journal of the Early Book Society* 21 (2018), 123–47.

Schutte, Valerie, 'Anne of Cleves: Survivor Queen', *Tudor and Stuart Consorts*, ed. by Aidan Norrie, Carolyn Harris, J.L. Laynesmith, Danna R. Messer, and Elena Woodacre (New York, NY: Palgrave Macmillan, 2022), 101–17.

Sharpe, Kevin, *Selling the Tudor Monarchy: Authority and Image in Sixteenth-Century England* (New Haven, CT: Yale University Press, 2009).

Shergold, N.D., *A History of the Spanish Stage: From Medieval Times until the End of the Seventeenth Century* (Oxford: Clarendon Press, 1967).

Sicca, Cinzia Maria, 'Fashioning the Tudor Court', in Maria Hayward and Elizabeth Kramer, eds., *Textiles and Text: Re-establishing the Links between Archival and Object-based Research* (London: Archetype Publications, 2007), 93–104.

Silec, Tatjana, 'Le Fou du Roi: Un Hors-la-Loi d'un Genre Particulier', *Camenulae* 2 (2008), 1–11.

Silleras-Fernández, Núria, 'Nigra Sum Sed Formosa: Black Slaves and Exotica in the Court of a Fourteenth-Century Aragonese Queen', *Medieval Encounters* 13 (2007), 546–65. https://doi.org/10.1163/157006707X222777

Southworth, John, *Fools and Jesters at the English Court* (Stroud: Sutton Publishing, 1998; Reprinted Stroud: History Press, 2011).

Sowerby, Tracey A., '"A Memorial and a Pledge of Faith": Portraiture and Early Modern Diplomatic Culture', *The English Historical Review* 129:537 (2014), 296–331. https://doi.org/10.1093/ehr/ceu070

Starkey, David, *Six Wives* (New York, NY: Harper Collins, 2003).

Stopes, C.C., *Shakespeare's Environment* (London: Bell and Sons, 1914).

Strong, Roy, *Art and Power: Renaissance Festivals, 1450–1650* (Woodbridge: The Boydell Press, 1984).

Struick, J.E.A.L., *Gelre en Habsburg, 1492–1528* (Utrecht: Smits, 1960).

Sutton, David C., 'Four and Twenty Blackbirds Baked in a Pie: A History of Surprise Stuffings', in Mark McWilliams, ed., *Wrapped and Stuffed Foods: Proceedings of the Oxford Symposium on Food and Cookery 2012* (Totness, Devon: Prospect Books, 2013), 285–94.

Styles, John, 'Fashion and Innovation in Early Modern Europe', in Evelyn Welch, ed., *Fashioning the Early Modern: Dress, Textiles, and Innovation in Europe, 1500-1800* (Oxford: Oxford University Press, 2017), 33–55.

Tammen, Björn R., 'A Feast of the Arts: Joanna of Castile in Brussels, 1496', *Early Music History* 30 (2011), 213–48. https://doi.org/10.1017/S0261127911000015

Taylor, Valerie, 'Banquet Plate and Renaissance Culture: A Day in the Life', *Renaissance Studies* 19:5 (2005), 621–33. https://doi.org/10.1111/j.1477-4658. 2005.00126.x

Thurley, Simon, 'The Sixteenth-Century Kitchens at Hampton Court', *Journal of the British Archaeological Association* 143:1 (1990), 1–28. https://doi.org/10. 1179/jba.1990.143.1.1

Tomasik, Timothy J., and Juliann M. Vitullo, eds., *At the Table: Metaphorical and Material Cultures of Food in Medieval and Early Modern Europe* (Turnhout: Brepols, 2007).

Tremlett, Giles, *Catherine of Aragon: Henry's Spanish Queen* (London: Faber and Faber, 2010).

Uytven, Raymond van, 'Showing off One's Rank in the Middle Ages', in Wim Blockmans and Antheun Janse (eds.), *Showing Status: Representations of Social Positions in the Late Middle Ages* (Turnhout: Brepols, 1999), 19–34.

Vandenbroeck, Paul, 'A bride amidst heroines, fools and savages. The Joyous Entry into Brussels by Joanna of Castile, 1496 (Berlin, Kupferstichkabinett, Ms. 78D5)', *Jaarboek Koninklijk Museum voor Schone Kunsten Antwerpen* (2012), 153–94.

Vanderjagt, Arjo, 'The Princely Culture of the Valois Dukes of Burgundy', in M. Gosman, A. MacDonald, and A. Vanderjagt, eds., *Princes and Princely Culture, 1450–1650*, volume 1 (Leiden: Brill, 2003), 51–79.

Van Pelt, Nadia T., 'Henry VIII Decapitating Ecclesiastics on Stage?' *Notes & Queries* 62:4 (2015), 534–36. https://doi.org/10.1093/notesj/gjv136

Van Pelt, Nadia T., 'John Blanke's hat in the Westminster Tournament Roll', *Notes & Queries* 68:4 (2021), 387–89, gjab156. https://doi.org/10.1093/notesj/ gjab156

Van Pelt, Nadia T., 'John Blanke's wages: No business like show business', *Medieval English Theatre* 44 (2023), 3–35.

Walker, Greg, 'Rethinking the Fall of Anne Boleyn', *The Historical Journal* 45:1 (2002), 1–29. https://doi.org/10.1017/S0018246X01002126

Walker, Greg, *Writing Under Tyranny: English Literature and the Henrician Reformation* (Oxford: Oxford University Press, 2005).

Warnicke, Retha M., *The Marrying of Anne of Cleves: Royal Protocol in Early Modern England* (Cambridge: Cambridge University Press, 2000).

Warnicke, Retha M., *The Rise and Fall of Anne Boleyn: Family Politics at the Court of Henry VIII* (Cambridge: Cambridge University Press, 1989).

Watanabe-O'Kelly, Helen, 'Early Modern European Festivals—Politics and Performance, Event and Record', in J.R. Mulryne and Elizabeth Goldring, eds., *Court Festivals of the European Renaissance: Art, Politics and Performance* (Aldershot: Ashgate, 2002), 15–25.

Watanabe-O'Kelly, Helen, 'The Early Modern Festival Book: Function and Form', in J.R. Mulryne, Helen Watanabe-O'Kelly, Margaret Shewring, eds., *Europa Triumphans: Court and Civic Festivals in Early Modern Europe*, volume 1 (Aldershot, Hampshire: Ashgate, 2004), 3–17.

Watanabe-O'Kelly, Helen, "True and Historical Descriptions'? European Festivals and the Printed Record', in Jeroen Duindam and Sabine Dabringhaus, eds., *The Dynastic Centre and the Provinces: Agents & Interactions* (Leiden: Brill, 2014), 150–59. https://doi.org/10.1163/9789004272095_010

Weigert, Laura, *French Visual Culture and the Making of Medieval Theatre* (Cambridge: Cambridge University Press, 2015).

Welch, Evelyn, ed., *Fashioning the Early Modern: Dress, Textiles, and Innovation in Europe, 1500-1800* (Oxford: Oxford University Press, 2017).

Welsford, Enid, *The Fool: His Social and Literary History* (London: Faber and Faber, 1935).

Wild, Benjamin, 'Clothing Royal Bodies: Changing attitudes to royal dress and appearance from the Middle Ages to Modernity', in Elena Woodacre et al., eds., *The Routledge History of Monarchy* (London: Routledge, 2019), 390–407.

Wilson, Katherine Anne, 'The Household Inventory as Urban 'Theatre' in Late Medieval Burgundy', *Social History* 40:3 (2015), 335–59. https://doi.org/10.1080/03071022.2015.1043179

Woodacre, Elena, ed., *Queenship in the Mediterranean: Negotiating the Role of the Queen in the Medieval and Early Modern Eras* (New York, NY: Palgrave Macmillan, 2013).

Woolgar, C.M., 'Gifts of Food in Late Medieval England', *Journal of Medieval History* 37 (2011), 6–18. https://doi.org/10.1016/j.jmedhist.2010.12.004

Woolgar, C.M., 'Food and the Middle Ages', *Journal of Medieval History* 36 (2010), 1–19. https://doi.org/10.1016/j.jmedhist.2009.12.001

Woolgar, C.M., D. Serjeantson, and T. Waldron, eds., *Food in Medieval England: Diet and Nutrition* (Oxford: Oxford University Press, 2006).

Yeoman, Victoria, 'Speaking Plates: Text, Performance, and Banqueting Trenchers in Early Modern Europe', *Renaissance Studies* 31:5 (2017), 755–79. https://doi.org/10.1111/rest.12280

Unpublished dissertations and PhD theses

Beer, Michelle, 'Practices and Performances of Queenship: Catherine of Aragon and Margaret Tudor, 1503–1533' (Unpublished doctoral thesis, University of Illinois at Urbana-Champaign, 2014).

Cantalapiedra, Pablo F., *Percusión en la Corte de los Reyes Católicos* (Unpublished dissertation, Universidad Autónoma de Madrid, 2015).

Dijk, Sara van, *'Beauty Adorns Virtue': Dress in Portraits of Women by Leonardo da Vinci* (Unpublished doctoral thesis, University of Leiden, 2015).

Doda, Hilary, *'Of Crymsen Tissue': The Construction of A Queen: Identity, Legitimacy and the Wardrobe of Mary Tudor* (Unpublished dissertation, Dalhousie University, Halifax, Nova Scotia, 2011).

Kaufmann, Miranda, *Africans in Britain, 1500–1640* (Unpublished doctoral thesis, University of Oxford, Christ Church, 2011).

Kosior, Katarzyna, *Becoming a Queen in Early Modern Europe: East and West* (Unpublished doctoral thesis, University of Southampton, 2017).

Nubia, Onyeka, *Blackamoores: Critical Assessment of PhD thesis* (University of East Anglia, 2016).

Sharpe Pearsall, Eileen, *Tudor Court Musicians, 1485–1547: Their Number, Status, and Function*, volume 1 (Unpublished doctoral thesis, New York University, 1986).

INDEX

For the benefit of digital users, indexed terms that span two pages (e.g., 52–53) may, on occasion, appear on only one of those pages.